Lecture Notes in Business Information Processing 407

Series Editors

More information about this series at http://www.springer.com/series/7911

Eriks Klotins · Krzysztof Wnuk (Eds.)

Software Business

11th International Conference, ICSOB 2020
Karlskrona, Sweden, November 16–18, 2020
Proceedings

Springer

Editors
Eriks Klotins
Blekinge Institute of Technology
Karlskrona, Sweden

Krzysztof Wnuk
Blekinge Institute of Technology
Karlskrona, Sweden

ISSN 1865-1348 ISSN 1865-1356 (electronic)
Lecture Notes in Business Information Processing
ISBN 978-3-030-67291-1 ISBN 978-3-030-67292-8 (eBook)
https://doi.org/10.1007/978-3-030-67292-8

This Springer imprint is published by the registered company Springer Nature Switzerland AG
The registered company address is: Gewerbestrasse 11, 6330 Cham, Switzerland

Preface

Welcome to the proceedings of the 11th International Conference on Software Business (ICSOB). This edition of the conference was hosted by the Software Engineering Research and Education Lab (SERL) at Blekinge Institute of Technology, Sweden. The host university conducts education and research at a high international level, focusing on IT integrated with other subjects such as engineering, industrial economics, spatial planning design, and health sciences. SERL is one of the top software engineering research groups in the world and recognized by extensive industry-academia collaboration. SERL industrial partners include Volvo, Ericsson, Spotify, Sony, IBM, and Telia among others.

The conference in 2020 was held in the midst of the global COVID-19 pandemic. Most organizations have been forced to adapt to the new reality of working and collaborating remotely. Thus, the conference was held fully online.

For ICSOB 2020, we received 39 submissions from a wide range of research groups. Each submission was reviewed by three independent expert reviewers. Considering the reviews, the program committee accepted 13 full papers and an additional 5 short papers. The papers were primarily selected for the quality of the presented work and relevance to the community.

The conference publications covered a range of topics including practices for engineering and marketing software-intensive products, extracting business value from machine learning-based software components, ethical considerations of the software business, software ecosystems, and pedagogy of teaching entrepreneurship and software business.

The conference offered two interesting keynotes: the first one by Prof. Martin Andersson from BTH about the Relationship Between Software Development and Innovation among companies in Sweden and the second by Carl-Eric Mols about Open Source Business Models.

As Program Committee chairs, we would like to thank the members of the Program Committee and the additional reviewers for their efforts in evaluating the submissions and ensuring the high quality of the conference. The efforts of the Steering and Organizing Committees and all the chairs were of enormous value in building a successful conference. We extend our gratitude to all the scholars who submitted papers to the conference, all the authors who presented papers, and to the audience, who participated in very inspirational discussions during the conference.

November 2020

Eriks Klotins
Krzysztof Wnuk

Organization

General Chairs

Pekka Abrahamsson	University of Jyväskylä, Finland
Pasi Tyrväinen	University of Jyväskylä, Finland

Program Committee Chairs

Eriks Klotins	Blekinge Institute of Technology, Sweden
Krzysztof Wnuk	Blekinge Institute of Technology, Sweden

Social Media Chair

Sonja M. Hyrynsalmi	University of Turku, Finland

Program Committee

Pekka Abrahamsson	University of Jyväskylä, Finland
Sergey Avdoshin	National Research University Higher School of Economics, Russia
Richard Berntsson Svensson	Chalmers University of Technology, Sweden
Jan Bosch	Chalmers University of Technology, Sweden
David Callele	University of Saskatchewan, Canada
João M. Fernandes	University of Minho, Brazil
Javier Gonzales-Huerta	Blekinge Institue of Technology, Sweden
Helena Holmström Olsson	Malmö University, Sweden
Sami Hyrynsalmi	LUT University, Finland
Slinger Jansen	Utrecht University, The Netherlands
Thomas Kude	ESSEC Business School, France
Johan Linåker	Lund University, Sweden
Dirk Riehle Friedrich-Alexander	University of Erlangen-Nürnberg, Germany
Matti Rossi	Aalto University, Finland
Kari Smolander	Lappeenranta University of Technology, Finland
Pasi Tyrväinen	University of Jyväskylä, Finland
Xiaofeng Wang	Free University of Bozen-Bolzano, Italy

Additional Reviewers

Michael Dorner
Darja Smite
Javier Gonzales-Huerta
Ehsan Zabardast

Contents

How SaaS Companies Price Their Products: Insights from an Industry Study

Andrey Saltan[1,2](✉) and Kari Smolander[1](✉)

[1] LUT University, Lappeenranta, Finland
{andrey.saltan,kari.smolander}@lut.fi
[2] HSE University, St. Petersburg, Russia

Abstract. Pricing is one of the business and product strategy elements to achieve both financial performance and competitive advantage. The transition towards the Software-as-a-Service model has unlocked new opportunities for pricing software products. Conflicting recommendations from existing studies and industry experts make it challenging for SaaS providers to design and implement the pricing of their services. SaaS providers have come a long way in adapting their pricing practices to the new paradigm that assumes the offering of service instead of selling software as a product. This paper explores how SaaS providers package and price their products by reviewing the pricing information of 220 SaaS providers. The study reveals that SaaS companies are relatively heterogeneous in the way they price their products and the pricing practices of SaaS providers within the same size and product type could differ sufficiently.

Keywords: Software-as-a-Service · SaaS · Pricing · Empirical research

1 Introduction

The transition towards the Software-as-a-Service (SaaS) licensing and delivery model has significantly impacted business and engineering practices and processes. The ability to provide customers with software solutions over the Internet, rather than selling distributable products, requires companies to reconsider their business model with a particular focus on pricing.

SaaS pricing has been addressed in recent academic studies and is also widely discussed by practitioners outside academia. Studies from different research domains, including economics, decision science, and software engineering, explored various SaaS pricing aspects. However, these studies include a range of views, and they are often separated from practice. As a result, we have a diverse range of SaaS pricing guidelines, solutions, and recommendations; but still, we do not know whether SaaS providers follow and implement them.

This paper presents the first results of an ongoing study to understand the status quo of SaaS pricing practices. Using data on 220 randomly selected SaaS companies, we empirically investigate contemporary SaaS pricing practices. More formally, the research question (RQ) that drives our research can be formulated as follows: *How do*

E. Klotins and K. Wnuk (Eds.): ICSOB 2020, LNBIP 407, pp. 1–13, 2021.
https://doi.org/10.1007/978-3-030-67292-8_1

SaaS companies price their solutions? To find an answer, we take a closer look at nine pricing aspects identified in a recent multivocal literature review, grouped into three levels: Strategic, Tactical, and Operational [20, 21]. Working with open data provided by SaaS companies on their pricing pages allow us to assess aspects of SaaS pricing that have never been raised in academic literature before.

2 Background

SaaS pricing gained traction at the end of the 2000s when scholars from various fields started to investigate the new service-oriented software model, later called software-as-a-service. From the very beginning, it was apparent that the new licensing and delivery model would change the way a product will be offered, positioned, and priced. However, the way companies should set the pricing of their products was not clear, which became a more critical problem to solve with the drastic spread of the SaaS model.

Evidence of this intense interest can be found in the rapid growth of online publications about SaaS pricing, with diverse recommendations and opinions usually grounded in personal experience and non-systematic observations. However, there is not an abundance of empirical studies investigating the pricing practices of existing SaaS companies, especially from the quantitative perspective.

Lehmann et al. [13] use data of 295 SaaS providers to investigate the disclosure of pricing information on the websites of SaaS providers and the use of value metrics in defining the price. They identify three characteristics of SaaS providers and SaaS solutions that might affect pricing-related decisions: company size, age, and product category. The study reveals the difference in disclosing pricing information by small/young and large/mature providers. However, no statistically significant results regarding the usage of the metrics were obtained.

Laatikainen et al. [10] assess the pricing models of 54 cloud service providers (including 33 SaaS providers). They adapt the five-dimension generic pricing framework SBIFT (Scope, Base, Influence, Formula, Temporal rights) proposed in [8], to the cloud context, by adding two more dimensions relevant for cloud solutions: the degree of discrimination, and dynamic pricing strategy. The developed seven-dimensional framework is further used to classify cloud computing pricing models and identify generic pricing models of cloud providers. The study demonstrates that SaaS providers tend to have similar pricing models regarding specific pricing model dimensions.

Like the previous paper, Wu et al. [26] also propose a pricing framework that is further used to assess pricing practices of 353 SaaS providers. The cluster analysis confirms that SaaS providers prefer value-based pricing over other pricing strategies. However, they still try to make it straightforward to target a broad market.

Finally, Laatikainen and Luoma [11] use data collected from a survey, rather than manual website screening, to assess the evolution of internal processes of pricing practices. A statistical analysis of 324 responses concludes that the adoption of cloud technologies implies changes in pricing. The study also identifies and evaluates factors affecting the decision-making process and provides a rationality for companies' behavior.

Besides research papers, several reports published outside academic venues overview SaaS pricing practices empirically. Using data collected from a large number of SaaS providers, Poyar, in his blog posts [17, 18], provides insights into how companies cope with SaaS pricing challenges and how pricing-related decision-making is organized. However, these publications are relatively narrow regarding the scope and the analysis of patterns discovered.

Brandall [2, 3] and Shelley [23, 24] use for their publications, in the form of blog posts, data collected by exploring pricing pages of SaaS providers. However, these reports focus on large numbers of different small features, which are often related to the visual representation (i.e., versions naming, color pallets used, version listing order, etc.) without specifying their importance or providing attempts to explain the rationale behind observed patterns.

Empirical publications authored by scholars and practitioners provide valuable insights into certain SaaS pricing aspects. However, all of them focus on a limited number of SaaS pricing aspects, while a full picture of how SaaS providers price their products is missing. This paper reports on the first results of ongoing research complementing existing studies in gaining a full picture of SaaS pricing.

3 Methodology

Multiple different ratings and listings of SaaS vendors, compiled with a wide range of criteria and goals (i.e., fastest-growing[1] or leading[2]), can be found on the Internet. We used the three most complete databases of SaaS companies available to define the sample of SaaS companies for the analysis. Table 1 contains information on these databases.

Table 1. Explored SaaS databases

Resource name	# of items	URL
Golden Research Engine	10 250	https://golden.com/list-of-software-as-a-service-companies/
GetLatka	4 369	https://getlatka.com
SaaS Mag	2 086	https://www.saasmag.com/saas-1000-2020/

The number of providers and solutions covered in these databases varies significantly, but partly this can be explained by the variety and blurred boundaries of the definitions of SaaS. Some of these databases include providers that develop and deliver software solutions and digital services that either could or could not be classified as SaaS, depending on the definition and criteria used. Examples of such services include IT managed services, proofreading and translation services, logistic and delivery services, and ride-sharing services.

We used data from these three databases to make a random sample of 220 SaaS providers for our research. For the purpose of our analysis, we considered only SaaS providers that meet the following criteria:

[1] https://clockwise.software/blog/top-ten-fast-growing-saas-startups-to-follow/.

[2] https://www.datamation.com/cloud-computing/50-leading-saas-companies.html.

- The SaaS solution meets the definition provided by NIST [16], which defines SaaS as the capability provided to a consumer to use a provider's applications running on cloud infrastructure. This study does not consider video-on-demand services, social networks, search engines, and digital marketplaces as examples of SaaS services.
- The SaaS solution has a dedicated pricing webpage. For SaaS solutions included in the sample, we manually collected data from their websites.

The descriptive statistics of the SaaS solutions included are presented in Table 2.

Table 2. Descriptive statistics for SaaS providers sample

Parameter	Value	Number (percentage)
SaaS provider age (years)	Less than 5	7 (3%)
	5–10	**104 (47%)**
	11–15	66 (30%)
	15–20	28 (13%)
	More than 20	15 (7%)
SaaS provider HQ country	USA	**153 (70%)**
	EU	20 (9%)
	UK	15 (7%)
	Canada	13 (6%)
	Australia	8 (3%)
	India	7 (3%)
	Others	4 (2%)
Ownership structure	Private	**196 (89%)**
	Public	24 (11%)
Number of employees	1–10	13 (6%)
	11–50	**74 (34%)**
	51–250	**86 (39%)**
	250–1000	34 (15%)
	More than 1000	13 (6%)
Types of Customers	B2B	**182 (83%)**
	B2B and B2C	36 (16%)
	Others	2 (1%)

4 Analysis and Results

A recently performed multivocal literature review [20, 21] identified nine SaaS pricing aspects grouped in three broad categories: strategic level, tactical level, and operational level. Our data analysis assesses SaaS pricing practices across these levels; however, the publicly available data provided on SaaS company websites sometimes reveals only part of these details.

4.1 Strategic Level of SaaS Pricing

The following three SaaS pricing aspects can be attributed to the strategic level:

(1) **Competitive research and market positioning:** how a SaaS company, through pricing, shapes consumer perception of their SaaS solution and distinguish their solution from the solutions of competitors, if they exist;
(2) **Market segmentation and value proposition:** how a SaaS company divides potential customers into segments and defines the benefits and value in the usage of their SaaS service with (or without) respect to these market segments;
(3) **Pricing structure, strategies, and models:** how a SaaS company determines the objectives, logic, and structure of SaaS pricing, its terms of usage and pricing evolution principles.

Pricing practices within all three strategic aspects are rarely openly communicated by companies and are often subject to commercial confidentiality. However, an evaluation of pricing pages allows us to make certain conclusions on pricing strategies and models employed by SaaS companies.

Pricing Strategies and Models
SaaS pricing strategy is a complex concept without a shared and formalized definition. The pricing strategy can be considered as a portfolio of certain strategic decisions. Two decisions mostly widely discussed in the academic and non-academic literature are associated with the long-term price evolution and the foundation for pricing strategy formation. The first decision can select the following dynamic pricing options (based on [10, 14, 19]):

- **Penetration pricing:** SaaS solution is introduced at the lowest possible prices and then increased over time.
- **Skimming pricing:** SaaS solution is introduced at the highest possible prices and then decreased over time.
- **Premium pricing:** SaaS solution maintains the highest price in relation to competitors' possible prices over time.
- **Economy pricing:** SaaS solution maintains the lowest price in relation to competitors possible prices over time.
- **Non-dynamic pricing:** does not imply any strategic principle in price changes over time.

The second crucial decision related to pricing is determining the foundation, selecting from the following options (based on [4, 6]):

- **Cost-based pricing:** SaaS prices are defined based on costs and the cost structure the company faces while developing and delivering SaaS solutions.

- **Value-based pricing:** SaaS prices are defined based on the value the SaaS solution provides to the customers.
- **Competition-based pricing:** SaaS prices are defined based on prices offered by competitions for similar SaaS solutions.
- **Market-based pricing:** SaaS prices are defined based on market demand, especially with a lack of competition and consumers willingness-to-pay.

Assessing both decisions is quite challenging, and analyses of pricing pages cannot reveal all the possible details of what pricing strategies are used. Companies may also implement hybrid strategies as combinations of the available options. However, the vast majority of companies (**91%**) specify the value/benefits gained by consumers as the basis for defining the price of SaaS solutions and implicitly communicate it on their pricing pages. This can mean that companies implement value-based pricing or hybrid pricing strategies.

The concept of SaaS pricing strategy is closely connected with the concept of SaaS pricing models. The SaaS pricing model aims to structure and provide a clear algorithm for the calculation of prices based on the selected pricing strategy and various internal and external factors. The number of identified pricing models vary across existing publications. Based on [4, 5] we distinguish between the following models:

- **Flat-rate pricing:** SaaS is offered for a fixed amount of money.
- **Pay-as-you-go pricing:** SaaS payments depend on the usage metrics of SaaS.
- **Tiered pricing:** SaaS is provided in the form of several price points with a fixed number of features and usage conditions (i.e., number of items, transactions).
- **User-based pricing:** SaaS payments depend on the number of SaaS users for the same account.
- **Feature-based pricing:** SaaS payments are based on the number of SaaS features available.
- **Variable pricing:** SaaS payments are individually discussed.

Similar to pricing strategy, these models can be merged into hybrid ones. Our empirical analysis reveals that tiered pricing (**54%**) is the most used pricing model. Additionally, **27%** of companies develop and use hybrid models largely based on the tiered pricing model.

4.2 Tactical Level of SaaS Pricing

The following three aspects can be attributed to the tactical level:

(1) **Offering design, versioning[3], and bundling:** how companies translate strategic decisions into a range of concrete offers for consumers, consisting of specific obligations related to the work of the proposed service, if the specified conditions, including financial ones, are fulfilled
(2) **Transparency, promotion, and communication:** how SaaS companies inform target customers about their SaaS offerings and perform activities aimed at increasing customer interest in using the SaaS solution
(3) **Customer acquisition, retention, and usage analytics:** how SaaS companies, by means of pricing, manage the processes related to customer acquisition and retention.

Offering Design and Versioning
The two core and closely related activities within offering design are the determination of the number and functions of offered SaaS versions, and the definition of the prices consumers will be charged for their usage.

Our empirical analysis reveals that the vast majority of SaaS providers offer 3 or 4 versions (Fig. 1, left). This number includes free versions offered by some SaaS providers but does not include the opportunity to directly contact SaaS providers if the available offerings do not match customer requirements. Mature and large companies tend to offer a high number of versions as do companies that aim at both B2B and B2C markets.

We also calculated the average price increase ratio between adjacent non-free versions. For more than half SaaS providers, the range for this average increase ratio is from 2 to 3 (Fig. 1, right). We did not assess the correspondence between the increase in prices between versions with the functional/quality propositions behind these versions.

As discussed earlier, companies tend to use pure value-based pricing or hybrid strategies. In many cases, SaaS providers do not limit themselves to one value metric and use multiple ones aligned with each other. Exploring the variety of metrics used by SaaS providers led us to propose the following five type classification:

- **User-based metrics:** the price of using a SaaS solution depends on the number of users/accounts requested by the consumer
- **Function-based metrics:** the price of using a SaaS solution depends on the number of features, options, and functions available for the consumer
- **Usage-based metrics:** the price of using a SaaS solution depends on the intensity/depth of usage (i.e., the amount of cloud storage required, or number of transactions performed)

[3] The notion of the SaaS version might mislead and require certain clarification as there are two different meanings and corresponding definitions for it. According to the first one, SaaS versions are identified as stages of the SaaS solution in a release lifecycle [22]. The second one defines versions as strategically developed configurations of SaaS solutions within the same lifecycle stage [14]. Within this study, we will follow the latter meaning and definition.

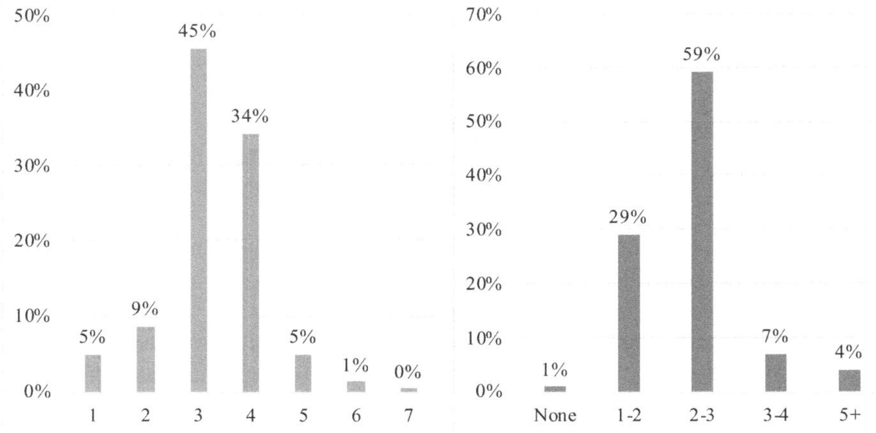

Fig. 1. Distribution of SaaS solution based on the number of offerings (left) and average price increase ratio between versions (right)

- **Consumer-based metrics:** the price of using a SaaS solution depends on the specific characteristics of the consumer (i.e., on the B2B market, consumer's revenue, or its size)
- **Outcome-based metrics:** the price of using a SaaS solution depends on the outcome achieved by using this solution (i.e., an increase in revenue or customer churn decrease).

Our empirical analysis reveals that the vast majority of SaaS providers use either user-based or function-based value metrics. The full picture of the distribution of SaaS solutions in our sample, with regard to the number of offerings, is presented in Fig. 2.

One particular type of versioning, called freemium, assumes offering the most basic version for free. This strategy has become popular and is widely employed in services targeted at the B2C market (i.e., music services, online games) [15].

Sixty-four SaaS providers (29%) implemented the freemium model by offering at least one version of their solution free of charge. Most of them operate in both the B2B and B2C market segments, and are large companies aiming to have a dominant market position. However, small- and medium-sized B2B SaaS providers do not implement freemium, giving a preference to free trial versions.

Unlike freemium, offering a free trial version also allows for generating purchase leads. The associated costs of a trial are less than in freemium due to the usage time constraints of the free trial version. The time constraint could be supplemented with limitations in the number of features or usage intensity. Our analysis showed that the vast majority (**81%**) of SaaS companies in the sample employ free trials.

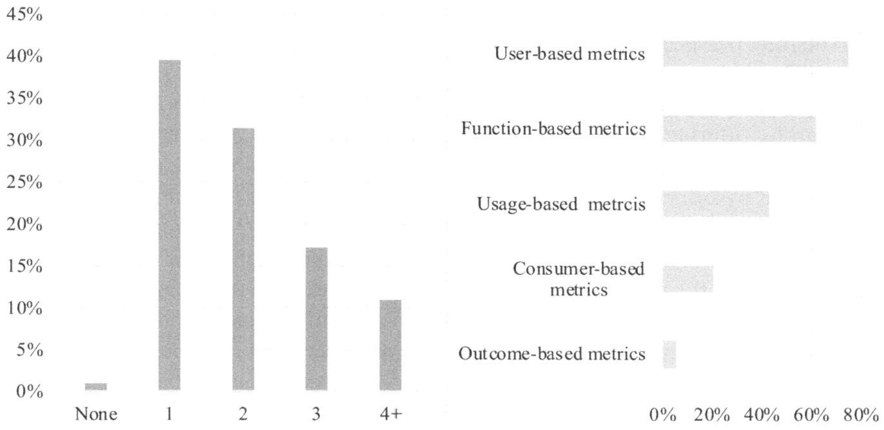

Fig. 2. Distribution of SaaS solution based on the number of value metrics used (left) and frequency of using different types of metrics (right)

4.3 Operational Level of SaaS Pricing

The following three aspects can be attributed to the operational level:

(1) **Ownership, control, and decision-making:** how pricing-related decision making is organized inside a SaaS company and how responsibility for decision making is dispersed among the management team
(2) **Performance measurement, testing, and evolution:** how a SaaS company assesses the performance and efficiency of their pricing and how the SaaS pricing changes over time and under internal and external factors and circumstances
(3) **Resources, costs planning and management:** how pricing is aligned with the planning and management of resources and costs.

The data do not allow us to assess any operational level aspects of SaaS pricing.

5 Discussion

We compared our findings with theoretical and empirical studies on similar issues. Our main result is about the pricing strategy and model. Value-based and tiered pricing are the most widely used pricing strategies and models of SaaS providers.

Another result is about the number of versions the SaaS provider should offer. There are two distinct perspectives on the issue of versioning/offering design in the academic literature. The first one, which could be called economic, has its roots in price discrimination theory (e.g., [25]). It can be beneficial for SaaS providers to use a price discrimination mechanism by offering several versions, targeting different market segments and customers. Software companies conventionally employ variations of second-degree price discrimination by offering additional versions to the flagship one, with different functions/conditions, including corresponding changes in pricing. Versioning based on price discrimination can lead to the problem of cannibalization and possible loss of revenue. Consumers choose the more affordable option when more than one version is available.

The second perspective, which can be called behavioral, has its roots in theories of predictable, bounded rationality (e.g., [1, 9]). Consumer bounded rationality has two important implications for the versioning design. First, offering too many versions can make the selection process for consumers too complicated and eventually lead to loss of customers. The second implication is related to the pattern of how consumers make decisions when facing several options. The most well-known and empirically verified example of such irrationality states that regardless of the circumstances, with the choice of two offerings, consumers tend to select the cheapest one, while with the choice of three – the middle one [1]. SaaS providers can take advantage of such irrationality while designing their offerings and predict which offer will be in demand for consumers.

The perspectives and theories discussed above are quite generic and do not take into account all conditions of the SaaS business model and the underlying engineering practices and processes. However, they suggest implementing versioning with a number of versions which should correspond to the targeted market segments and take into account behavioral patterns. The observed pricing practices regarding the number of offered versions seem to be reasonable and correspond with these theoretical recommendations. The issue of using value metrics looks similar to the issue of versioning: SaaS providers need to find the optimal number and types of metrics that can estimate the value consumers gain from using a SaaS service. Studies on value-based pricing do not provide solid advice that supports or questions the appropriateness of the observed practices.

Finally, one of our observations is related to offering free options, primarily in the form of the freemium strategy. Table 3 summarizes the core advantages and disadvantages of following this strategy [7, 12, 15]. While there are promising benefits of implementing the freemium model, it might work only with SaaS providers that offer generic solutions targeting a broad market and different market segments.

Table 3. Advantages and disadvantages of using the freemium model

Advantages	Disadvantages
Purchase lead: In the long run, consumers who are using the free version might become paid ones	**Cannibalization:** there is a risk that consumers will not migrate to the paid version, being satisfied with the free one
Network effect activation: offering a free version might increase the value of the SaaS service for paying consumers and the price a SaaS provider might charge	**Higher costs:** freemium requires higher prices for paying consumers to cover costs associated with free ones
Better analytics: with a more extensive user base, SaaS providers obtain more usage data that can be used to increase the quality of the service	
Extra revenue options: freemium and the subsequently more extensive user base can be beneficial if a SaaS provider's revenue model assumes cash flows from supplementary services or advertising	

6 Conclusion

This paper reports ongoing empirical research on contemporary SaaS pricing practices. We overview existing pricing practices and supplement our results to discuss how they correspond with current pricing theories. We focused on aspects where conclusions can be made based on publicly available data presented on SaaS company websites. Our conclusions are related primarily to pricing tactics. Most strategic and operational aspects are unlikely to be reliably evaluated and assessed using open data from company websites.

The study reveals that SaaS companies are relatively homogeneous in the way they price their products. SaaS providers have come a long way in adapting their pricing practices to the new paradigm that assumes offering a service instead of selling software as a product. There is a shared vision of how SaaS solutions should be priced, and it is shared by most SaaS providers, which, however, does not lead to identical pricing practices. In this paper we concentrated on versioning design, the selection of value metrics, the usage of the freemium model, and offering users free-trial options. When compared to the limited number of existing empirical studies, all of which were published more than five years ago, we can observe and state that SaaS pricing is becoming more and more sophisticated. Most SaaS providers are offering multiple versions, designed and priced based on consumer value metrics. With all the promising benefits, the freemium model has not become widespread; most companies that employ this model operate on both B2B and B2C markets and offer generic solutions for a broad audience.

The study has limitations. We limit our analysis to regular descriptive statistics. Further steps after this descriptive analysis include performing a correlation analysis to determine how different SaaS pricing mechanisms influence each other, a regression analysis to assess factors that might explain selected SaaS pricing practices, and a cluster analysis to develop a taxonomy of SaaS pricing practices.

The second limitation is associated with the sample. Based on the inclusion criteria, we did not consider SaaS providers that do not have a dedicated pricing webpage for their products. A lack of a pricing page can result from offering a SaaS solution for free or with an advertising-supported revenue model, or there can be an intention to initiate a negotiation with potential consumers and provide a unique value proposition to each consumer. Studies show that up to 50% of SaaS providers do not publicly disclose pricing information on their solutions [2, 13].

References

1. Ariely, D., Jones, S.: Predictably Irrational. Harper Perennial, New York (2008)
2. Brandall, B.: I Analyzed 250 SaaS Pricing Pages — Here's What I Found. https://www.process.st/saas-pricing-pages/
3. Brandall, B.: Insightful Study of 386 SaaS Startup Pricing Pages. http://www.onstartups.com/learn-by-example-38-saas-startup-pricing-pages-analyzed
4. Campbell, P.: The Anatomy of SaaS Pricing Strategy (2017)
5. Harmon, R., et al.: Pricing strategies for information technology services: a value-based approach. In: Hawaii International Conference on System Sciences (HICSS) Proceedings, pp. 1–10 (2009)
6. Harmon, R., et al.: Value-based pricing for new software products: strategy insights for developers. In: Portland International Conference on Management of Engineering and Technology (PICMET) Proceedings, pp. 1–24 (2004)
7. Holm, A.B., Günzel-Jensen, F.: Succeeding with freemium: strategies for implementation. J. Bus. Strategy **38**(2), 16–24 (2017). https://doi.org/10.1108/JBS-09-2016-0096
8. Iveroth, E., et al.: How to differentiate by price: proposal for a five-dimensional model. Eur. Manag. J. **31**(2), 109–123 (2013)
9. Kahneman, D.: Maps of bounded rationality: psychology for behavioral economics. Am. Econ. Rev. **93**(5), 1449–1475 (2003). https://doi.org/10.1257/000282803322655392
10. Laatikainen, G., Ojala, A., Mazhelis, O.: Cloud services pricing models. In: Herzwurm, G., Margaria, T. (eds.) ICSOB 2013. LNBIP, vol. 150, pp. 117–129. Springer, Heidelberg (2013). https://doi.org/10.1007/978-3-642-39336-5_12
11. Laatikainen, G., Luoma, E.: Impact of cloud computing technologies on pricing models of software firms – insights from Finland. In: Lassenius, C., Smolander, K. (eds.) ICSOB 2014. LNBIP, vol. 182, pp. 243–257. Springer, Cham (2014). https://doi.org/10.1007/978-3-319-08738-2_17
12. Lee, C., et al.: Designing freemium: strategic balancing growth and monetization. SSRN Electron. J. (2016). https://doi.org/10.2139/ssrn.2767135
13. Lehmann, S., Draisbach, T., Buxmann, P., Dörsam, P.: Pricing of software as a service – an empirical study in view of the economics of information theory. In: Cusumano, M.A., Iyer, B., Venkatraman, N. (eds.) ICSOB 2012. LNBIP, vol. 114, pp. 1–14. Springer, Heidelberg (2012). https://doi.org/10.1007/978-3-642-30746-1_1
14. Lehmann, S., Buxmann, P.: Pricing strategies of software vendors. Bus. Inf. Syst. Eng. **1**(6), 452–462 (2009)
15. Liu, C.Z., et al.: Effects of freemium strategy in the mobile app market: an empirical study of google play. J. Manage. Inf. Syst. **31**(3), 326–354 (2014). https://doi.org/10.1080/07421222.2014.995564

16. Mell, P.M., Grance, T.: The NIST Definition of Cloud Computing (2011)
17. Poyar, K.: Pricing Insights from 1,800 SaaS Companies. https://labs.openviewpartners.com/saas-pricing-insights/#.XDzVHC2B1QI
18. Poyar, K.: Survey of 1,000 SaaS Executives Reveals Major Blind Spot Around Pricing. https://openviewpartners.com/blog/survey-of-1000-saas-executives-reveals-major-blind-spot-around-pricing
19. Saltan, A., Nikula, U., Seffah, A., Yurkov, A.: A dynamic pricing model for software products incorporating human experiences. In: Maglyas, A., Lamprecht, A.-L. (eds.) Software Business. LNBIP, vol. 240, pp. 135–144. Springer, Cham (2016). https://doi.org/10.1007/978-3-319-40515-5_10
20. Saltan, A.: Do we know how to price saas: a multivocal literature review. In: ACM SIGSOFT International Workshop on Software-Intensive Business: Start-ups, Platforms, and Ecosystems (IWSiB) Proceedings, pp. 7–12 (2019). https://doi.org/10.1145/3340481.3342731
21. Saltan, A., Smolander, K.: Towards a SaaS pricing cookbook: a multi-vocal literature review. In: Hyrynsalmi, S., Suoranta, M., Nguyen-Duc, A., Tyrväinen, P., Abrahamsson, P. (eds.) Software Business. ICSOB 2019. Lecture Notes in Business Information Processing, vol 370, pp. 114–129. Springer, Cham (2019). https://doi.org/10.1007/978-3-030-33742-1_10
22. Schneider, M., Uhle, J.: Versioning for Software as a Service in the context of Multi-Tenancy (2013)
23. Shelley, E.: 5 key learnings from analyzing top B2B SaaS pricing pages. https://blog.chartmogul.com/b2b-saas-pricing/
24. Shelley, E.: B2B SaaS pricing pages in 2017: lessons from 100+ top businesses. https://blog.chartmogul.com/saas-pricing-pages-2017/
25. Varian, H.R.: Price discrimination. In: Handbook of Industrial Organization, pp. 597–654. Elsevier (1989). https://doi.org/10.1016/S1573-448X(89)01013-7
26. Wu, S. et al.: A pricing framework for software-as-a-service. In: International Conference on the Innovative Computing Technology (INTECH) Proceedings, pp. 152–157 (2014)

Architecting AI Deployment: A Systematic Review of State-of-the-Art and State-of-Practice Literature

Meenu Mary John[1(✉)], Helena Holmström Olsson[1], and Jan Bosch[2]

[1] Malmö University, Malmö, Sweden
{meenu-mary.john,helena.holmstrom.olsson}@mau.se
[2] Chalmers University of Technology, Gothenburg, Sweden
jan.bosch@chalmers.se

Abstract. Companies across domains are rapidly engaged in shifting computational power and intelligence from centralized cloud to fully decentralized edges to maximize value delivery, strengthen security and reduce latency. However, most companies have only recently started pursuing this opportunity and are therefore at the early stage of the cloud-to-edge transition. To provide an overview of AI deployment in the context of edge/cloud/hybrid architectures, we conduct a systematic literature review and a grey literature review. To advance understanding of how to integrate, deploy, operationalize and evolve AI models, we derive a framework from existing literature to accelerate the end-to-end deployment process. The framework is organized into five phases: Design, Integration, Deployment, Operation and Evolution. We make an attempt to analyze the extracted results by comparing and contrasting them to derive insights. The contribution of the paper is threefold. First, we conduct a systematic literature review in which we review the contemporary scientific literature and provide a detailed overview of the state-of-the-art of AI deployment. Second, we review the grey literature and present the state-of-practice and experience of practitioners while deploying AI models. Third, we present a framework derived from existing literature for the end-to-end deployment process and attempt to compare and contrast SLR and GLR results.

Keywords: Machine learning · Deep learning · Deployment · Systematic literature review · Grey literature review · Practices · Challenges

1 Introduction

Most embedded system companies have been progressively integrating ML/DL (Machine Learning/Deep Learning) techniques [1,2] into their systems due to advancements in hardware and big data explosions. Developing, deploying and maintaining a complex ML-based business system is a daunting challenge [3,4].

E. Klotins and K. Wnuk (Eds.): ICSOB 2020, LNBIP 407, pp. 14–29, 2021.
https://doi.org/10.1007/978-3-030-67292-8_2

Although a significant number of studies on how to design and train models are published each year, there is noticeably less research on how to manage and deploy these models once they have been trained [5]. In addition, the effort needed to go beyond the prototype stage and to deploy and keep it in production is known to be exceptionally high [3]. The need to consider and adapt well-established Software Engineering (SE) practices that have typically been overlooked or had a minor impact on ML literature is important to the real implementation [3,6,7]. Hence it is important to advance understanding of how AI models can be deployed, monitored and evolved.

The contribution of paper is threefold. First, we conduct a systematic literature review in which we review the contemporary scientific literature and offer a detailed overview of the state-of-the-art of AI deployment. Second, we review the grey literature and present the state-of-practice and experience of practitioners. Third, we present a framework derived from current literature for end-to-end deployment process and try to compare and contrast SLR and GLR results. The rest of the paper is set out in six sections. Section 2 introduces the research methodology employed in carrying out the study. Section 3 describes the threats to validity. In Sect. 4, we focus on the results of the study. We present the derived framework in Sect. 5 and discussions in Sect. 6. Section 7 summarizes the related works. Finally, Sect. 8 provides conclusions and future work.

2 Research Method

The study aims to advance understanding of how to integrate, deploy, monitor and evolve ML/DL models in the context of edge/cloud/hybrid architectures. We believe that this research initiative has the potential to accelerate the transition of ML/DL models from the prototyping stage to the deployment stage within companies. In order to accomplish this objective, the following research questions have been formulated:
RQ1: What is the state-of-the-art regarding the deployment of AI models as published in contemporary scientific literature?
RQ2: What is the state-of-practice in deploying AI models as experienced and reported in grey literature?

In the context of edge/cloud/hybrid architectures, we conducted SLR (RQ1) [8,9] and GLR (RQ2) [10,11] to address different and complementary RQs. We restricted our study during the recent time frame from January 1, 2010 to August 31, 2020 in order to obtain recent results, since most companies are currently at the prototyping stage and are slowly moving towards the deployment stage.

2.1 Systematic Literature Review (SLR)

The SLR is designed to identify, analyze, and interpret al.l relevant studies on the topic of interest [8,9]. This is the proposed methodology for aggregating empirical studies. To answer RQ1, we have defined search strings that included both research objective as well as research question terms, as suggested by [8]. We

Table 1. Search query used to retrieve relevant studies from selected libraries

Scientific library	Search query	Filters
IEEE Xplore	"All Metadata": software AND (deploy* OR production) AND (integrat* OR inference OR serv* OR monitor* OR scale OR evol*) AND (edge OR cloud OR hybrid) AND ("machine learning" OR "deep learning")	Conferences & Journals
ACM Digital Library	software AND (deploy* OR production) AND (integrat* OR inference OR serv* OR monitor* OR scale OR evol*) AND (edge OR cloud OR hybrid) AND ("machine learning" OR "deep learning")	PDF
Scopus	TITLE-ABS-KEY (software AND (deploy* OR production) AND (integrat* OR inference OR serv* OR monitor* OR scale OR evol*) AND (edge OR cloud OR hybrid) AND ("machine learning" OR "deep learning")	Conferences & Journals
ScienceDirect	software AND (deployment OR production) AND (edge OR cloud OR hybrid) AND ("machine learning" OR "deep learning")	Conference & Journals
Web of Science	TS = (software AND (deploy* OR production) AND (integrat* OR inference OR serv* OR monitor* OR scale OR evol*) AND (edge OR cloud OR hybrid) AND ("machine learning" OR "deep learning"))	Article or Proceeding paper

queried five popular scientific libraries to retrieve the relevant studies. The search queries and the retrieved studies of each scientific library are listed in Table 1. The retrieved studies were integrated and exported into the excel sheet. As an inclusion criteria, we defined (a) Studies that report the deployment of ML/DL models within the context of edge/cloud/hybrid architectures. We excluded (a) Duplicate versions (b) Not written in English (c) Not a peer-reviewed scientific research and (d) Not available electronically through web. Figure 1 outlines the overall SLR process adopted in the study. [12–24] represent primary studies.

2.2 Grey Literature Review (GLR)

Researchers are increasingly using GLR in their study. As reported in [10], although the SLR and the Systematic Mapping Study (SMS) provide comprehensive descriptions of the state-of-the-art, they typically lack the state-of-practice. This state-of-practice is critical in a more practice-oriented field of study such as SE. There is also a disconnect between studies reported by researchers and practitioners, as practitioners hardly involve in and display interest in scientific literature publications. Using GLR [11] in studies can (a) Eliminate publication bias (b) Offer contextual knowledge (c) Allow SE researchers to understand solutions to a specific existing SE challenge, perform evaluations and identify areas where further evaluation and improvement are required.

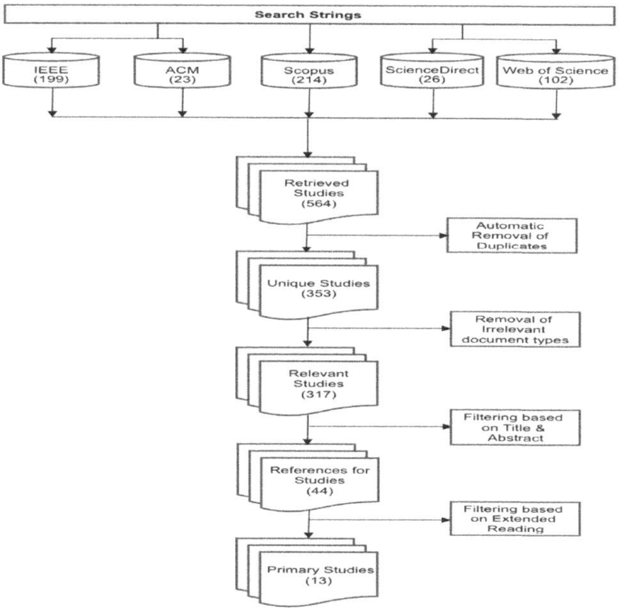

Fig. 1. Research process for SLR

Grey literature may offer practitioner perspectives on key topics relevant to practice and research, as well as encourage the voice of practitioners. Grey literature is suitable for this study, as it reflects the state-of-practice and experience of practitioners when deploying AI into cloud/edge/hybrid architectures. As part of conducting the GLR, we included studies that (a) Focus on integration, deployment, operationalization and evolution of ML/DL models in companies within limited time frame (b) Written in English (c) PDF file format and (d) Included documents from companies by filtering site as ".com". We excluded (a) Peer-reviewed scientific articles and (b) Other sources of information such as blogs, posts, etc. to increase the reliability of results. We explored Google search engine using the below query, which resulted in sixteen studies referring to RQ2. Among these sixteen studies, we selected six studies [25–30] that benefit our research.

(deploy* OR production) AND (integrat* OR inference OR monitor* OR evol* OR scal* OR operation*) AND (machine learning OR deep learning) AND (edge OR cloud OR hybrid) site:.com filetype:pdf

3 Threats to Validity

Potential threats to validity are taken into account and minimized in the study [31]. They are as follows: (a) Construct Validity - Enhanced by conducting SLRs and GLRs to identify the state-of-art and the state-of-practice to better study AI deployment from multiple perspectives. A considerable threat is that two of the thirteen primary studies extracted from SLR included studies that had the participation of practitioners in companies. Hence, there could be a potential possibility of conflict between the results of SLR and GLR. This threat is inevitable, because some practitioners seldom publish their work in peer-reviewed scientific articles. To accurately collect primary studies using SLR and GLR, we defined search process, search query, inclusion and exclusion criteria. (b) Internal Validity - Threats caused by author bias when selecting and interpreting data leads to internal validity threats. The SLR results are complemented by the GLR results to provide a clear overview of the subject under study. (c) External validity - Results can be extended to all software-intensive companies deploying ML/DL models as the study encompasses both state-of-art and state-of-practice reported in the literature.

4 Results

Based on the state-of-the-art and state-of-practice reported in SLR and GLR for deploying AI in the context of edge/cloud/hybrid architectures, we extract the practices and challenges. According to the findings from the literature, they are grouped into five phases i.e. Design, Integration, Deployment, Operation and Evolution. Each phase consists of two tasks. These phases have been chosen based on the literature review. In addition, most phases represent the keywords used in our search query. The phases and tasks extracted from SLR and GLR are shown in Table 2, 3 and 4. The hybrid architecture referred to in the study consists of a combination of cloud and edge architectures to deploy ML/DL models.

5 Framework

Based on the insights gained by synthesizing practices extracted from SLR and GLR, we derive a framework to facilitate the end-to-end deployment process of ML/DL models. Figure 2 shows an illustration of the framework. The overall framework is structured into five phases and consists of two tasks for each phase. They are: (a) Design - Validation & Tracking (b) Integration - Resource Discovery & Rewrite/Package (c) Deployment - Target Environment & Launching (d) Operation - Inference & Monitoring (e) Evolution - Retrain & Redeploy. Below, we detail each of the phases:

A. **Design**: When the models are properly *validated* [26] and offer confidence in results, the model is ready for placing into production. At this stage, the training process is terminated and all associated computing resources are released [14]. Before bringing the models into production, ensure that necessary *burn-in tests* are carried out to avoid initial model failures when put into production [17]. *Proper planning* of deployment process [28] can ensure a smooth transition from prototyping to deployment phase. Models, dependencies, artifacts, etc. need to be tracked and versioned to ensure reproducibility [17,28]. For instance, GitHub hashtags can be used for code versioning [28]. It is highly recommended

Table 2. Practices and challenges extracted from SLR and GLR [1/3]

Phases	Tasks	Practices	Challenges
Design	Validation	- Execute validation techniques: modelling, training and test error and cross-validation [26] - Terminate training process and release occupied computing sources [14] - Understand collected features with effect on outcome [28] - Compare experiments and run burn-in tests [17] - Plan model deployment [28]	- Data scientists need new ways of knowledge sharing [28] - Data scientists prefer to develop models alone [28]
	Tracking	- Track models, dependencies [28], experiments [17], versions [13] (eg: GitHub hash tags [28]), etc. - Maintain registry for model status and artifacts [17,28]	- Failure to version models leads to undesired situations [17]
Integration	Resource discovery	- Store models in a single format for ease of use [13] - Execute resource discovery and set up resources [18]	- Difference in prototype and production environment in terms of hardware, OS, library, etc.[17,28]
	Rewrite/ Package	- Two ways for integrating models: (a) Rewrite from data analysis to industrial development language (b) Equip with web interface [22] - Rewrite model for integrating to reports/applications or to share insights and prediction with analytic products [28] - For web interface, package image (eg: docker image [12,17]) with frameworks and libraries [19,22,23] - For reproducibility, use standard run time and configuration files [13] - Technology for packaging different applications: (a) Containers [12,13] [18,19,22,27] (b) Serverless computing [19] (c) Hypervisor-based virtualization [18]	- Difficulty in integrating ML models into existing or new applications [28,30] - Lack of docker containers optimized for accelerator [13] - Implementing same model in different frameworks need time and efforts [13,29] - Support code updates due to change in API framework [13]

(contniued)

Table 2. *(contniued)*

Phases	Tasks	Practices	Challenges
		- Existing containerization solutions: (a) Docker [12,13,15,17–19] (b) Singularity [13,15] (c) LXC [19] - Abandon usage of hypervisor-based virtualization [18] - Provide integration with existing data infrastructure and ensure data access and storage [17] - Apply compression before deploy, if needed [15,23] - Select ML solution fully integrated with databases to reduce efforts [28]	- Converted model performs bad compared with model implemented using native API framework [13]

Table 3. Practices and challenges extracted from SLR and GLR [2/3]

Phases	Tasks	Practices	Challenges
Deployment	Target environment	- Host model to invoke and get predictions [29] - Run workloads in [19,27,28] (a) Public cloud (b) On-premise (c) Hybrid cloud (d) Edge - Use cloud for compute-intense tasks, otherwise opt edge [16,19] - If edge is incapable to process, forward the request to cloud [19] - Minimize deploy cost while giving good QoE to users [19]	- Difficulty in deploying neural networks in edge devices due to limiting sparabreak computation and memory resources [21] - Most DL packages (Caffe, TensorFlow, etc.) focus on cloud and not on edge [21] - Human experts lack GPU configuration knowledge for device placement [24]
	Launching	- Decompress unpack image[15] - Expose deployed application as services to external users via communication channel [12,18] - Provide REST API to pipeline [17,21,22,28] (e.g..flask API [19]) - Need support from data scientists, engineering teams [17], ML engineers [23] data engineers, domain experts, infrastructure professionals and end users [28,29]	- Complicated process to deploy and configure DL framework and AI models execution on edge [21] - EU financial institutions are not yet al.lowed to move to cloud by EU regulators

(contniued)

Table 3. *(contniued)*

Phases	Tasks	Practices	Challenges
			- Lack of skills among data scientists to deploy REST API endpoint [28] - Inability of ML models to stay on laptops of data scientists [28]
Operation	Inference	- Ensure proper deployment of inference pipelines to pass, pre-process, predict and post-process raw data to serve batch and real-time requests [28,29] - Provide simple API for serving prediction [29] - For processing online inference request for features computed offline [17], take values: (a) End -of-day (b) Start-of-day - Needs to be elastic in response to traffic changes [17,26,29] - Ensure good data is used in both prototyping and production setup [28] - For latency critical and accuracy insensitive tasks, use low-latency mode with fog configuration else use high accuracy mode [16] - Response time, jitter and power usage[16] is: (a) Low, if send to fog nodes (b) High, if send to cloud	- Companies find difficulty in operationalizing [28] - Ensure data consistency across environments of offline training and online inference [17,28] - Scalability and security are major concerns [17,28] - Network latency is the bottleneck in end-to-end latency [19] - Difficulty in serving each user with separate edge computing instance when number of users increase - To reduce latency, lot of packages sacrifice memory for execution on edge [21] - Inference cost goes up when multiple models are deployed with different endpoints [29] - Mostly GPU instances are oversized for inference [29]

Table 4. Practices and challenges extracted from SLR and GLR [3/3]

Phases	Tasks	Practices	Challenges
	Monitoring	- Ensure monitoring system for querying, visualising and deeper understanding of metrics and event logging [12] - Monitor status and performance [17] and compare to business expectation [29] -Deploy initial model and boost traffic incrementally if it works well [28] - Determine concept drift, [28] memory consume by production environment and errors returned by models - Measure inference accuracy of deployed model to ensure data drifts noticed and actions taken [29] -Automatic roll back and forward capability to recover from degraded model performance [27,29]	- ML is deemed valuable by companies until it begin to improve profit [28] - Models performing well during training might not perform well during production [28]
Evolution	Retrain	- Employ Agile, DevOps-style work flows [26] - Ability of teams to re-evaluate the models quickly and use CI/CD to keep updated and prevent decay [26,29] - Retrain model when changes in model performance occur [28,29] - Apply automation to trigger model retraining which reduces effort and human error [29] - Retraining model on personal data outperform general models - Update model with latest data instead of retraining on historical data [14] - Create more model instances by: (a) Periodically [14] (b) Accuracy lower than threshold	- Most early users of ML models (a) Do not refresh [28] or replace models when accuracy degrades (b) Do so at each fixed intervals rather than continuously
	Redesign	- Choose tools and a broad set of diagnostics and monitoring ability to check if model under-performs and redesign from scratch [28] - Refine and scale solution as new technology is available [26,28] - Use blue/green deployment, canary deployment technique to deploy new version of model to production [29] - Deploy different versions of same application based on different needs. For instance, by utilizing A/B test [12,29] or take a multi-armed bandit approach [28]	

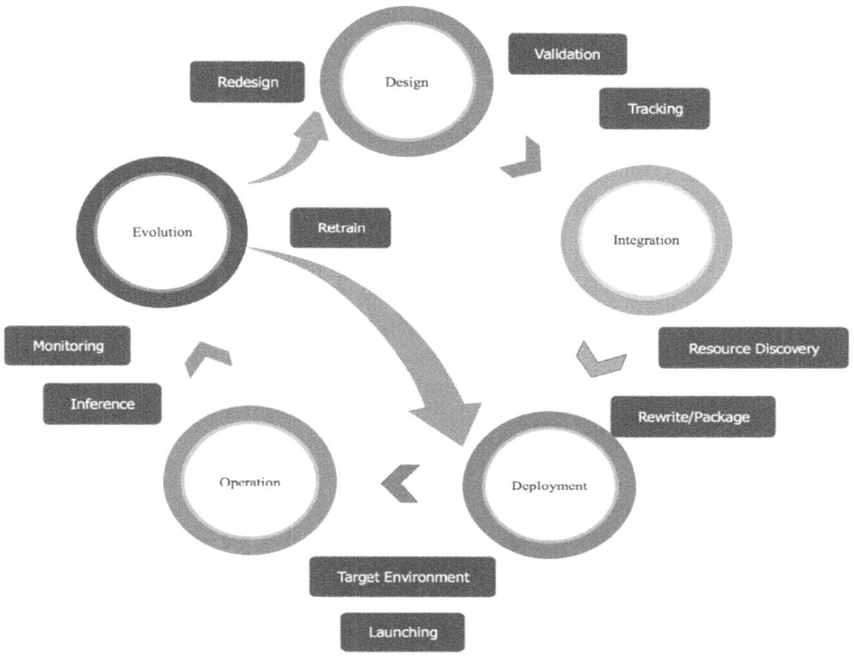

Fig. 2. End-to-end deployment framework

to maintain a registry containing entries for status of model life cycle and artifacts [17,28].

B. **Integration**: After validating and versioning the models properly, save them for reuse. Next, *discover and set-up* the necessary resources to put the model into production. Models can be incorporated into the application logic in two primary ways. These are: (a) *Rewrite models* from the data analysis language (for instance, R or Python) to industrial development language (for instance, Java or C++). Models are often rewritten to integrate into applications or reports or to share knowledge and predictions with analytical products. (b) Provide *web-interface* to the models. In the latter case, the model images are *packaged* with the required frameworks and libraries. One of the most popular technologies for packaging is *containerization*. It is important to ensure that the model integrate well with existing infrastructure and also verify appropriate data access and storage. Models are *compressed* based on use case requirements and resource availability prior to deployment.

C. **Deployment**: The compressed models are *decompressed* and unpacked in the target environment [15], if necessary. These target environments can be cloud, edge or hybrid cloud-edge collaboration, according to the use case [19,27,28]. For instance, more computation-intensive and less safety critical tasks need to be migrated to the cloud for processing. In contrast, process all latency critical requests at the edge device [16,19]. The deployment phase deals in particular with the *initial model deployment.* Proper consideration should be devoted to minimize the *deployment costs as low* as possible while at the same time guaranteeing *quality of experience* to end-users. The deployed application is provided to users through a communication channel [12,18]. Introducing the model into production demands *close collaboration* between data scientists, ML engineers, engineering teams, data engineers, domain experts, infrastructure professionals, etc. [17,23,28,29].

D. **Operation**: Companies perceive operationalization as the most challenging phase. Ensure proper deployment of models, inference pipelines, monitoring and event logging mechanisms before serving models [28,29]. In this phase, the deployed model consumes raw data to serve either *batch or real time inference requests* [28,29]. Model performance can be improved by deploying the initial model and slowly increasing the traffic to the model instead of allowing it to serve all requests at the beginning [28]. It should be noted that most of the GPU resources used in training DL models are oversized for inference [29]. The deployed model undergoes *continuous monitoring* to determine data drifts, concept drifts, returned errors from model, etc. [28]. As model performance degrades, introduce *roll back mechanisms* for quicker recovery [27,29].

E. **Evolution**: The evolution phase deals with subsequent model deployment. As the models are placed in production, performance degrades over time [28,29]. If so, select one of the two mechanisms: (a) Retrain (b) Redesign. Teams may employ CI/CD (Continuous Integration/Continuous Deployment) to keep the model up-to-date. Provisions to automatically trigger retraining will lessen both human errors and efforts [29]. Instead of retraining the entire model, updating the model with the latest information [14] is a good option. Techniques such as A/B test [12,29] and multi-armed bandit [28] can be selected for deploying different versions of the same model to determine the best performing model. On the other hand, blue/green deployments can be used to deploy new model versions in production [29]. An iteration is triggered from the evolution phase to the deployment phase when it is necessary to retrain the model. If redesigning the model is appropriate, an iteration is triggered from the evolution to design phase where we experiment with the current models for better performance or from scratch [28]. Teams that evaluate model performance needs to be very quick to prevent model decay as soon as possible [26].

6 Discussion

The study highlights the fact that ML/DL model deployment is gaining momentum over the last two to three years, since most primary studies cover the period 2017–2020. In addition, only two of the thirteen SLR studies involve participation from companies. This emphasizes that GLR is a valuable source to advance our knowledge about practices and challenges practitioners face in companies. Below, we compare and contrast SLR and GLR findings to provide further insights on AI deployment and illustrated in Fig. 3.

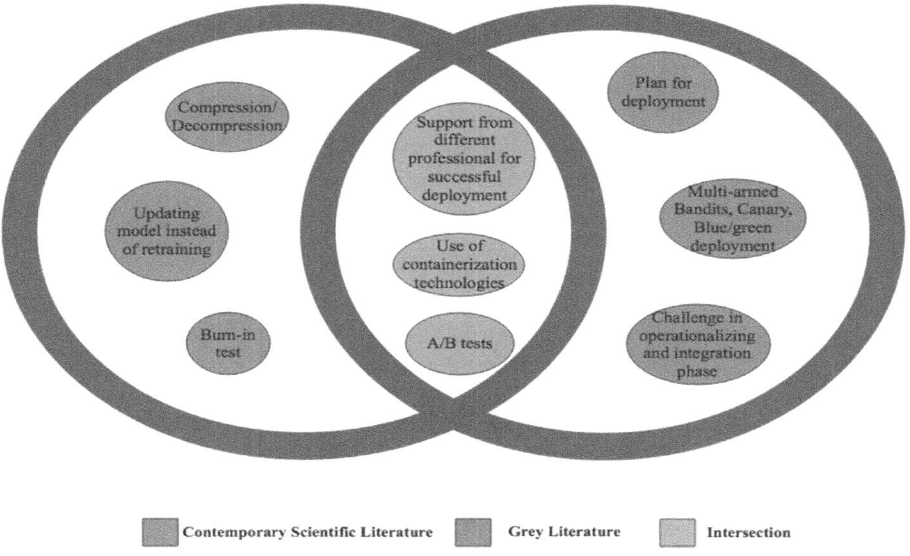

Fig. 3. Comparison/contrast between literature review findings

Compare Findings: Below, we compare the findings of literature review:
A. *Support among Professionals*: Both SLR and GLR sources suggest that successful deployment of ML/DL models *requires support* from data scientists and other experts such as data engineers, domain experts, infrastructure professionals and end-users. For instance, lack of data scientist skills to deploy REST API slows down the deployment process. Deployment can also be postponed due to prioritization and limitation of experts.
B. *Use of Containerization Technologies*: Containerization has been identified as the most popular packaging technology. Implementation of same model in different frameworks result in a loss of time and effort. For instance, models often need to be completely rewritten in production preferred languages. Since companies only find ML/DL valuable until they start producing value and profit, it is *not acceptable to delay production* because they want their product to reach markets more rapidly. This is perhaps one of the reasons for increasing demands for containerization.
C. *A/B Test*: Once the model is deployed into production, it is obvious that both SLR and GLR sources recommend adoption of A/B testing technique *to deploy multiple versions* of the best performing model. It can be concluded that fraction of academia projects that proceed into production utilize A/B testing. Besides A/B test, GLR confirms the use of other techniques for deploying new versions. For instance, blue/green deployment.

Contrast Findings: Below, we contrast findings between SLR and GLR:
A. *Compression/Decompression*: Models are *compressed* prior to deployment and *decompressed* after deployment as stated in SLR based on use case requirements and resource constraints. This is generally used for deploying models at edge by making minimal compromise on accuracy.
B. *Updating Models*: According to SLR, we find technique of *updating* models when the performance degrades with entire historical data *instead of retraining.* For instance, update the model every two hours with the latest up-to-date information or as performance degrades. This technique suits to non safety-critical applications where accuracy is insensitive.
C. *Burn-in Test*: Based on SLR, burn-in tests are executed before real deployment to *stop initial model failures* when deployed on target devices. On the other hand, as per GLR, the models are put in the pilot phase prior to deployment. Although burn-in test is identified from SLR in our study, it is part of one of the two scientific peer-reviewed company-based paper.
D. *Plan for Deployment*: In accordance with GLR, companies always plan beforehand for deployment compared to SLR. Studies show that companies have difficulty in integrating models into existing or new applications, deploying models on edge devices, operationalizing models, etc. Therefore, *proper planning* makes the deployment process even easier with less overhead and resource utilization.
E. *More Deployment Techniques*: Although A/B test is widely used in companies, techniques such as multi-armed bandits, canary and blue/green deployments are employed in companies based on GLR to deploy new model versions. These techniques are absent in contemporary literature, which may be due to the immaturity of deployment process employed in academia.
F. *Challenges in Operationalizing phase*: GLR provides more information about different practices, techniques and challenges in relation to monitoring and evolution compared to SLR. Most models in scientific literature experience only initial deployment and are not constantly replaced/refreshed as performance degrades over time.

7 Related Work

ML benefits can only be harnessed when models move from prototyping to deployment stage [32]. According to [33,34], deployment is an underestimated area where companies are struggling with model testing, trouble shooting, glue code for running the system, and, monitoring and logging mechanisms. Moreover, ML/DL model deployment demands significant change in the overall system architecture as it needs to be integrated to a software-intensive system. In addition to the components that care for model deployment in production, it is recommended that additional components be provided for model validation prior to deployment, model evaluation and monitoring [35,36]. Deployed models are dedicated to serve real data [37]. If the model fail to meet expectations, roll back and restore the previous model version. Federated learning requires a specialized deployment framework to address changes in edge [38].

8 Conclusions

Most companies are placing lot of models into production compared to previous years. To better understand design, integration, deployment, operation and evolution of AI models, we analyze both SLR and GLR in the context of edge/cloud/hybrid architectures. Based on these findings, we list various practices and challenges practitioners face when deploying ML/DL models. We derive a framework on the basis of literature review for the end-to-end deployment process and also attempt to compare and contrast the findings of SLR and GLR. We look forward to validate the framework in various software-intensive domain companies to better understand the deployment process.

References

1. Amershi, S., et al.: Software engineering for machine learning: a case study. In: 2019 IEEE/ACM 41st International Conference on Software Engineering: Software Engineering in Practice (ICSE-SEIP), pp. 291–300. IEEE, May 2019
2. Bernardi, L., Mavridis, T., Estevez, P.: 150 successful machine learning models: 6 lessons learned at booking. com. In: Proceedings of the 25th ACM SIGKDD International Conference on Knowledge Discovery & Data Mining, pp. 1743–1751, July 2019
3. Sculley, D., et al.: Hidden technical debt in machine learning systems. In: Advances in Neural Information Processing Systems, pp. 2503–2511 (2015)
4. Dahlmeier, D.: On the challenges of translating NLP research into commercial products. In: Proceedings of the 55th Annual Meeting of the Association for Computational Linguistics (Volume 2: Short Papers), pp. 92–96, July 2017
5. Crankshaw, D., Gonzalez, J., Bailis, P.: Research for practice: prediction-serving systems. Commun. ACM **61**(8), 45–49 (2018)
6. Hill, C., Bellamy, R., Erickson, T., Burnett, M.: Trials and tribulations of developers of intelligent systems: a field study. In: 2016 IEEE Symposium on Visual Languages and Human-Centric Computing (VL/HCC), pp. 162–170. IEEE, September 2016
7. Provost, F., Kohavi, R.: Guest editors' introduction: on applied research in machine learning. Mach. Learn. **30**(2–3), 127–132 (1998)
8. Keele, S.: Guidelines for performing systematic literature reviews in software engineering, vol. 5. Technical report, Version 2.3 EBSE Technical Report, EBSE (2007)
9. Kitchenham, B.A., Budgen, D., Brereton, P.: Evidence-Based Software Engineering and Systematic Reviews, vol. 4. CRC Press, Boca Raton (2015)
10. Garousi, V., Felderer, M., Mäntylä, M.V.: The need for multivocal literature reviews in software engineering: complementing systematic literature reviews with grey literature. In: Proceedings of the 20th International Conference on Evaluation and Assessment in Software Engineering, pp. 1–6, June 2016
11. Williams, A.: Using reasoning markers to select the more rigorous software practitioners' online content when searching for grey literature. In: Proceedings of the 22nd International Conference on Evaluation and Assessment in Software Engineering 2018, pp. 46–56, June 2018
12. Xiaojing, X.I.E., Govardhan, S.S.: A service mesh-based load balancing and task scheduling system for deep learning applications. In: 2020 20th IEEE/ACM International Symposium on Cluster, Cloud and Internet Computing (CCGRID), pp. 843–849. IEEE, May 2020

13. Serebryakov, S., Milojicic, D., Vassilieva, N., Fleischman, S., Clark, R.D.: Deep learning cookbook: recipes for your AI infrastructure and applications. In 2019 IEEE International Conference on Rebooting Computing (ICRC), pp. 1–9. IEEE, November 2019
14. Li, J., Li, J. and Zhang, H., 2018, August. Deep learning based parking prediction on cloud platform. In: 2018 4th International Conference on Big Data Computing and Communications (BIGCOM), pp. 132–137. IEEE
15. Brayford, D., Vallecorsa, S., Atanasov, A., Baruffa, F., Riviera, W.: Deploying AI frameworks on secure HPC systems with containers. In: 2019 IEEE High Performance Extreme Computing Conference (HPEC), pp. 1–6. IEEE, September 2019
16. Tuli, S., Basumatary, N., Buyya, R.: EdgeLens: deep learning based object detection in integrated IoT, fog and cloud computing environments. In: 2019 4th International Conference on Information Systems and Computer Networks (ISCON), pp. 496–502. IEEE, November 2019
17. Brumbaugh, E., et al.: Bighead: a framework-agnostic, end-to-end machine learning platform. In: 2019 IEEE International Conference on Data Science and Advanced Analytics (DSAA), pp. 551–560. IEEE, October 2019
18. Salza, P., Hemberg, E., Ferrucci, F., O'Reilly, U.M.: Towards evolutionary machine learning comparison, competition, and collaboration with a multi-cloud platform. In: Proceedings of the Genetic and Evolutionary Computation Conference Companion, pp. 1263–1270, July 2017
19. Gupta, N., Anantharaj, K., Subramani, K.: Containerized architecture for edge computing in smart home: a consistent architecture for model deployment. In: 2020 International Conference on Computer Communication and Informatics (ICCCI), pp. 1–8. IEEE, January 2020
20. Cartas, A., et al.: A reality check on inference at mobile networks edge. In: Proceedings of the 2nd International Workshop on Edge Systems, Analytics and Networking, pp. 54–59, March 2019
21. Zhang, X., Wang, Y., Lu, S., Liu, L., Shi, W.: OpenEI: an open framework for edge intelligence. In 2019 IEEE 39th International Conference on Distributed Computing Systems (ICDCS), pp. 1840–1851. IEEE, July 2019
22. Rovnyagin, M.M., Timofeev, K., Elenkin, A.A., Shipugin, V.A.: Cloud computing architecture for high-volume ML-based solutions. In: 2019 IEEE Conference of Russian Young Researchers in Electrical and Electronic Engineering (EIConRus), pp. 315–318. IEEE, January 2019
23. Pääkkönen, P., Pakkala, D.: Extending reference architecture of big data systems towards machine learning in edge computing environments. J. Big Data **7**, 1–29 (2020). https://doi.org/10.1186/s40537-020-00303-y
24. Li, Y., Han, Z., Zhang, Q., Li, Z., Tan, H.: Automating cloud deployment for deep learning inference of real-time online services. In: IEEE INFOCOM 2020-IEEE Conference on Computer Communications, pp. 1668–1677. IEEE, July 2020
25. Data blueprint - IOA Knowledge Base. https://ioakb.com/fileattachment?file=b3O7X9NGQKO2OrG8ohmRvw%3D%3D&v=3
26. Machine Learning Based Advanced Analytics using Intel Technology. https://media.bitpipe.com/io_14x/io_147787/item_1954603/machine-learning-based-advanced-analytics-using-intel-ForDistribution-2.pdf
27. Next Generation Hybrid Cloud Data Analytics Solution. https://builders.intel.com/docs/datacenterbuilders/next-gen-hybrid-cloud-data-analytics-solution.pdf
28. Getting Started with Machine Learning in the Cloud. https://www.oracle.com/a/ocom/docs/machine-learning-goes-to-the-cloud-ebook.pdf

29. Machine Learning Lens-AWS Well-Architected Framework. https://d1.awsstatic.com/whitepapers/architecture/wellarchitected-Machine-Learning-Lens.pdf.Move the Algorithms, Not the Data
30. https://www.oracle.com/technetwork/database/options/advanced-analytics/oml19c-white-paper-5601561.pdf
31. Easterbrook, S., Singer, J., Storey, M.-A., Damian, D.: Selecting empirical methods for software engineering research. In: Shull, F., Singer, J., Sjoberg D.I.K. (eds.) Guide to Advanced Empirical Software Engineering, pp. 285–311. Springer, London (2008). https://doi.org/10.1007/978-1-84800-044-5_11
32. Crankshaw, D., et al.: The missing piece in complex analytics: low latency, scalable model management and serving with velox. arXiv preprint arXiv:1409.3809, September 2014
33. Bosch, J., Olsson, H.H., Crnkovic, I.: Engineering AI systems: a research agenda. In: Artificial Intelligence Paradigms for Smart Cyber-Physical Systems, pp. 1–19. IGI Global (2020)
34. Arpteg, A., Brinne, B., Crnkovic-Friis, L., Bosch, J.: Software engineering challenges of deep learning. In: 2018 44th Euromicro Conference on Software Engineering and Advanced Applications (SEAA), pp. 50–59. IEEE, August 2018
35. Baylor, D., et al.: TFX: a tensorflow-based production-scale machine learning platform. In: Proceedings of the 23rd ACM SIGKDD International Conference on Knowledge Discovery and Data Mining, pp. 1387–1395 (2017)
36. Crankshaw, D., et al.: The missing piece in complex analytics: low latency, scalable (2014)
37. Olston, C., et al.: Tensor flow-serving: flexible, high-performance ml serving. In: Workshop on ML Systems at NIPS (2017)
38. Breck, E., Cai, S., Nielsen, E., Salib, M., Sculley, D.: What's your ML test score? A rubric for ML production systems (2016)

Autonomously Improving Systems in Industry: A Systematic Literature Review

Rolf Green[1], Jan Bosch[1(✉)], and Helena Holmström Olsson[2]

[1] Chalmers University of Technology, Gothenburg, Sweden
{rolf.green,jan.bosch}@chalmers.se
[2] Malmö University, Malmö, Sweden
helena.holmstrom.olsson@mau.se

Abstract. A significant amount of research effort is put into studying machine learning (ML) and deep learning (DL) technologies. Real-world ML applications help companies to improve products and automate tasks such as classification, image recognition and automation. However, a traditional "fixed" approach where the system is frozen before deployment leads to a sub-optimal system performance. Systems autonomously experimenting with and improving their own behavior and performance could improve business outcomes but we need to know how this could actually work in practice. While there is some research on autonomously improving systems, the focus on the concepts and theoretical algorithms. However, less research is focused on empirical industry validation of the proposed theory. Empirical validations are usually done through simulations or by using synthetic or manually alteration of datasets. The contribution of this paper is twofold. First, we conduct a systematic literature review in which we focus on papers describing industrial deployments of autonomously improving systems and their real-world applications. Secondly, we identify open research questions and derive a model that classifies the level of autonomy based on our findings in the literature review.

Keywords: Autonomously improving systems · Machine learning · Industrial application · AI engineering · Empirical validation

1 Introduction

Today software are used to solving increasingly complex and dynamic with the introduction of machine learning (ML) and Deep learning (DL). Applications of ML and DL in autonomous systems play an increasingly important part in several areas, from industrial robots, self-driving vehicles to insulin delivery systems [1]. These systems operate in increase non-stationary environments where the systems need to adapt to keep their performance. A traditional static approach where the system is frozen before deployment leads to a sub-optimal system performance in dynamic environment. However, a non-static approach where system is able experiment with its own behaviour and improve performance will improve

E. Klotins and K. Wnuk (Eds.): ICSOB 2020, LNBIP 407, pp. 30–45, 2021.
https://doi.org/10.1007/978-3-030-67292-8_3

business outcomes. The flexibility in non-stationary systems could improve performance post-deployment for a fixed task or be used for mass customization. As an example consider having software products that are able to autonomously customize its response based on each user's preferences to give the optimal user experience for each individual user. This would make it possible to maximize value for each customer/user in the entire lifetime of the product while keeping the human resources to manage the improvement as low a possible. Systems autonomously experimenting with and improving their own behavior and performance could improve business outcomes but we need to know how this could actually work in practice. Hence this SLR.

Autonomy in systems such as self-management was put forward as a viable solution to deal with challenge of complexity in deployed systems without investing a lot of human resources [2]. These are intelligent systems that are able to observe their own behaviour and can adapt autonomously to achieve goals or improve performance based on a high level objective [2]. Autonomously improving systems are deployed systems which autonomously try to improve performance by learning from experiments with the systems own parameters while ensuring a minimum level of performance.

Key components in improving the performance of a system while keeping systems stability is monitoring of the environment the system is deployed in and the performance of the system [3]. Although post-deployment data is collected by several companies, it is not as widely used in industry [4].

Automated experiments using A/B/n testing is an example of using a data-driven and structured approach to experiment with different configurations and their performance levels in deployed systems [5]. Machine learning can be used to improve the efficiency of A/B/n testing [6]. Multi-armed bandits is a search strategy that reduces the number of experiments needed to ideally find the best solution among multiple possibilities [7]. However, in practice there is no guaranty that the found solution is in fact the best solution without performing an exhaustive search.

Systems based on ML models such as multi-armed bandits can help companies deliver mass customization or specific domain adaption, since the systems can adapt and improve with little or no human resources involved [8]. The ability to learn over time can be used for improving performance in a static environment or to adapt to changes in a dynamic environment. In general, training of ML models can be divided into two different phases, offline and online [9]. Offline learning relies on a large dataset with all data available at the start of training. Online learning learns from a continuous and sequenced stream of data. To improve performance and reduce the human-interaction, the ML system has to continuously learn based on monitoring the environment and its own performance by continuously evaluating, training and deploying updated ML models [10]. Implementing an autonomously improving system based on ML in an industrial systems context imposes several challenges in the design, development, and deployment of the system [11]. However, the challenge is that most previously published research does not deal with real-world industry applications and often only experiment with synthetic data or limited datasets [12].

The purpose of our study is to provide an overview of existing research as a basis for future research in the area of autonomously improving systems with focus on software engineering and real-world industrial application that in the end can improve business outcomes.

The contribution of this paper is twofold. First, we conduct a systematic literature review (SLR) in which we focus on papers describing industrial deployments of autonomously improving systems and their real-world applications. The purpose is to discover the existing academic literature with empirical work and identifying challenges within the field of industrial autonomously improving systems. Secondly, we identify open research questions and derive a model that classify the level of autonomy based on our findings in the literature review.

The remaining of the paper is structured as follows. In Sect. 2, we provide the background around the autonomously improving systems and existing research on this. In Sect. 3, we present the research method for the systematic literature. In Sect. 4 we present the findings from the literature review. Section 5 and 6 contains the discussion and conclusion of this paper.

2 Background

This section introduces existing concepts of autonomously improving system and related topics such as controlled experimentation and multi-armed bandits which can be used to implement sub-components of an autonomously improving system. The topics in this section represents the different autonomy levels integrated into the experimentation process to improve system performance.

2.1 A/B/n Experiments

A/B experiments or split tests is a group of experiments techniques that relies on hypotheses testing. In A/B experiments, also called A/B tests, tests two different variants of a feature using a control variant and an altered variant called the treatment. Users are randomly assigned to the two variants [13]. When more than one split-test variation is being tested against the same control variant it is called A/B/n tests. Data from these experiments are collected and based on this the best treatment/variant can be selected [14]. Many companies perform A/B experiments to explore parameters and test these to find parameters that increases system performance [5,15]. A/B tests are used by many large companies such as Microsoft, Booking.com, Netflix to improve their services [5]. However, the A/B tests are limited by the amount of data that is received. To ensure that the result is statistically significant a certain amount of data must be received [16]. Also, variations in the population, e.g.. users, needs to be considered to be sure that the sub-group used for the experiments is representing the global population of users [16]. Performing A/B experimentation sequentially can also be expensive since there is no dynamic prioritization based on live feedback data between individual experiments and their excepted outcome, since this involves running tests that might not perform well and waiting on those to complete before switching to the next [17].

2.2 Multi-Arm and Contextual Bandits

Multi-armed bandits (MAB) is a sub-field in reinforcement learning (RL) specifically for the problem of choosing between exploration and exploitation. MAB tries to minimize the cost of running experiments by running multiple experiments at the same time by switching between different treatments and selecting the most promising. This minimizes "regret" caused by the selection of a non-optimal alternative of the multiple arms available in the multi-arm bandit experiment [17]. If resource constraints are a concern, the MAB can be used to lower the overall cost of experimentation by sacrificing some statistical significance [17]. The policy that implements the selection between different arms is a MAB algorithm. The trade-off between exploration and exploitation is determined by the MAB algorithm. Besides the user-selected policy, MAB have requirements for the environment they work in such as the reward feedback for selecting an arm and that the experiments do not affect each other [17]. If the limitations of the MAB is not addressed correctly, companies risk making decisions based on wrong information [7].

2.3 Autonomously Improving System

Systems that continuously learn tasks and improve by fine-tuning policies have been studied for decades. The idea of the autonomously improving systems e.g.. robots able to change and generalize on different tasks, were already proven by simplified lab experiments in 1995 [18]. The online or incremental learning in an autonomously improving systems can be implemented in many different ways depending on the context [10,12,19]. Once a new model is developed or an existing model is retrained the performance must be compared against the existing to decide if the model should be used. However, the true real-world performance can only be found by performing experiments in an already deployed system. Training of the ML models can be divided into two different approaches, i.e. offline and online, determined by the algorithm or model.

Offline learning involves data collection and storage of a dataset for training the ML model [11]. Training of offline models usually uses a big dataset with labelled data for training or is retrained multiple times on a re-sampled training set. This requires a lot of resources for storage and data preparation [10]. If the system itself or the task of the system changes over time, the dataset that has been collected, processed, and labelled might become outdated and over time useless. There exist several ML models that use offline training e.g. object detection YOLO [20] and MobileNet [21]. Big ML frameworks are mainly focused on offline learning.

Online learning or incremental learning is where the ML model is trained using a potentially infinite stream of data and does not require all data to be available at one time. The motivation for online learning is the ability to improve or adapt to changes addressing concept drift which is due to changes in a non-stationary environment or goal of the system. Concept drift can be a gradual change over time, a recurring or cyclical change, or a sudden or abrupt change.

Problems with concept drift will benefit for the continuous learning of the system, since the model can be trained with new data and therefore adapt to the concept drift [19,22]. Besides system adaption or optimization, online learning can also reduce the required size of the dataset and labelling needed for the initial training, because the systems are continuously learning. This approach can be used to deal with resource constrain if the dataset is too big for offline learning [23].

Several literature reviews have been performed within online/offline learning, Self-* systems and concept drift primarily but not specifically focused on industrial deployment [12,19,24–26]. A significant amount of work goes into describing the techniques and algorithms in theory. Many of the studies compare performance between the different techniques and algorithms by using simulations, synthetic datasets or modified real world datasets [12]. However, few of these studies deploy the systems in an industrial context to perform empirical validation in the real-world.

3 Method

This literature review follows the guidelines proposed by [27]. Originally the "Systematic literature review" (SLR) was used within medical research but the method has also been widely adopted in other research domains [28–30], including the software engineering domain. The SLR provides a systematic approach to perform a review of existing literature by specifying guidelines for how to perform the search, select and review selected papers.

The purpose of this literature review is to provide an overview of existing research as a basis for future research in the area of autonomously improving systems. We identify papers, with focus on software engineering and real-world industrial application, that describe systems supporting machine learning as an integrated part. In the literature review we look to answer the following research questions:

- *RQ1: What techniques are used to deploy industrial autonomously improving systems?*
- *RQ2: In what domains are these systems implemented and deployed in industry?*

3.1 Search Strategy

Our literature search focuses on providing an overview of existing research as a basis for future research in the area of autonomously improving systems. We identified papers that describe systems supporting machine learning with focus on software engineering and real-world industrial application. The search started by selecting key words used in the research area. We conducted a pilot search on *Autonomously Improving Systems*, using Scopus, we collected more keywords and broadened the search to ensure relevant studies would be included. We also used the *software* to focus on papers involving software and *industr* OR "case study" OR "case studies" OR empirical* to limit results to studies with empirical work with industrial relevance. Several different search strings were explored based on the pilot search.

The following two search queries was constructed and used on 28.02.2020 for the literature review: *TITLE-ABS-KEY ("software") AND TITLE-ABS-KEY (autonomous OR intelligent OR self- OR learning) AND TITLE-ABS-KEY ("concept drift" OR lifelong OR continual OR online) AND TITLE-ABS-KEY ("machine learning" OR ml OR ai OR "artificial intelligence" OR dl OR "deep learning") AND TITLE-ABS-KEY(industr* OR "case study" OR empirical)* and *TITLE-ABS-KEY ("A/B/n testing" OR "online controlled experiments") AND TITLE-ABS-KEY (industr* OR "case study" OR "case studies" OR empirical)* The bibliography search was conducted on Scopus, IEEE, and ACM digital library. The search was adapted to the different search engines to use the same settings except searches in the ACM digital library was done on only the abstract due to the limitations of the search engine.

3.2 Exclusion and Inclusion Criteria

As a step in the original process as proposed by [27], each paper in the search was reviewed first by the title and keywords, then by abstract. Papers with non-related title and keywords were excluded from the result. The remaining papers were reviewed by the abstract. Finally, the body of the remaining papers were used to verify the empirical work. As the focus in our SLR is real-world application in industry, the papers included in the SLR must contain empirical evaluation of the proposed theory in an industrial context.

3.3 Data Collection

As a part of the SLR process the data collected should be defined as proposed by [27]. For each of the studies the approach to the autonomously improving system and the type of learning method was extracted and noted and the focus of studies was determined. The type of data e.g. dataset, simulation or data from real-world deployment and the method of the empirical work was also extracted.

3.4 Results

The search resulted in a total of 1345 papers. After the process of removing duplicates 1305 papers remained. The 1305 papers were filtered down to 95 papers based on the title and keywords to remove unrelated papers. Finally, the 95 papers were filtered based on abstract containing information about empirical validation e.g. case study and real-world application. If there were any doubt about the inclusion or exclusion of the papers based on the abstract, the papers were examined further by reading the body of the paper. Based on the previous filtering and the full body text the papers were filtered down to 21. The final 21 papers are from the period 2010 to 2020.

4 Results

4.1 Techniques for Autonomously Improvement of Systems

Previous studies present many different customized approaches for realizing some type of an autonomously improving system with little standardization of software components or implementation details. In Fig. 1 the distribution between the different types on learning approaches used in the papers are shown. Most of the ML papers apply an online learning approach [31–39], a few use offline [40–42], or a hybrid [43–46] which is a combination of both online and offline approaches, but the industrial deployed systems tends to have a lower level of autonomy or specifically focuses on a few numbers of challenges. A/B/n testing papers [5,47–50] simple adaption is done online in deployed systems. Figure 2 shows the distribution between dataset [32,34–36,41–43,45,46], simulation [33,37–39], and deployment [31,40,44] used for empirical validation of the systems. Most of the papers use datasets and simulation for validation and few deploy a system.

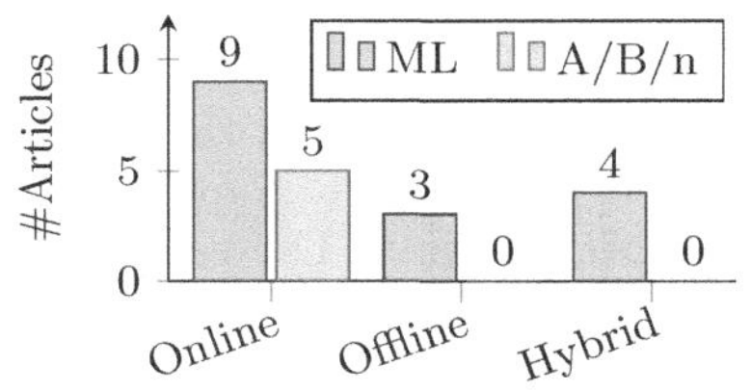

Fig. 1. Types of adaption

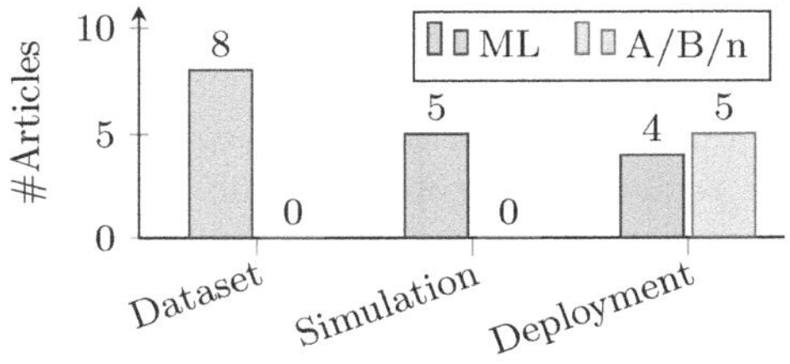

Fig. 2. Methods used for empirical validation

A/B experiments are already used in industry to improve performance. Several big companies perform A/B experimentation as a part of the development process to improve their systems [5]. Most often the data from A/B experimentation is used as basis for data-driven decision support. Before an A/B experiment is performed, human experts have determined the goal for the experiment and then find metrics that measure the performance in relation to the goal. Based on the goal and the metric, one or more experiments are designed that are believed to have an impact [50]. The next step is to deploy the experiments and then monitor and collect data about the system performance. The data collected during experimentation is analysed in comparison to the goal to conclude outcome. The deployment of experiments and the data-collection should be automated to be able to gather feedback from the experiments in an effective way. To perform successful experiments, resources must be invested in finding the different variants. The strategy on how to find the next variant highly affects the cost and efficiency of the experimentation process. The most basic strategy involves an exhausted search e.g. system parameters and settings.

Using machine learning to improve the system performance has been suggested in literature especially in the form of reinforcement learning used to minimize the cost of experimentation [51]. But also, genetic programming has been suggested as a candidate [38]. Reinforcement learning has been used to make computers learn how to play complex video games with human level performance which shows its potential [52]. Moving away from controlled simulations, such as games, into real-world system is difficult as real-world systems impose many considerations and limitations. One of the reinforcement learning techniques, multi-armed bandits (MAB), has been applied to optimize the search problems to find a solution with a lower cost.

In the literature two different types of approaches are used for dealing with deteriorating performance. The systems use either passive or active techniques to handle decreasing performance through additional experimentation.

Systems using a passive technique often rely on update of the ML model or parameters either based on the number of samples, a certain time span or by a human expert. Several approaches has been proposed that are based on the passive adaption [37]. Systems using passive adaption do not need to have the ability to detect changes since they are updated periodically. This technique is a more "open-loop" approach to adaption and requires resources to perform updates even though the system performance do not improve. This could be scheduled batch training of normal offline ML models [40] or learning based on each new data sample in system [43].

Systems using an active technique on the other hand relies on methods for detecting change in the environment or system and to react based on that knowledge [32] Online techniques are usually based on monitoring current systems statistics and model performance. A sub-sample or window of data is used to compute statistics required to determine if additional adaption is needed [45]. Supervised and unsupervised learning has been proposed as techniques for performing online learning by experimenting with model updates [51]. Unsupervised learning is used to provide labels for the supervised learning [46]. Concept drift detection can also be based on a combination of the two techniques [32].

4.2 Industry Domains

Autonomously improving systems and experimentation have a wide field of application for real-world problems but only few have actually been deployed in real-word systems. The literature in this review describe real-world application of their techniques. These cover many domains and various stages of maturity regarding deployment.

In Table 1 all the studies are grouped into different application areas. The focus of many studies is mainly on describing the theoretical solution based on a control loop with only little focus on how the system performs in a real context. However, studies often describe situations in which systems are deployed as simple test set-ups and do not involve practitioners from industry to invest real-world validation efforts [53]. The methods used for validation can be seen in Fig. 2. First, solutions use datasets to represent the system behaviour as a rough way to implement the system. Datasets are a good basis for a proof-of-concept but not ideal for a real-world deployment as challenges of integration and deployment is not considered. Second, simulation provides a basis for implementing a

Table 1. Previous studies categorized into application areas

Domain	Papers
Online services/Web	[5,33,46–49,51]
Data mining	[32,34,39,41,50]
Manufacturing	[36–38]
Network/Communication	[31,44]
Finance, fraud detection	[43]
Healthcare	[42]
Software development	[45]
Transportation	[34]
Water distribution	[40]

"real-world" system. However, in practice a simulation does not cover all possible variation in a non-stationary environment and noise of the real-world.

4.3 Challenges and Limitations

There are several challenges and limitations with the techniques and approaches that were identified in the literature review. In general, with more advanced techniques, such as reinforcement learning, limited testing is done with deployed real-world systems. As a result the challenges of deployment in real-world is not properly addressed [11,34]. Many techniques are proposed and tested with datasets or simulations. However, since datasets and simulators only estimate parts of real-world scenarios, real-world deployment is necessary to gain knowledge of system performance in a real scenario. Taking the next step from an experimental setup to a real-world setup requires more effort and work but it is necessary to increase the real-world impact.

5 Discussion

The purpose of this study is to provide an overview of existing research with focus on software engineering and real-world industrial application in the area of autonomously improving systems. In this section, we discuss the results of the review. Additionally, we summarize our findings in a structured model that provides an overview of existing techniques and their levels of autonomy.

When analysing the papers and the different techniques they develop or use, we see characteristics and trends in relation to the level of autonomy and focus on the methods. First, very few studies in academic literature addresses industrial autonomously improving systems in a holistic way including development, deployment, and maintenance of systems. Second, most studies use datasets or simulations for development and verification the solutions do not cover all limitations and challenges in a real-world industrial context such as operational cost, wear and tear, and lifetime of a system. The studies where the solution is deployed is often done in a simple or incomplete context that only addresses a limited set of conditions and do not generalize. Third, the correct use and application becomes increasingly harder when systems move from A/B testing to more complex machine learning techniques such as reinforcement learning, since the systems take on tasks that was previously solve be human experts. Additionally, the studies describing complex techniques often focus less on software engineering and production grade AI required for use in an industrial system. Therefore, it is important building on top of knowledge from a structured approach such as A/B/n testing when increasing the autonomy of a system by using machine learning.

5.1 Towards Industrial Autonomously Improving Systems

In Fig. 3, we present a model that presents activities for autonomously improving systems mapped with existing techniques with different levels of autonomy, techniques and ideas presented in literature in our literature review. The model defines autonomy levels based on existing techniques and how to integrate changes in a deployed system be leveraging existing techniques e.g. A/B experiments, Concept drift and multi-armed bandits.

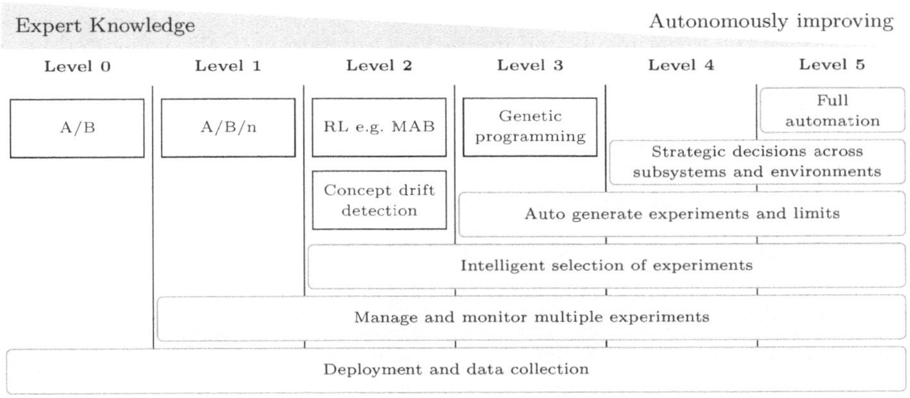

Fig. 3. Towards autonomously improving systems

At level 0, data collection and deployments must be automated as the basis of effective experimentation. This is the foundation for increasing the level of automation and autonomy. Triggered by a request the system will automatically deploy A/B experiments and collect data needed for evaluation of the experiments. This level does not include management or monitoring of the experiments, which makes it inefficient when running multiple experiments. At this level human experts must ensure that experiments do not affect each other, since this will make the test result invalid. This level of automation makes it feasible to run a limited amount of A/B experiments.

At level 1, the system is extended to include managing and monitoring of the experiments. The system manages multiple experiments simultaneously, with experiments deployed on one or distributed on several sub-systems. The system ensures that there are no conflicts between different experiments e.g. two tests controlling the same parameter. Besides direct conflicts based on parameters, experiments might conflict if two processes have indirect hidden dependencies. The system can handle multiple experiments supplied to the system but have no way of prioritizing between them. This level of automation support running many tests efficiently with less manual tasks, hence making A/B/n feasible. Levels 0 and 1 relates to the experimentation growth model for A/B experiments describing steps needed to increase the level of experimentation [5].

At level 2, the overall cost of performing experiments are minimized by providing an intelligent prioritization or selection of the experiments. One way of minimizing the cost is to reduce the amount of experiments and tasks that does not improve the system performance. Multi-armed bandits could be used to decrease the cost as the technique aims to optimize the search for a better solution. Also concept drift detection can detect when it is necessary to initiate or stop the experimentation process because of changes in the environment [32]. This level of automation supports running many experiments in an optimized way for a predefined sub-system under specified conditions and limitations for the operating environment.

At level 3, the experiments and limitations are automatically generated for a predefined sub-part of the whole system. The experiments should help generate new data and insights to improve the system without compromising the system performance. Hence, the experiments and parameters should be within system limits to avoid any permanent damage. An example is using machine learning to experiment with adaptation to different traffic and load scenarios with 78 pre-selected features while trying to increase 8 goal metrics without violating the goals during the experimentation [33].

At level 4, the system should be able to work without predefined sub-systems of the system. Fewer predefined parameters are needed for the system to perform experimentation compared to lower levels, since the system can adapt to and generalize knowledge, across different systems and environments using machine learning.

At level 5, the system is autonomously improving without or with only limited supervision from experts. The system can handle new environments and autonomously adjust to new situations with limited human expert knowledge and supervision.

5.2 Future Work

Autonomously improving systems is a field of active research, trying to improve and increase the level of autonomy in systems. Different domains develop new solutions and algorithms and validate the improved performance on datasets or simple setups. To increase and demonstrate real-world impact industry practitioners should be included in the validation efforts [53]. However, to demonstrate industrial impact an unified view of whole process and problems must be considered from low to high levels of autonomy proposed in our proposed model. We present the following research challenges:

1. *How to autonomously generate alternatives e.g. parameters and features for experiments?*
2. *How to ensure a minimum level of performance for each alternative?*
3. *How to deploy experiments with alternatives in an already deployed system?*
4. *How to improve capacity and efficiency of an expensive experimentation process while keeping the quality?*
5. *How to generalize goals across subsystems and different environments?*
6. *How to include indirect effects e.g. lifetime, effects on other systems that are not easily measured or monitored?*
7. *How to increase the level of industry collaboration for industrial validation with companies?*

6 Conclusion

To autonomously improve performance in deployed systems, companies need to continuously collect system data and perform experiments. Today several companies already perform non-autonomous experimentation to make decisions based on data. Although there are several recent studies in algorithms to implement autonomously improving systems, companies struggle to implement the systems and how to choose which techniques to use due to the lack of research concerning software engineering and holistic evaluation of algorithms. Our research reveals overall techniques for autonomously improving system from simple experiments e.g. A/B experimentation, to more complicated machine learning approaches such as multi-armed bandits. Within machine learning, reinforcement learning is the most promising candidate for improving system performance with experimentation.

A correctly implemented autonomously improving system will improve business outcomes by being able to offer performance improvements or adaptation to changes without increasing the need of human-resources. This would make it possible to provide highly customized systems for customers based upon their preferences and priories at reduced effort and cost for the companies.

We summarize our finding in a model that helps mapping the current automation levels in the context of autonomously improving systems. Based on the findings in this paper we also identify the main research challenges in relation to implementation and industrial deployment of autonomously improving systems.

References

1. Benhamou, P.Y., et al.: Closed-loop insulin delivery in adults with type 1 diabetes in real-life conditions: a 12-week multicentre, open-label randomised controlled crossover trial. Lancet Digit. Health **1**(1), e17–e25 (2019)

2. Chess, D.M., Kephart, J.O.: The vision of autonomic computing. Computer **36**(1), 41–50 (2003)
3. IBM: An architectural blueprint for autonomic computing. IBM White Pap. **36**(June), 34 (2006). https://doi.org/10.1021/am900608j. ISSN 19448244
4. Olsson, H.H., Bosch, J.: Post-deployment data collection in software-intensive embedded products. Contin. Softw. Eng. **9783319112**, 143–154 (2014). https://doi.org/10.1007/978-3-319-11283-1-12
5. Fabijan, A., Dmitriev, P., McFarland, C., Vermeer, L., Olsson, H.H., Bosch, J.: Experimentation growth: evolving trustworthy A/B testing capabilities in online software companies. J. Softw. Evol. Process **30**(12), 1–23 (2018). https://doi.org/10.1002/smr.2113
6. Tamburrelli, G., Margara, A.: Towards automated A/B testing. In: Le Goues, C., Yoo, S. (eds.) SSBSE 2014. LNCS, vol. 8636, pp. 184–198. Springer, Cham (2014). https://doi.org/10.1007/978-3-319-09940-8_13
7. Mattos, D.I., Bosch, J., Olsson, H.H.: Mult-armed bandits in the wild: pitfalls and strategies in online experiments. Inf. Softw. Technol. **113**(April 2018), 68–81 (2019)
8. Koulouriotis, D.E., Xanthopoulos, A.: Reinforcement learning and evolutionary algorithms for non-stationary multi-armed bandit problems. Appl. Math. Comput. **196**(2), 913–922 (2008). https://doi.org/10.1016/j.amc.2007.07.043. ISSN 00963003
9. Krawczyk, B., Minku, L.L., Gama, J., Stefanowski, J., Woźniak, M.: Ensemble learning for data stream analysis: a survey. Inf. Fusion **37**, 132–156 (2017). https://doi.org/10.1016/j.inffus.2017.02.004. ISSN 15662535
10. Parisi, G.I., Kemker, R., Part, J.L., Kanan, C., Wermter, S.: Continual lifelong learning with neural networks: a review. Neural Netw. **113**, 54–71 (2019). https://doi.org/10.1016/j.neunet.2019.01.012. ISSN 18792782
11. Dulac-Arnold, G., Mankowitz, D., Hester, T.: Challenges of Real-World Reinforcement Learning (2019). http://arxiv.org/abs/1904.12901
12. Lu, J., Liu, A., Dong, F., Feng, G., Gama, J., Zhang, G.: Learning under concept drift: a review. IEEE Trans. Knowl. Data Eng. **31**(12), 2346–2363 (2019). https://doi.org/10.1109/TKDE.2018.2876857. ISSN 15582191
13. Kohavi, R., Longbotham, R., Sommerfield, D., Henne, R.M.: Controlled experiments on the web: survey and practical guide. Data Min. Knowl. Disc. **18**(1), 140–181 (2009). https://doi.org/10.1007/s10618-008-0114-1. ISSN 13845810
14. Mattos, D.I., Bosch, J., Holmström Olsson, H.: ACE: easy deployment of field optimization experiments. In: Bures, T., Duchien, L., Inverardi, P. (eds.) ECSA 2019. LNCS, vol. 11681, pp. 264–279. Springer, Cham (2019). https://doi.org/10.1007/978-3-030-29983-5_18
15. Schermann, G., Cito, J., Leitner, P., Zdun, U., Gall, H.C.: We're doing it live: a multi-method empirical study on continuous experimentation. Inf. Softw. Technol. **99**(February), 41–57 (2018)
16. Kohavi, R., Longbotham, R.: Online controlled experiments and A/B testing. In: Sammut, C., Webb, G.I. (eds.) Encyclopedia of Machine Learning and Data Mining. Springer, Boston (2017). https://doi.org/10.1007/978-1-4899-7687-1_891
17. Burtini, G., Loeppky, J., Lawrence, R.: A Survey of Online Experiment Design with the Stochastic Multi-Armed Bandit, pp. 1–49 (2015)
18. Thrun, S., Mitchell, T.M.: Lifelong robot learning. Robot. Auton. Syst. **15**(1–2), 25–46 (1995). https://doi.org/10.1016/0921-8890(95)00004-Y. ISSN 09218890
19. De Lange, M., et al.: Continual learning: A comparative study on how to defy forgetting in classification tasks, pp. 1–23 (2019)

20. Redmon, J., Divvala, S., Girshick, R., Farhadi, A.: You only look once: unified, real-time object detection. In: Proceedings of the IEEE Computer Society Conference on Computer Vision and Pattern Recognition, December 2016, pp. 779–788 (2016). https://doi.org/10.1109/CVPR.2016.91. ISSN 10636919
21. Howard, A.G., et al.: MobileNets: Efficient Convolutional Neural Networks for Mobile Vision Applications (2017)
22. Diethe, T., Borchert, T., Thereska, E., Balle, B., Lawrence, N.: Continual Learning in Practice, (Nips) (2019). http://arxiv.org/abs/1903.05202
23. Song, H., Triguero, I., Özcan, E.: A review on the self and dual interactions between machine learning and optimisation. Prog. Artif. Intell. **8**(2), 143–165 (2019). https://doi.org/10.1007/s13748-019-00185-z
24. Grua, E.M., Malavolta, I., Lago, P.: Self-adaptation in mobile apps: a systematic literature study. In: ICSE Workshop on Software Engineering for Adaptive and Self-Managing Systems, May 2019, pp. 51–62 (2019). https://doi.org/10.1109/SEAMS.2019.00016. ISSN 21567891
25. Muccini, H., Weyns, D.: Self-adaptation for cyber-physical systems: a systematic literature review. In: 2016 IEEE/ACM 11th International Symposium on Software Engineering for Adaptive and Self-Managing Systems (SEAMS), pp. 75–81 (2016). https://doi.org/10.1109/SEAMS.2016.016
26. Gama, J., Zliobaite, I., Bifet, A., Pechenizkiy, M., Bouchachia, A.: A survey on concept drift adaptation. ACM Comput. Surv. **46**(4), 1–37 (2014). https://doi.org/10.1145/2523813. ISSN 15577341
27. Kitchenham, B.: Procedures for Performing Systematic Reviews, Keele University 33, 1–26, Keele, UK (2004)
28. Kroll, A.: Drivers of performance information use: systematic literature review and directions for future research. Public Perform. Manage. Rev. **38**(3), 459–486 (2015). https://doi.org/10.1080/15309576.2015.1006469. ISSN 15579271
29. Gaudette, M., Roult, R., Lefebvre, S.: Winter Olympic games, cities, and tourism: a systematic literature review in this domain. J. Sport Tour. **21**(4), 287–313 (2017). https://doi.org/10.1080/14775085.2017.1389298. ISSN 10295399
30. Fischer, K., Ekener-Petersen, E., Rydhmer, L., Björnberg, K.E.: Social impacts of GM crops in agriculture: a systematic literature review. Sustain. (Switz.) **7**(7), 8598–8620 (2015). https://doi.org/10.3390/su7078598. ISSN 20711050
31. Kasten, E.P., McKinley, P.K.: MESO: supporting online decision making in autonomic computing systems. IEEE Trans. Knowl. Data Eng. **19**(4), 485–499 (2007). https://doi.org/10.1109/TKDE.2007.1000. ISSN 10414347
32. Minku, L.L., White, A.P., Yao, X.: The impact of diversity on online ensemble learning in the presence of concept drift. IEEE Trans. Knowl. Data Eng. **22**(5), 730–742 (2010). https://doi.org/10.1109/TKDE.2009.156. ISSN 10414347
33. Esfahani, N., Elkhodary, A., Malek, S.: A learning-based framework for engineering feature-oriented self-adaptive software systems. IEEE Trans. Softw. Eng. **39**(11), 1467–1493 (2013). https://doi.org/10.1109/TSE.2013.37. ISSN 00985589
34. Moreira-Matias, L., Gama, J., Mendes-Moreira, J.: Concept neurons – handling drift issues for real-time industrial data mining. In: Berendt, B., et al. (eds.) ECML PKDD 2016, Part III. LNCS (LNAI), vol. 9853, pp. 96–111. Springer, Cham (2016). https://doi.org/10.1007/978-3-319-46131-1_18
35. Filho, R.R., Porter, B.: Defining emergent software using continuous self-assembly, perception, and learning. In: ACM Transactions on Autonomous and Adaptive Systems, vol. 12. Association for Computing Machinery (2017). https://doi.org/10.1145/3092691

36. Mayer, C., Mayer, R., Abdo, M.: Grand challenge: StreamLearner - distributed incremental machine learning on event streams. In: DEBS 2017 - Proceedings of the 11th ACM International Conference on Distributed Event-Based Systems, pp. 298–303. Association for Computing Machinery Inc. (2017). https://doi.org/10.1145/3093742.3095103. ISBN 9781450350655
37. Carvajal Soto, J.A., Tavakolizadeh, F., Gyulai, D.: An online machine learning framework for early detection of product failures in an industry 4.0 context. Int. J. Comput. Integr. Manuf. **32**(4–5), 452–465 (2019)
38. del Campo, I., Martínez, V., Echanobe, J., Asua, E., Finker, R., Basterretxea, K.: A versatile hardware/software platform for personalized driver assistance based on online sequential extreme learning machines. Neural Comput. Appl. **31**(12), 8871–8886 (2019). https://doi.org/10.1007/s00521-019-04386-4
39. Ren, S., et al.: Selection-based resampling ensemble algorithm for nonstationary imbalanced stream data learning. Knowl.-Based Syst. **163**, 705–722 (2019)
40. Mounce, S.R., Boxall, J.B.: Implementation of an on-line artificial intelligence district meter area flow meter data analysis system for abnormality detection: a case study. Water Sci. Technol. Water Supply **10**(3), 437–444 (2010). https://doi.org/10.2166/ws.2010.697. ISSN 16069749
41. Schölkopf, B., Janzing, D., Peters, J., Sgouritsa, E., Zhang, K., Mooij, J.: On causal and anticausal learning.In: Proceedings of the 29th International Conference on Machine Learning, ICML 2012, vol. 2, pp. 1255–1262 (2012)
42. Sutton, J.R., Mahajan, R., Akbilgic, O., Kamaleswaran, R.: PhysOnline: an open source machine learning pipeline for real-time analysis of streaming physiological waveform. IEEE J. Biomed. Health Inform. **23**(1), 59–65 (2019)
43. Artikis, A., et al.: Industry paper: a prototype for credit card fraud management. In: DEBS 2017 - Proceedings of the 11th ACM International Conference on Distributed Event-Based Systems, pp. 249–260 (2017). https://doi.org/10.1145/3093742.3093912
44. Appelt, D., Nguyen, C.D., Panichella, A., Briand, L.C.: A machine-learning-driven evolutionary approach for testing web application firewalls. IEEE Trans. Reliab. **67**(3), 733–757 (2018). https://doi.org/10.1109/TR.2018.2805763. ISSN 00189529
45. Kabir, M.A., Keung, J.W., Benniny, K.E., Zhang, M.: Assessing the significant impact of concept drift in software defect prediction. In: Proceedings - International Computer Software and Applications Conference, vol. 1, pp. 53–58 (2019). https://doi.org/10.1109/COMPSAC.2019.00017. ISSN 07303157
46. Washha, M., Qaroush, A., Mezghani, M., Sedes, F.: Unsupervised collective-based framework for dynamic retraining of supervised real-time spam tweets detection model. Expert Syst. Appl. **135**, 129–152 (2019)
47. Belluf, T., Xavier, L., Giglio, R.: Case study on the business value impact of personalized recommendations on a large online retailer. In: RecSys'12 - Proceedings of the 6th ACM Conference on Recommender Systems (2012)
48. Fabijan, A., Dmitriev, P., Olsson, H.H., Bosch, J.: The benefits of controlled experimentation at scale. In: Proceedings - 43rd Euromicro Conference on Software Engineering and Advanced Applications, SEAA 2017 (2017)
49. Fabijan, A., Dmitriev, P., Olsson, H.H., Bosch, J.: Effective online controlled experiment analysis at large scale. In: Proceedings - 44th Euromicro Conference on Software Engineering and Advanced Applications, SEAA 2018 (2018)
50. Fabijan, A., Dmitriev, P., Olsson, H.H., Bosch, J.: The online controlled experiment lifecycle. IEEE Softw. **PP**(1), 1 (2018)
51. Filho, R., Porter, B.: Defining emergent software using continuous self-assembly, perception, and learning. ACM Trans. Auton. Adapt. Syst. **12**(3), 1–25 (2017)

52. Mnih, V., et al.: Human-level control through deep reinforcement learning. Nature **518**(7540), 529–533 (2015)
53. Weyns, D.: Software engineering of self-adaptive systems: an organised tour and future challenges. In: Handbook of Software Engineering, pp. 1–41 (2017)

Industrial Agile Transformations Lacking Business Emphasis: Results from a Nordic Survey Study

Petri Kettunen[1(✉)], Maarit Laanti[2], Fabian Fagerholm[3], Tommi Mikkonen[1], and Tomi Männistö[1]

[1] University of Helsinki, Helsinki, Finland
{petri.kettunen,tommi.mikkonen,tomi.mannisto}@helsinki.fi
[2] Nitor Delta, Helsinki, Finland
maarit.laanti@nitor.com
[3] Aalto University, Espoo, Finland
fabian.fagerholm@aalto.fi

Abstract. In agile transformations, agile principles and practices are applied across the organization – ultimately for an agile enterprise. Such company-wide changes are not straightforward and there are research needs to understand how they are successfully conducted and sustained. We have recently done an industrial agile survey in Finland (2018) and in Sweden (2019). The findings suggest that there are many goals for companies to become (more) agile. Operational goals (productivity, quality) and responsiveness to customer/market changes are the most often reported ones, but higher-level business goals (new product development, new business innovations) appear to be less common. There are many ways to conduct agile transformations. Not all companies display a clear strategy. Operational goals appear to be more in focus than the business strategic ones and the overall agility of the company. Overall, our survey results suggest that companies put more emphasis on operational and organizational agility than business and enterprise agility. We suggest that each company should declare a clear purpose and well-defined business goals for the agile transformation.

Keywords: Agile transformation · Agile software development · Business agility · Enterprise agility · Survey

1 Introduction

Agile transformations can in general range from small-scale, local changes and transitions to full-scale enterprise transformations. In software organizations, such developments mean typically advancing from agile adoptions in software teams to R&D organization (e.g., product management) and related business functions and – ultimately – to transforming the entire company [1, 2]. Agile principles and practices are then applied across the organization. Still, the terminology and conceiving of agile transformations in software-related organizations vary [3]. Current active research themes and

E. Klotins and K. Wnuk (Eds.): ICSOB 2020, LNBIP 407, pp. 46–54, 2021.
https://doi.org/10.1007/978-3-030-67292-8_4

topics include continuous operations (CI, CD, delivery) and DevOps [4]. More research has been called for large-scale agile transformations and enterprise agility [5].

In this paper, we present current results about agile transformations in industry organizations based on our recent survey study done in Finland in 2018 and in Sweden in 2019. Previously, we have published selected overall results of the survey, focusing on questions about agile transformation and SAFe adoption in Finland [6–8]. The key contribution of this continuation paper is in aggregating a combination of the distinct survey questions for answering a higher-level research question: *What types of agility do companies approach with their agile transformations?* In addition, we include new data from Sweden and previously unpublished results from the Finnish survey data.

2 Background and Method

This research effort started in Finland in 2018 from the industrial stance. Different companies may approach agile development and agility in different ways. Hence, we were interested in examining how agile companies really are nowadays and how they currently practice agile software development. Moreover, we wanted to go beyond team levels to large-scale agile and enterprise agility. We were also interested in the future. In all, we targeted to investigate not just ICT companies but industries in general.

The research method was descriptive survey with no one particular theory or maturity model as the underlying basis. The questionnaire included agile transformation elements. The questions and the predefined answer choices were compiled by referring to selected prior surveys and by deriving from own industrial experiences and prior research. Most of the questions were closed type with an open free-text choice. The final version consisted of total of 50 questions (including background items). All content questions were non-mandatory and had a N/A option. For data collection, the survey was implemented with a commercial web-based online questionnaire tool.

In 2018 in Finland, the questionnaire was distributed with one Finnish consulting company mailing list mass postings and with social media. In 2019, we repeated the survey in Sweden. The original questionnaire in Finnish/English was extended with a Swedish choice. The survey call was distributed in the same manner as in Finland.

3 Results

We received 118 finished responses in Finland (2018) and 15 in Sweden (2019). Not everyone responded to every question. Below we report based on the provided data.

Figure 1 presents the key demographics. ICT was the most frequently reported sector (line of business). Notably, 70% of the respondents represented other industries.

Company's State of Agile. The first section of the questionnaire included the following question item: (Q0) *When has there been executed or planned agile transformation in Your company most recently?* One of the answer choices was 'Not done/planned agile transformation'. In Finland 16% (19/118) and in Sweden 33% (5/15) respondents reported so, respectively. In the following result tables (Table 1, 2, 3, 4 and Table 5), we have included also those respondents.

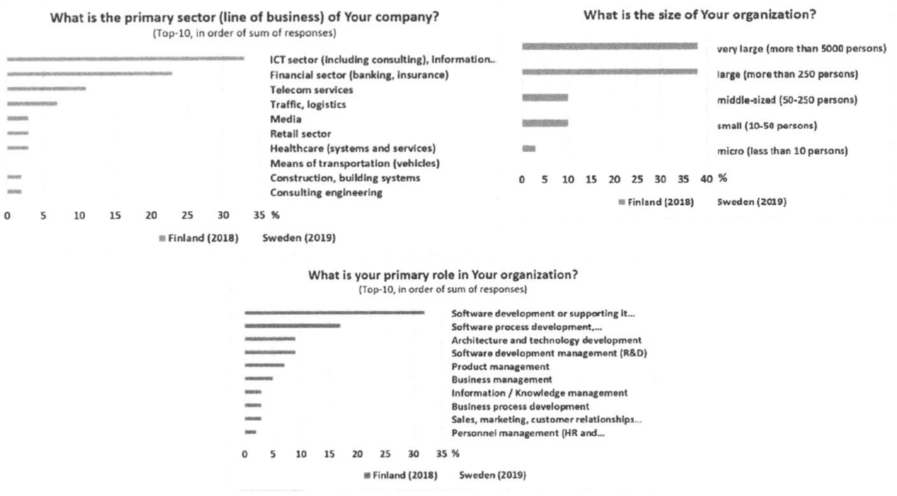

Fig. 1. Demographical information of the organizations and respondents.

Agile Company Transformation. The questionnaire section of agile transformations comprised the following questions:

- Q1: *Why does Your company want to become more agile?*
- Q2: *How is Your company/has Your company been executing agile transformation?*
- Q3: *What results and experiences does the company have of agile development?*
- Q4: *Where is the current overall focus of agility in Your company?*

There are different needs and goals for companies to become (more) agile as shown in Table 1. Operational goals (productivity, quality) and responsiveness to customer/market changes are typical reasons for companies to improve their performances. However, higher-level business goals (new product development, new business innovations) appear to be less common.

There are many ways of conducting agile transformations, as indicated in Table 2. Not all display a clear strategy. This could possibly mean that companies do not address agility fully strategically from a company-level business perspective. When the changes are not decisively initiated top-down, the transformations may lack established leadership supported by the top management. External consultants may then not be able support the changes most effectively.

Agile development can bring various, even company-wide effects and outcomes. Three biggest benefits/advantages/improvements reported for the question Q3 (open comment) were transparency and visibility, speed, and manageability and controllability. Business benefits were not highlighted, indicating an operational emphasis.

In principle, agile transformations involve all areas and elements of the organizations. Companies may be focusing on changing different aspects at different times as shown in Table 3. Operational goals appear to be more emphasized than the business strategic ones and the overall agility of the company.

Table 1. (Q1) Why does Your company want to become more agile?

ANSWER CHOICES (multi choice allowed) In order of sum of responses, N:# of responses including N/A answers	*Finland* (2018) % out of N (N = 86, N/A = 2)	*Sweden* (2019) % out of N (N = 8, N/A = 0)
Productivity and quality (operative)	72	50
Responsiveness to customer/market changes (new features)	65	75
Job satisfaction	53	38
Fast/continuous organizational learning in rapidly changing operating environments	51	50
Competitive and desirable products (new product development)	48	50
Project manageability	48	38
Strategic and organizational flexibility	44	63
Customer experience	44	50
Customer satisfaction	43	50
New business (product and service innovation)	33	25
User experience (UX)	31	25
Employer brand	29	13
Continuous budgeting, resourcing	21	25
Company image	21	0
Customers require/wish (agile development)	15	13
Other	3	29

Agile Future of the Company. In this section of the questionnaire, the respondents were asked to view the future (until 2020) with four questions including the following ones:

- Q5: *What changes does Your company plan about the use of agile methods, practices or models in the future?*
- Q6: *What factors are important when Your company recruits software development talents?*

Continuous adaptation is inherent in agile journeys. Changes in use of agile methods (adopting new methods, practices or models/abandoning or replacing methods, practices or models in use) are planned in some cases, but companies also report no planned changes. Table 4 presents, what particular changes the respondents described in open comments considering new methods, practices or models. The companies may possibly have be many different reasons for adopting the SAFe framework and the Spotify model apart from distinct business improvements.

Table 2. (Q2) How is Your company/has Your company been executing agile transformation?

ANSWER CHOICES (multi choice allowed) In order of sum of responses, N: # of responses including N/A answers	*Finland* (2018) % out of N (N = 85, N/A = 2)	*Sweden* (2019) % out of N (N = 8, N/A = 0)
The company has had external consultants (subcontracting) to assist in the change	61	38
There is a dedicated agile support team in the company	45	38
The company has initiated the change bottom-up (from teams) in the organization	40	25
The company has initiated the change top-down in the organization	29	25
The company has a strategy for adopting agile ways of working and practices	27	38
Self-made transformation in the company	15	50
In other ways	6	13

Table 3. (Q4) Where is the current overall focus of agility in Your company?

ANSWER CHOICES (multi choice allowed) In order of sum of responses, N: # of responses including N/A answers	*Finland* (2018) % out of N (N = 86, N/A = 2)	*Sweden* (2019) % out of N (N = 8, N/A = 0)
Operative goals (e.g., internal efficiency)	51	50
Organizational means (e.g., self-organizing teams)	48	50
Scaling agile development	41	38
Technological means (e.g., improved work methods)	40	25
Overall agility of the company	31	13
Strategic goals (e.g., speed advantage in the business sector)	23	50
No particular focusing	5	0
Other	2	13

There are many potential considerations for hiring software people in agile organizations as presented in Table 5. Software technical competence is the most important factor in recruitment. Suitability for an agile organization also weighs strongly. The value judgements appear to be less important, which may possibly indicate that business-orientation is not so emphasized for software operations.

Table 4. (Q5) What changes does Your company plan about the use of agile methods, practices or models in the future? – Our company plans to take into use new methods, practices or models.

ANSWERS (open comment) In order of sum of occurrences, N: # of responses	*Finland* (2018) % out of N (N = 35)	*Sweden* (2019) % out of N (N = 2)
SAFe	20	0
In-house model, suitable practices	14	0
Spotify (model)	9	50
Tribes	9	0
Automation (test, release)	9	0
Customers, business development, other units	9	0
Portfolio management	6	0
MISC. (several nominations, other than the ones above)	29	50

Table 5. (Q6) What factors are important when Your company recruits software development talents? – Appraise the 3 most important ones.

ANSWER CHOICES (multi choice allowed) In order of sum of responses, N: # of responses including N/A answers	*Finland* (2018) % out of N (N = 111, N/A = 12)	*Sweden* (2019) % out of N (N = 11, N/A = 1)
Software technical competence	78	64
Suitability of the recruited person's character for agile organization (e.g., self-directing)	48	45
Practical competence of agile methods	41	27
Value judgements of the recruited person are in alignment with the values of our company	39	36
Domain competence	16	0
Value judgements of the recruited person are in alignment with the agile values	14	27
Agile methods certificates	4	0
Other	1	9

4 Discussion

Having presented the direct results in Sect. 3, we are in a position to analyze them further in order to gain deeper reflective insights and suggestions. Our survey questionnaire offers many possibilities for that. One obvious elaboration is to refine the summarized results in Table 1, 2, 3, 4 and Table 5 according to the demographical variables in Fig. 1.

One potentially insightful filter is to compare management and developer perspectives on agility. Figure 2 presents the summary results in Table 1 according to those roles. For contrasting, there are also software process/organization developers (agile coaches). Interestingly enough, managers put more weight on external business aims (New business (product and service innovation), Competitive and desirable products (new product development)) than the developers. This may indicate that the business emphasis is inherent for the managers, but it is not necessarily well-established organization-wide. Note, however, that since our data does not distinguish organizations, the respondents in Fig. 2 may be in different organizations.

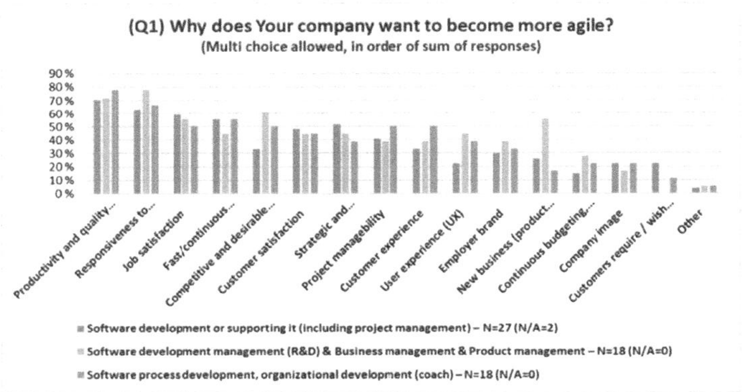

Fig. 2. (Q1) Why does Your company want to become more agile? (By roles).

In a similar vein, Fig. 3 refines the results in Table 3 according to the industry sectors. Interestingly, the overall agility of the company was reported as the primary focus area by the financial sector respondents. Strategic goals were stressed most in the ICT sector while scaling agile appeared to be most important in the telecom sector. These could possibly be explained by the current business trends in those sectors.

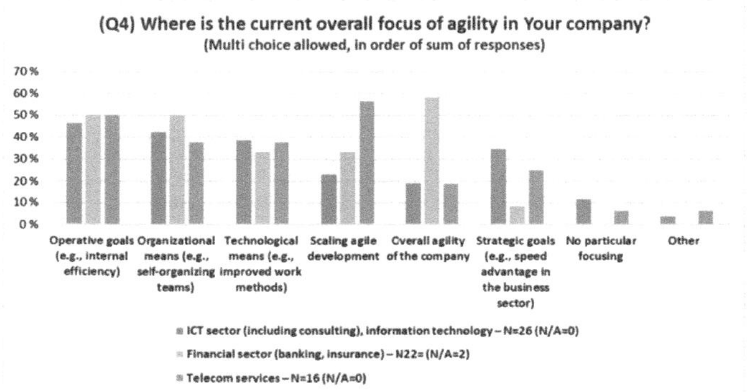

Fig. 3. (Q4) Where is the current overall focus of agility in Your company? (By sectors).

Agile transformation is currently a relevant and growing research field, and there are many possible reasoned viewpoints of agile transformations [3]. Conceptually, there are different types of agility: operational, organizational, strategic and business, and enterprise agility. Our survey results suggest that companies – at the time of responding – put more emphasis on operational and organizational agility than business and enterprise agility. However, achieving a well-functioning agile global software organization requires the inclusion of agility on the strategic business level and an organization-wide perspective. Agility is required beyond the software development functions and should cover product and service development and the inclusion of partner organizations and customers. There should be a clear purpose and well-defined rationale for the transformation (Q1). The strategy should fit for the purpose taking into account the particular organizational contingencies (Q2). The transformation should be continuously monitored and aligned with the strategic intent (Q3, Q4; Q2). Sustainable agility requires continuous adjustments and proactive preparation for the futures (Q5, Q6; Q3, Q4).

Finally, we have rationalized our industry-oriented questionnaire and the constraints and limitations of the survey research design earlier [7]. Most notably, we cannot tell the number of different organizations in our respondent population, and we refrain from judging how representative our sample is. Due to such statistical validity limitations, we make no attempt at generalizing the findings.

5 Conclusions

In this paper, we have presented industrial agile transformation findings based on Nordic agile survey data collected in Finland (2018) and in Sweden (2019) for answering a higher-level research question: *What types of agility do companies approach with their agile transformations?* Overall, the responses suggest that companies tend to put more emphasis on improving operational agility than on attaining higher-level business goals with strategic and business agility as agile enterprises.

Because of the significant disparity of the number of respondents in Finland and in Sweden, it was not feasible to compare the two countries here. The differences between the Finnish and Swedish industries and business environments could be taken into account for further reasoning about our results with respect to business goals [9, 10].

In the future, we plan to continue our survey research by collecting more data by repeating the survey possibly annually in Nordic countries. That would support longitudinal analysis with respect to our results so far in 2018–2019.

References

1. Olsson, H.H., Bosch, J.: Going digital: disruption and transformation in software-intensive embedded systems ecosystems. J. Softw. Evol. Process **32**, e2249 (2019)
2. Mancl, D., Fraser, S.D.: XP 2019 panel: business agility. In: Hoda, R. (ed.) XP 2019. LNBIP, vol. 364, pp. 149–153. Springer, Cham (2019). https://doi.org/10.1007/978-3-030-30126-2_18

3. Barroca, L., Dingsøyr, T., Mikalsen, M.: Agile transformation: a summary and research agenda from the first international workshop. In: Hoda, R. (ed.) XP 2019. LNBIP, vol. 364, pp. 3–9. Springer, Cham (2019). https://doi.org/10.1007/978-3-030-30126-2_1
4. Rodríguez, P., Mäntylä, M., Oivo, M., Lwakatare, L., Seppänen, P., Kuvaja, P.: Advances in using agile and lean processes for software development. In: Advances in Computers, vol. 113, pp. 135–224 (2019)
5. Prikladnicki, R., Lassenius, C., Carver, J.C.: Trends in agile: business agility. IEEE Softw. **37**(1), 78–80 (2020)
6. Kettunen, P., Laanti, M., Fagerholm, F., Mikkonen, T.: Agile in the era of digitalization: a finnish survey study. In: Franch, X., Männistö, T., Martínez-Fernández, S. (eds.) PROFES 2019. LNCS, vol. 11915, pp. 383–398. Springer, Cham (2019). https://doi.org/10.1007/978-3-030-35333-9_28
7. Kettunen, P., Laanti, M., Fagerholm, F., Mikkonen, T., Männistö, T.: Finnish enterprise agile transformations: a survey study. In: Hoda, R. (ed.) XP 2019. LNBIP, vol. 364, pp. 97–104. Springer, Cham (2019). https://doi.org/10.1007/978-3-030-30126-2_12
8. Laanti, M., Kettunen, P.: SAFe adoptions in Finland: a survey research. In: Hoda, R. (ed.) XP 2019. LNBIP, vol. 364, pp. 81–87. Springer, Cham (2019). https://doi.org/10.1007/978-3-030-30126-2_10
9. Pohjola, M.: Technology, investments, structural change and productivity – Finland in international comparison. Ministry of Economic Affairs and Employment, Helsinki, Finland (2020)
10. Ek, J.: Sector report for the software sector for 2020. Ministry of Economic Affairs and Employment, Helsinki, Finland (2020)

Essential Approaches to Dual-Track Agile: Results from a Grey Literature Review

Stefan Trieflinger[1(✉)], Jürgen Münch[1], Bernd Heisler[2], and Dominic Lang[3]

[1] Reutlingen University, Alteburgstraße 150, 72762 Reutlingen, Germany
{stefan.trieflinger,juergen.muench}@reutlingen-university.de

[2] Royal Dutch Shell, Schepersmaat 2, 9400HH Assen, The Netherlands
b.heisler@shell.com

[3] Robert Bosch GmbH, Hoferstraße 30, 71636 Ludwigsburg, Germany
Dominic.lang2@bosch.com

Abstract. Context: Nowadays, companies are challenged by increasing market dynamics, rapid changes and disruptive participants entering the market. To survive in such an environment, companies must be able to quickly discover product ideas that meet the needs of both customers and the company and deliver these products to customers. Dual-track agile is a new type of agile development that combines product discovery and delivery activities in parallel, iterative, and cyclical ways. At present, many companies have difficulties in finding and establishing suitable approaches for implementing dual-track agile in their business context. **Objective**: In order to gain a better understanding of how product discovery and product delivery can interact with each other and how this interaction can be implemented in practice, this paper aims to identify suitable approaches to dual-track agile. **Method:** We conducted a grey literature review (GLR) according to the guidelines to Garousi et al. **Results**: Several approaches that support the integration of product discovery with product delivery were identified. This paper presents a selection of these approaches, i.e., the Discovery-Delivery Cycle model, Now-Next-Later Product Roadmaps, Lean Sprints, Product Kata, and Dual-Track Scrum. The approaches differ in their granularity but are similar in their underlying rationales. All approaches aim to ensure that only validated ideas turn into products and thus promise to lead to products that are better received by their users.

Keywords: Product management · Dual-track agile · UX design · Product discovery · Agile development · Kata · Software engineering · Scrum

1 Introduction

Nowadays, companies are facing increasing market dynamics, rapidly evolving technologies and shifting user expectations. In addition, new market participants are trying to force established market participants out of the market through disruptive approaches. Therefore, it is increasingly difficult to plan and predict in advance which products, features or services should be developed in the future, especially long term. This situation

E. Klotins and K. Wnuk (Eds.): ICSOB 2020, LNBIP 407, pp. 55–69, 2021.
https://doi.org/10.1007/978-3-030-67292-8_5

often leads to the development of products, services or features that customers either do not want or cannot use [1, 2]. Cagan [3] points out that the reason for the former is mainly that the outputs do not deliver sufficient value to the customer, while for the latter the product is too complicated (i.e. insufficient usability), which means more trouble for the user than it is worth. Hence, companies are facing the challenge of quickly discovering the products/features to be built, and then delivering those products/features to the market as soon as possible.

Dual-track agile is a new type of agile development that combines product discovery (i.e., the ability of a company to validate products, services or features before implementation) and product delivery (i.e., the technical implementation and deployment of the identified outputs of product discovery) in parallel.

As a result, product delivery generates validated product backlog items, which are then implemented and deployed by product delivery (see Fig. 1) [4].

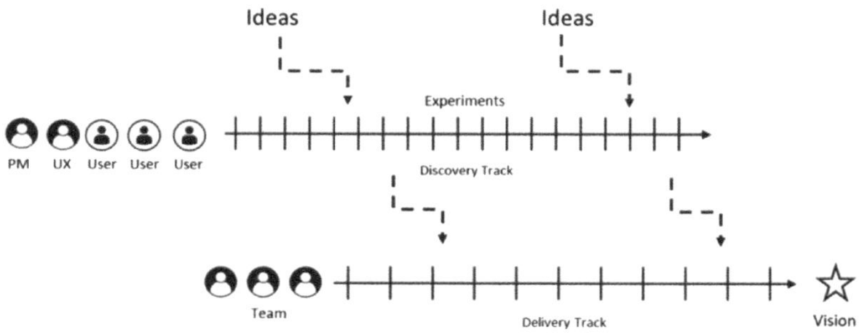

Fig. 1. Dual-track agile (based on [5])

The aim of dual-track agile is to ensure that only validated concepts for products, features and services are included into the product backlog, thus avoiding that outputs are developed that do not have the expected effects. Moreover, the simultaneous execution of product discovery and delivery allows the product team to adapt the solution to the needs of the customer more quickly. This leads to faster development and release cycles and reduces waste [6]. A recent study has shown that many companies see product discovery as a necessity but struggle in finding an approach to conduct product discovery and integrate it with delivery activities [7]. The scientific literature provides only little knowledge about how to integrate product discovery activities with product delivery activities. In order to close this gap, the aim of this paper is to identify suitable approaches that help companies to align product discovery with product delivery based on the analysis of the so-called 'grey literature' (e.g., white papers, articles, blogs, business books etc.). The rest of this paper is organized as follows: Sect. 2 discusses related work. Section 3 presents the research approach including a description of the chosen search strategy, the research questions and scope of the study, the applied selection process as well as the quality assessment we performed. In the following, the results of the study are described and the threats to validity are discussed. Finally a summary is given.

2 Related Work

In the scientific literature we have identified several studies that deal with the topic of dual-track agile in the context of the product management. First, Sedano et al. [8] conducted a study at one case company to use dual-track agile in order to reconcile human-centered development with agile methods. Therefore, the authors used two tracks: one that generates feature ideas and loads them into the backlog, while the second track unloads these ideas from the product backlog and delivers them as part of a software product. The authors point out that there exists a metaphorical gulf between both tracks. In this study, the two tracks were led by people from different backgrounds and involve different kinds of work and knowledge. Therefore, the authors recommend that the product manager should span the gap by aligning everyone on the business value. All observed teams used the product backlog as a bridge between the two tracks to facilitate the exchange of knowledge and for coordination purposes.

Shim and Lee [9] defined six criteria for developing an agile requirements engineering process and propose a lightweight agile requirements engineering approach to support continuous learning and improving effectively. The authors point out that an agile requirements engineering approach should support the following principles: 1) hypothesis (or assumption) oriented, 2) customer- and goal-driven, 3) external and internal goal modeling, 4) dual-track (concurrent with development and reflecting feedback regularly), 5) deriving test cases by specifying concrete scenarios, and 6) the enrichment of collaboration and communication. Based on these six criteria, the authors suggest an iterative requirements management approach consisting of the track's 'discovery' and 'delivery'. Within the discovery track, impact maps are used in order to identify customer needs and to formulate hypotheses. The delivery track focuses on the validation of these hypotheses and on the delivery of solutions. The authors suggest that the development team should use a Kanban Board. Moreover, the outputs of the two tracks are synchronized at the beginning and end of each iteration.

Besides this, we have identified some related literature in the context of 'continuous experimentation', which is described in the following. Fragerholm et al. [10] propose the RIGHT model for setting up an experimentation system for continuous customer experiments. The model describes an experimentation process in which assumptions for product and business development are derived from the business strategy and systematically tested. The results are used as a basis for further development of the strategy and the products. The authors point out that a suitable experimentation system requires at least 1) the ability to release minimum viable products or features with suitable instrumentations, 2) design and manage experiment plans, 3) link experiment results with a product strategy, and 4) manage a flexible business strategy. Bosch [11] presents a software development model, which focuses on three different aspects. First, the model addresses the continuous evolution of the software by frequently deploying new versions. Second, customers and customer usage data play a central role throughout the development process. Finally, the development is focused on innovation and testing as many ideas as possible with customers in order to drive customer satisfaction and hence increase revenue. Besides this, the authors mention that the development of software-intensive products includes the constant development of new hypotheses (ideas) and test these with groups of customers. Lindgren and Münch [12] performed semi-structured interviews and conducted a thematic data analysis in order to explore the state of the practice, challenges and success factors of experimentation in the software industry. The study revealed that although the principles of continuous experimentation resonated with industry practitioners, the state of the practice is not yet mature. Key challenges often relate to changing organizational culture, accelerating development cycle speed, and measuring customer value and product success. In particular, experimentation is rarely systematic and continuous, as companies do not use product user data to learn about customer needs. Further, the collaboration between R&D, product management and customers sometimes appears to be insufficient for supporting an innovative, experimental approach. Success factors include a supportive organizational culture, deep customer and domain knowledge as well as the availability of the relevant skills and tools to conduct experiments. Finally, Olsson et al. [13] developed the 'Hypothesis Experiment Data Driven Development' (HYPEX) model in order to support companies to close the open feedback loop to customers. In this context, features are being considered as hypotheses to be tested by using experiments. The usage of the model helps product management to get access to timely and accurate customer feedback. It helps to understand the customer value of features and to inform decisions as part of the roadmapping and prioritization process.

The existing scientific literature covers several aspects of dual-track agile such as methods and best practices or challenges related with this process. However, to the best of our knowledge studies which focus on approaches to conduct dual-track agile do not exists. An exception is the study conducted by Shim and Lee, which deals with the development of a dual-track agile approach. On the one hand, this study forms a good basis for our study. On the other hand, the present study offers practitioners alternative possibilities to the approach of Shim and Lee and can therefore be seen as an extension of this knowledge.

3 Research Approach

As this study aims to gain new insights it was designed exploratively. In order to conduct the study in a systematic and repeatable manner it follows the guidelines according to Garousi et al. [14], which consider three main phases: 1) planning the review, 2) conducting the review and 3) reporting the review (see Table 1).

3.1 Planning the Review

Identification of the Need of a GLR: First we assessed whether a GLR is the appropriate method for our study. Therefore we used the checklist according to Garousi et al. [14] as shown in Table 2. The authors of the checklist propose that if one or more questions can be answered positively, the conduction of a GLR is recommended, otherwise a Systematic Literature Review should be performed. Table 2 shows our answers regarding this study. The first question has been answered by a systematic literature review that is closely related to dual-track agile [15]. This review revealed that none of the identified papers addressed the relationships between product discovery activities and product delivery activities. Based on the checklist, a grey literature review is an appropriate research

Table 1. Design of the grey literature review [14]

Planning the review	• Identification of the need of a GLR
	• Formulation of the research questions and scope of the study
	• Definition and refinement of the search string
	• Determination of the inclusion and exclusion criteria
Conducting the review	• Usage of the search string
	• Performance of the study selection process
	• Conduction of the quality assessment
	• Data extraction
Reporting the review	• Writing down the findings as documentation

approach. Moreover, the conduction of expert interviews in previous research [2, 7] indicates that there is a high level of interest on the 'integration of product discovery with product delivery'. Therefore, a grey literature review can contribute to the transfer of practical knowledge to the scientific community and practitioners in industry. Besides this, a main side purpose of this systematic review of the grey literature is to provide background for positioning future research.

Table 2. Checklist according to Garousi et al. [14] to decide whether a grey literature review should be performed

ID	Question	Answer
1	Is the subject 'complex' and not solvable by considering only the formal literature?	Yes
2	Is there a lack of volume or quality of evidence, or a lack of consensus of outcome measurement in the formal literature?	No
3	Is the contextual information relevant to the subject under study?	Yes
4	Is it the goal to validate or corroborate scientific outcomes with practical experiences?	No
5	Is it the goal to challenge assumptions or falsify results from practice using academic research or vice versa?	No
6	Would a synthesis of insights and evidence from the industrial and academic community be useful to one or even both communities?	Yes
7	Is there a large volume of practitioner sources indicating high practitioner interest in a topic?	Yes

Research Question and Scope of the Study: Our study focuses on identifying suitable approaches for dual-track agile. In order to meet our objectives we have defined the following research question.

- RQ1: Which approaches are reported in the grey literature in order to conduct dual-track agile?

Identification of the Search String: In order to obtain appropriate results, we have tested the search terms and evolved them iteratively. After evaluating various options, we have defined the following search string.

(product discovery AND continuous) OR (product discovery AND dual track)

Inclusion/Exclusion Criteria: In order to filter relevant from irrelevant articles, we defined the inclusion and exclusion criteria as shown in Table 3.

Table 3. Inclusion and exclusion criteria

Inclusion	• The topic of the article is closely connected with the research question
	• The article was published in English
	• The URL is working and freely available
	• The publishing date is not older than one year
Exclusion	• The source is non text-based
	• The article contains duplicated content of a previously examined article
	• The article is not related to software development

3.2 Conducting the Review

Study Selection Process: The data retrieval process was performed by using the predefined search string and applying it to the Google search engine (google.com). The search was conducted on April 16th, 2020. Before starting the search, the browsers' search history was deleted, as selected language 'English' was chosen and any region as the region filter. The intention of these steps is that a minimum of influence of historical search could affect the results. In order to keep the scope of work manageable, we limited the analysis to the first 200 identified articles. The results of the search were exported to an Excel sheet and duplicates were filtered out. In addition to the search process, we conducted snowballing (i.e., considering further articles that are recommended in the article) and applied our inclusion and exclusion criteria. This led to one further article. Our applied search process is shown in Fig. 2.

Quality Assessment: The essential criterion for the quality assessment was that the reviewers were able to understand the suggested approach based on their practical experience. All steps of the selection process were carried out by one reviewer. Afterwards the results were discussed by three researchers in order to make a final inclusion and exclusion decision.

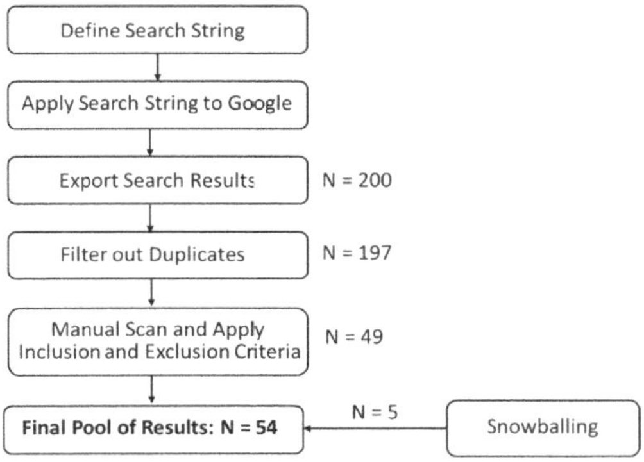

Fig. 2. Study selection process

4 Results

In order to answer our research question, we analyzed the relevant articles and identified suitable approaches for the conduction of dual-track agile. A list of the resulting 54 articles can be found on Figshare [16]. From this list, the authors have selected five essential approaches. These five approaches cover main aspects of the overall findings (such as proposed processes, interfaces between discovery and delivery, organizational aspects, and different granularity levels). These approaches are described in the following.

4.1 Discovery-Delivery Cycle: Pay to Learn/Pay to Build

One suggestion to practice dual-track agile is the conduction of discovery-delivery cycles (see Fig. 3) [17]. Within this method product discovery is conducted in the cycle "pay to learn", while product delivery is carried out in the cycle "pay to build". The process starts in the cycle "pay to learn" with the collection of ideas, for example by conducting interviews with potential customers and all relevant internal stakeholders. Based on these ideas, one or several hypotheses are defined in order to validate each idea. Experiments are used to test the hypotheses. Ideas that can be considered as successful based on the experiment results can go into the product backlog. They are thus handed over to product delivery, i.e., the "pay to build" cycle. Here, a first version of an idea is implemented and delivered it to the customers. The delivery team refines the idea into small timeboxed activities, resulting for example in a beta launch for a small pool of customers in order to test it in the real world. The product team receives continuous feedback from the customers. Thus, it learns not only after the launch of the final product, but also during the development stage. Moreover, this feedback serves as input for the ideation of new ideas in order to improve or extend the current version of the product. These ideas are input for the next discovery cycle.

4.2 Now-Next-Later Product Roadmap

Another approach to integrate product discovery activities with product delivery is to use product roadmaps. A well-suited structure for this integration is the 'now-next-later

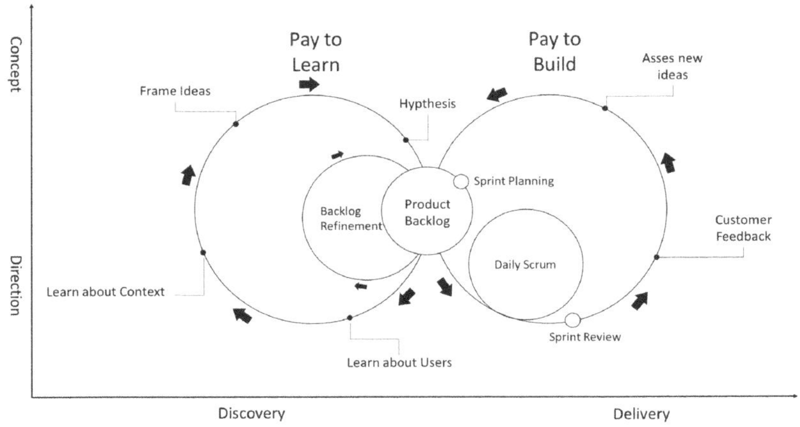

Fig. 3. Discovery-delivery cycle (based on [17])

product roadmap' format, often also referred to as 'outcome-driven product roadmap' or 'theme-based product roadmap'. Now-next-later product roadmaps support the delivery of products, features or services based on customer and business value. In comparison to outcome-driven roadmaps, theme-based roadmaps provide an addition layer of aggregation (themes), from which the outcomes to be achieved are derived. Usually both roadmap formats indicate the time horizon by the three columns 'now', 'next' and 'later' (in contrast to time-based roadmaps). The 'now' column describes the tasks the product team is currently working on, the 'next' column is about discovering the tasks the product team will work on in the near future, and the 'later' column shows which themes the product team would like to work on in the long-time horizon.

The now-next-later roadmap supports dual-track agile in the following ways: in the 'now' phase, features and products are implemented for which there is a high degree of certainty that they fulfill the underlying assumptions and have the expected effects. They have already gone through the discovery phase. Thus, in the delivery track mainly things are implemented that have been tested in the discovery track. In parallel, the discovery track determines which features are to be developed in the 'next' phase. For this purpose, experiments are usually conducted to see how the planned outcomes can be achieved. Often, prototypes or so-called minimum viable products (MVPs) are developed to support the conduction of experiments. For the so-called 'later' phase, themes are defined that are not further detailed. This task affects both, the delivery track and the discovery track and it is usually performed by strategic product management.

In more detail, dual-track agile starts with the decision of the product team which theme or outcome should be tackled. Then hypotheses are formulated by deriving possible solutions (outputs) in order to satisfy the previously selected themes or outcomes. An example of a hypothesis would be: "by introducing the payment method 'PayPal', we will increase our conversion rate by 15% by the end of the year". In order to validate the hypothesis (i.e. whether the outputs contribute to achieving the outcomes), prototypes are used to conduct one or several experiments. An example experiments to validate the hypothesis mentioned above could be to perform an A/B test to validate whether the number of checkouts is increased by adding the payment method 'PayPal' and those contributes to the increase of the conversion rate. In case the hypothesis is validated positively (i.e. the experiment shows that the output contributes to achieving the desired result), the corresponding outputs are moved to the 'now column' and thus handed over to the product delivery for implementation. This ensures that only validated outputs enter the product backlog and are released for implementation. In case the hypothesis is validated negatively, the corresponding output must be reconsidered, and alternatives may have to be validated. The 'now-next-later product roadmap' can be seen as a document and mechanism, that helps to synchronize the different tasks of the delivery and the discovery track and to integrate these tasks into a flexible product planning process [1, 18] (Fig. 4).

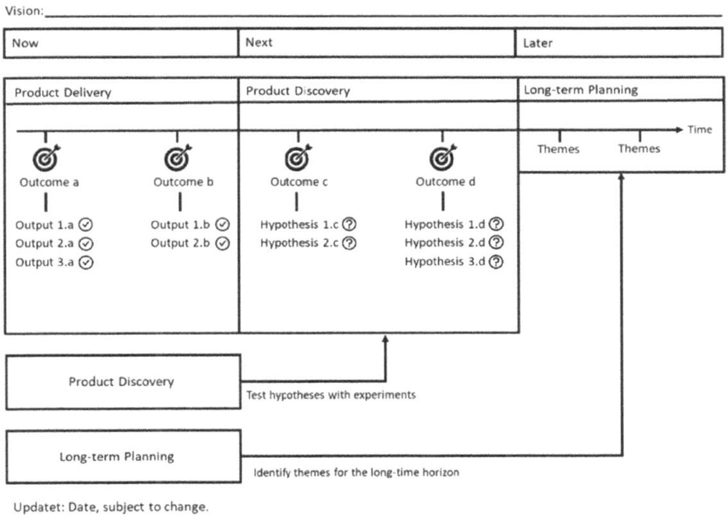

Fig. 4. Now-next-later-roadmap (based on [18])

4.3 Lean Sprint

The lean sprint developed by Maurya [19] can be seen as another approach to conduct dual-track agile. A lean sprint (see Fig. 5) is a time-boxed iteration cycle in order to generate, rank and test new ideas [19]. The sprint starts with a 'sprint planning meeting' and ends with a 'sprint review meeting'. The focus of both meetings is that the involved persons come together in order to plan activities regarding the strategic direction, future experiments as well as to share results. During the sprint, the team meets regularly to coordinate tasks by using a short daily stand-up meeting. A lean sprint consists of five phases including product discovery and product delivery activities, which are described in the following.

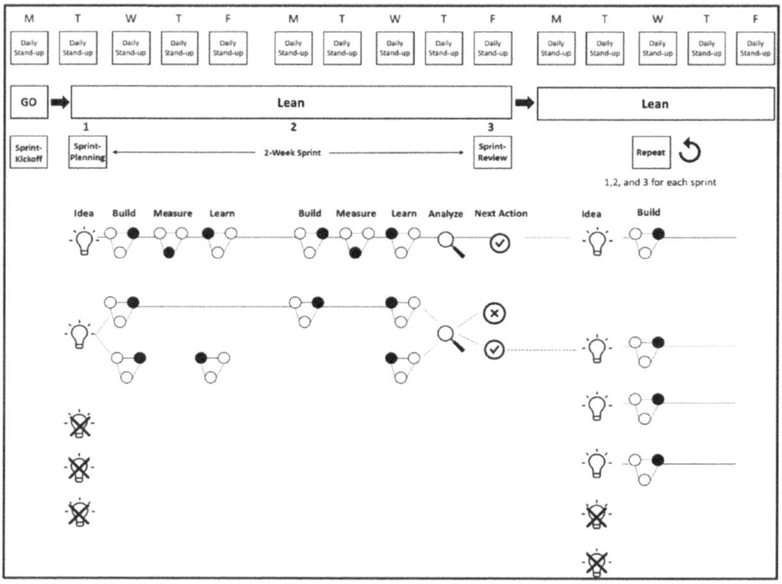

Fig. 5. Lean sprint (based on [19])

Within this model product discovery starts in the first phase 'expose problems'. This includes the composition of a team that must be small, multidisciplinary, and semi-autonomous. The author recommends building a cross-functional team including designers, developers and marketers in order to develop a variety of ideas. In addition, a sprint master should be introduced, who leads and steers the sprints. After the team composition, it is recommended to conduct a 'lean-sprint-kick-off meeting' in order to align and orient the team as well as to share goals. Ideally, this meeting should focus on the following issues: 1) set the context (e.g., how did the problem to solve arise, what has been done so far or how much time should be invested to solve the problem), 2) describe the traction model (what are significant milestones from idea to scale), 3) identify the constraint in the business model, and 4) set expectations (assign the team with big goals under tight constraints). In the phase 'define solutions' the team works on formulating a validation plan, i.e., a plan for achieving the formulated goal. This should be done individually by each team member in order to avoid group thinking and to obtain a wider diversity of ideas. After the generation of possible validation plans it is necessary to rank and shortlist these proposals as well as to define experiments for the current sprint. This is executed in the phase 'short-list solutions', more specifically within the 'sprint planning meeting'. The 'sprint planning meeting' officially starts the sprint. At this point the handover from product discovery to product delivery takes place. The reason is that for the conduction of the previously defined experiments, MVPs or prototypes are required, which are provided by product delivery. In the phase 'test solution', each experiment goes through a 'build-measure-learn-cycle'. 'Build' means the development of a prototype or MVP (as described in the phase short-list solutions), 'measure' indicates the identification of appropriate metrics in order to obtain at which point in time progress has been made and 'learn' refers to the analysis of the results of the experiments against the goals. Moreover, it is possible to run more than one experiment per validation plan during a sprint, but all experiments need to complete within a sprint time-box window. Finally, a sprint review meeting is held, where the results of the experiments are presented, and appropriate next actions are decided. The 'sprint review meeting' officially ends the sprint. During the sprint review the team votes on one of four possible next actions to take with the validation plan based on the results of the experiments. In this context possible options are: 1) retire (i.e., move on to a new idea), 2) persevere (i.e., stay the course), 3) pivot (i.e., change direction) and 4) reset (i.e., kill the idea). Overall, the Lean Sprint can be seen as a process that integrates discovery and delivery activities on the team level [19].

4.4 Product Kata

Another approach for integrating product discovery with delivery activities is the iterative method Product Kata [20]. Product Kata is a four-step approach that aims at helping product teams to align around a goal, to learn about customer needs, and to uncover the right solution to build. It starts with the phase 'understanding of the right direction' in order to agree on an overriding goal to be achieved as well as to align all relevant stakeholders. For this purpose, the product vision, the strategic intend of the company or product KPI's are suitable inputs. Next, product discovery starts with the analysis of the current state of the practice in order to identify the current customer behaviours as well as the working status in relation to the product vision. It also reflects the current state with respect to reaching the outcomes, including the current measurements of those outcomes. Subsequently, goals are defined, which represent the outcomes to be achieved in order to make progress towards the achievement on the overriding goal. Then, the last phase 'choose step of product process' takes place, which includes activities from product discovery as well as from product delivery. Product discovery is conducted through exploring and identifying problems in order to understand the needs of the customers. The next step focuses on developing a solution in order to solve these identified problems. Finally, these solutions are tested within the phase 'solution optimization' in order to identify improvement potentials. After this step, the overall process repeats. Product Kata integrates dual-track agile in the overall strategic product development process and helps to assure, that product discovery and delivery are aligned with the company vision [20, 21] (Fig. 6).

4.5 Dual-Track Scrum

Ciecholewski [22] suggests a dual-track scrum approach with 'discovery' and 'delivery' tracks. The aim of the discovery track is to validate ideas quickly and efficiently, to feed these findings into the delivery track for implementation, testing and deployment. This process continuously repeats during the entire life cycle of the product (see Fig. 7).

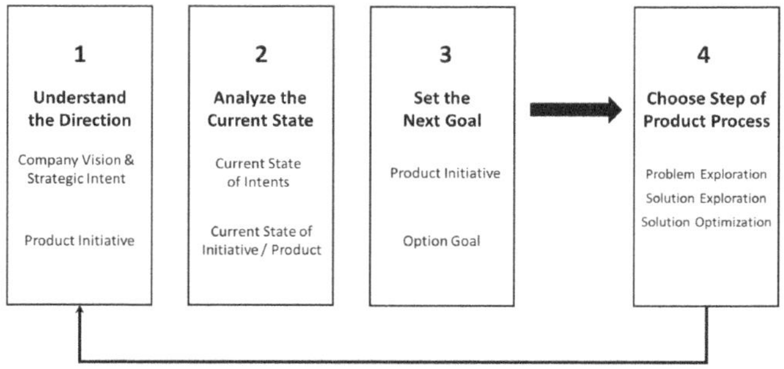

Fig. 6. Product Kata (based on [20])

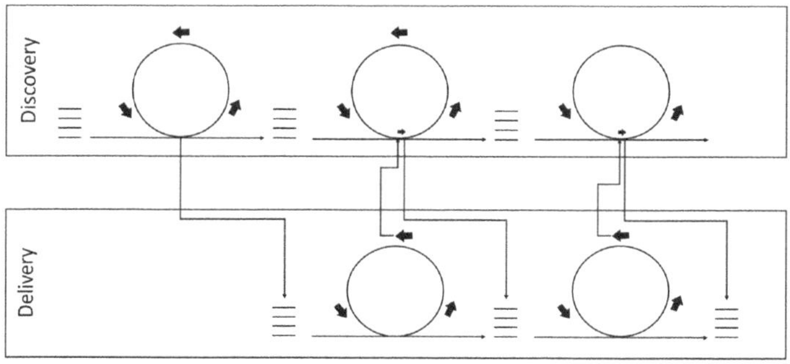

Fig. 7. Dual-track scrum (based on [22])

In the 'Dual-Track Scrum' approach, each track has its own team. The discovery team usually consists of lead designers and developers, while the delivery team consists of developers and software testers. It is recommended that a product owner is part of both teams in order to facilitate the coordination and workflow between the two teams. The discovery team conducts user research, builds prototypes and validates ideas (see Fig. 8). Usually the product discovery team operates in a Kanban fashion. Based on the result of the validation test, an idea is classified as either mature or immature. Immature ideas are neither considered valuable by the user nor viable by the development team. In the case that an idea has been validated as mature, it is planned in the scrum backlog of the delivery team and subsequently implemented. Dual-track scrum can be seen as an approach for integrating discovery and delivery into the Scrum framework.

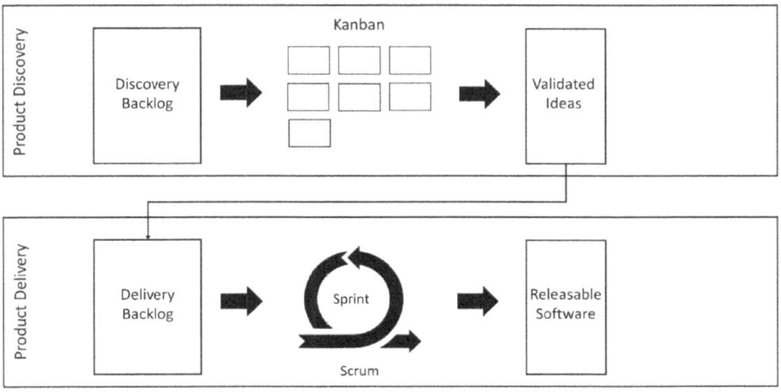

Fig. 8. Dual-track scrum process (based on [22])

5 Threats to Validity

We use the framework based on Wohlin et al. [23] as the basis for the discussion of the validity of our study. **Construct validity**: First, the construct validity is threatened by the Google search engine regarding the accessibility of search results. This means that Google does not allow the access to all identified articles. Therefore, it is not known whether the articles returned by Google is representative of the total population of search results. Moreover, the search strings itself poses a threat to the construct validity. There may be articles that deal with the research topic but use terms that were not covered by the selected search strings. It should be mentioned that a bias with regards to the search history due to the Google's identity tracking mechanisms cannot completely be excluded. This can lead to different results in the case that the search is repeated with our search string. **Internal validity**: In order to mitigate this threat, the findings were discussed by three researchers in order to limit conformation bias and interpretation bias. **External validity**: The results and conclusions relate to methods in order to conduct dual-track agile, which is designed for a dynamic market environment with high uncertainties. Therefore, the results are not directly transferable to other market environments. **Conclusion validity:** In order to mitigate this risk, we have presented and discussed our findings with practitioners of the software-intensive business. In this context no major ambiguities or consistencies were found [23, 24].

6 Summary

In this study, we conducted a grey literature review that aims at identifying suitable approaches for the implementation of dual-track agile. The results provide a better understanding of how the two components product discovery and product delivery can interact with each other and how this interaction can be implemented in practice. A list of all articles found in the Grey Literature Review can be found on FigShare (see [16]). We selected five essential approaches that might help to implement dual-track agile in practice.

The presented approaches show different possibilities for the integration of the two tracks 'discovery' and 'delivery'. On the one hand, an integration can be done via an artifact that serves as interface, for example via a product backlog or a product roadmap. On the other hand, the integration can be primarily process-oriented, such as with the discovery-delivery cycle or with dual-track scrum. The integration of the discovery and delivery track can also be carried out with a focus on organizational aspects, e.g., through a cadence of joint meetings as in the lean sprint. Above all, the integration of the two tracks should be done by means of a common vision and a focus on common goals. This becomes clear in the Product Kata approach. The Product Kata illustrates how product development can be directed towards a vision, even though you are moving through unknown and uncertain territory. All in all, the approaches for implementing dual-track agile are still very rudimentary. One reason for this may be that many companies have so far prioritized the establishment of agile practices. Product management or product discovery is still been largely decoupled and done by business development or similar roles. Therefore, a close integration of both tracks in the dual-track agile was not yet in the foreground. However, this dovetailing is becoming more and more important as development will be increasingly continuous and customer-centric. It is therefore to be expected that further companies and researchers will deal with the implementation of dual-track agile in practice. Currently, many companies are trying to gain first experiences with it. Therefore, more experience will probably be gained over time and more concrete approaches to implementing dual-track agile in practice will be published. It can also be assumed that there will be different approaches. Possible variation factors for different approaches could be the difficulty to obtain usage data from customers, the criticality of the solutions to be developed, or the company culture.

Future research could address a multivocal literature study with refined search strings in order to gain more detailed insights into the topic 'dual-track agile'. In addition, future research in this area could go in the following directions: Which factors influence the implementation? Which prerequisites must be fulfilled in order to implement dual-track agile successfully? How can the effectiveness and efficiency of dual-track agile be further increased by a suitable infrastructure (e.g. DataOps, MLOps, ProductOps, DesignOps)? Which variants of dual-track agile are necessary? What are the consequences of dual-track agile for strategic and operational management? Results of this research should be interesting for practitioners as well as for researchers, since on the one hand competitiveness depends essentially on modern product development methods and on the other hand many fundamental research questions are raised.

References

1. Lombardo, C.T., McCarthy, B., Ryan, E., Conners, M.: Product Roadmaps Relaunched - How to Set Direction While Embracing Uncertainty. O'Reilly Media, Inc., Sebastopol (2017)
2. Münch, J., Trieflinger, S., Lang, D.: Why feature-based roadmaps fail in rapidly changing markets: a qualitative suvey. In: Proceedings of the International Workshop on Software-Intensive Business: Start-Ups, Ecosystems and Platforms (SiBW 2018), Aachen, Germany, pp. 202–219 (2018)
3. Cagan, M.: Inspired: How to Create Tech Products Customer Love, 1st edn. Wiley, Hoboken (2018)

4. Albrecht, K.: Dual Track Agile: Focusing on Customer Value. https://medium.com/kevin-on-code/dual-track-agile-focusing-on-customer-value-a2e39312585b. Accessed 14 Sep 2020
5. Product Discovery Methods: Definition of Continuous Discovery. https://pdmethods.com/product-discovery/what-is-continuous-product-discovery/. Accessed 14 Sep 2020
6. Airfocus: Dual-Track Agile. https://airfocus.com/glossary/what-is-dual-track-agile/. Accessed 14 Sep 2020
7. Münch, J., Trieflinger, S., Lang, D.: What's hot in product roadmapping? Key practices and success factors. In: Franch, X., Männistö, T., Martínez-Fernández, S. (eds.) PROFES 2019. LNCS, vol. 11915, pp. 401–416. Springer, Cham (2019). https://doi.org/10.1007/978-3-030-35333-9_29
8. Sedano, T., Ralph, P., Peraire, C.: Dual-track development. IEEE Softw. **37**, 58–64 (2020)
9. Shim, W., Lee, S.W.: An agile approach for managing requirements to improve learning and adaptability. In: Proceedings of the 25th International Requirements Engineering Conference Workshops (REW), pp. 435–438. IEEE (2017)
10. Fagerholm, F., Guinea, F., Mäenpää, H., Münch, J.: The RIGHT model for continuous experimentation. J. Syst. Softw. **123**, 292–305 (2017)
11. Bosch, J.: Building products as innovation experiment systems. In: Cusumano, Michael A., Iyer, B., Venkatraman, N. (eds.) ICSOB 2012. LNBIP, vol. 114, pp. 27–39. Springer, Heidelberg (2012). https://doi.org/10.1007/978-3-642-30746-1_3
12. Lindgren, E., Münch, J.: Raising the odds of success: the current state of experimentation in product development. Inf. Softw. Technol. **77**, 80–91 (2016)
13. Olsson, H.H., Bosch, J.: From opinions to data-driven software R&D: a multi-case study on how to close the 'open loop' problem. In: IEEE 40th EUROMICRO Conference on Software Engineering and Advanced Applications, pp. 9–16. IEEE (2014)
14. Garousi, V., Felderer, M., Mäntylä, M.V.: Guidelines for including grey literature and conducting multivocal literature reviews in software engineering. Inf. Softw. Technol. **106**, 101–121 (2019)
15. Münch J., Trieflinger S., Lang, D.: Product roadmap – from vision to reality: a systematic literature review. In: ICE/IEEE ITMC: International Conference on Engineering, Technology and Innovation. IEEE (2019)
16. Published on Figshare. https://figshare.com/s/91da1dfc4314b721f005. Accessed 14 Sep 2020
17. Hodgson, M.: Better together: Agile + Lean UX. https://zenexmachina.com/better-together-agile-lean-ux/. Accessed 14 Sep 2020
18. Münch, J., Trieflinger, S., Bogazköy, E., Eißler, P., Roling, B., Schneider, J.: Product roadmap formats for an uncertain future: a grey literature review. In: Proceedings of the Euromicro Conference on Software Engineering and Advanced Applications. IEEE (2020)
19. Maurya, A.: Scaling Lean. Penguin Random House, New York (2016)
20. Perri, M.: Escaping the Build Trap. O'Reilly, Sebastopol (2018)
21. Perri, M.: The Product Kata. https://melissaperri.com/blog/2015/07/22/the-product-kata. Accessed 14 Sep 2020
22. Ciecholewski, J.: How to set up Dual-Track Scrum in Jira. https://www.devbridge.com/articles/how-to-set-up-dual-track-scrum-in-jira/. Accessed 14 Sep 2020
23. Wohlin, C., Runeson, P., Hörst, M., Ohlsson, B., Regnell, B., Wesslen, A.: Experimentation in Software Engineering: An Introduction. Kluwer Academic Publishers, Dordrecht (2000)
24. Runeson, P., Höst, M.: Guidelines for conducting and reporting case study research. Empirical Softw. Eng. **14**(2), 131–164 (2009)

Using Blockchain in Digitalizing Enterprise Legacy Systems: An Experience Report

Taija Kolehmainen[1(✉)], Gabriella Laatikainen[1], Joni Kultanen[1], Erol Kazan[2], and Pekka Abrahamsson[1]

[1] University of Jyväskylä, Jyväskylä, Finland
{taija.s.kolehmainen,gabriella.laatikainen,joni.m.kultanen, pekka.abrahamsson}@jyu.fi
[2] IT University of Copenhagen, Copenhagen, Denmark
erka@itu.dk

Abstract. Blockchain technology and distributed ledger technology (DLT) offer a secure, distributed, and tamper-proof way to store and exchange information. However, apart from standard cryptocurrency-based networks, innovations and process improvements based on the blockchain technology have mostly remained on the conceptualizing stage and have not yet reached mass adoption. There is a high demand for practical experiences from developing blockchain and DLT based systems in various domains outside FinTech. This work seeks to contribute to this gap by presenting real-world experiences from developing a proof of concept for automatizing conditional payments in social benefits and healthcare domains. We found that the key conditions for making these blockchain-based solutions viable are (1) attaining technological maturity and competences, (2) ecosystem thinking and adequate governance of these ecosystems, and finally (3) achieving legal and regulatory predictability. Furthermore, we discuss technological choice, business, and ethical considerations relevant to practitioners and research communities.

Keywords: Blockchain technology · Distributed ledger technology · Smart contract · Smart money

1 Introduction

Blockchain and distributed ledger technology (DLT) are often described as disruptive. They are frequently used synonymously; however, these are separated technologies. DLT presents a solution for creating distributed, peer-to-peer communication and interaction networks that do not have a single central authority [1]. Blockchain technology is one type of DLT that supports the safety of distributing a ledger by enabling an unmodifiable and interconnected list of ledger entries [1]. These technologies have enabled new kinds of innovations and infrastructure changes, most prominently in the financial industry [2, 3].

One of the key features of blockchain technology is that it enables process automation and transparency. This is provided through smart contracts: they are digital contracts

E. Klotins and K. Wnuk (Eds.): ICSOB 2020, LNBIP 407, pp. 70–85, 2021.
https://doi.org/10.1007/978-3-030-67292-8_6

that include executable program code lines and are both stored and run on the top of a blockchain [4–6]. Thus, in blockchain, rules for facilitating, verifying, and enforcing conditions on transactions are embedded into code that executes themselves on a condition-based principle.

In a DLT/blockchain-based ecosystem, information is shared across the network and stored by the actors. Based on the actors' roles and the rules for information sharing, we can divide blockchains into permissionless and permissioned infrastructure [7]. In permissionless blockchains, the actors are unknown to each other and have open access to the data. Trust is built on incentives that positively impact participants' behavior that plays an essential role in reaching consensus [8]. In contrast, in a permissioned ecosystem, the actors are invited and validated before joining the network. Furthermore, the actors are identifiable, and as a consequence, there is more trust among them as compared to the permissionless blockchain protocols with anonymous actors.

While blockchain technology has largely been proven to be eligible to automate processes and provide various benefits, it has not yet reached mass adoption. Some of the reasons behind this are identified lately in the literature (e.g. [2, 9, 10]); however, yet only a few commercial-grade blockchain application exist [11, 12], and we lack technology awareness and practical use case experiences in industries outside of cryptocurrencies (e.g. [11, 13]). These observations could guide the practitioners' possible adoption decisions and help researchers understand the viability of these technologies in a real-world context. Thus, with this study, we aim to bridge the gap between practitioners and academics and present lessons learned from a blockchain adoption experience.

In joint work with an IT services and software company and its partners, we studied the suitability of permissioned blockchain in transferring an asset from one entity to another in a business ecosystem. We developed a proof of concept for blockchain-based conditional payments to eliminate the need for manual issuance and verification of different payment guarantees, such as lunch coupons, vouchers, and bus tickets, among others[1]. In this process, we integrated insights from academic and grey literature and discussions with blockchain practitioners, attended technology-related events, and followed the national and global discussions concerning DLT/blockchain technology development. Furthermore, we considered ethics during development using the guidelines for the development of Trustworthy AI by the European Commission [14].

In this study, we present the key lessons learned during this process with the following main research question in mind: *"What adoption barriers do practitioners meet in real-world settings when digitalizing and automating processes in enterprise legacy systems by utilizing distributed ledger technology and blockchain?"* Besides identifying the barriers, we also aim to answer empirical questions, such as the requirements of a blockchain-based solution and what technological choices have been made and why. In addition to technological perspectives, we also consider business and ethical issues. Simply put, we aim to provide a realistic picture of the viability of automating and digitalizing enterprise legacy processes.

The structure of this article is as follows. In the next section, we present earlier work on this research domain from academic and grey literature. In the Findings section, we

---

[1] https://medium.com/kelalab/distributed-ledger-a-revolution-in-conditional-payments-fa92e6ec4747 https://medium.com/kelalab/experimenting-with-smart-money-f645512aeb8e.

give an overview of the developed proof of concept, the technological choices for its development, and the lessons learned in the form of key experiences. Finally, we discuss the findings and present our conclusions.

2 Recent Work

In this section, we give an overview of recent work. In the first subsection, we overview earlier research on adoption factors of DLT/blockchain technology. In the second subsection, we present two production stage projects whose experiences in value tokenization and conditional payments we used during the development of proof of concept.

2.1 Adoption of DLT/Blockchain Technology

Extant literature recognizes the technical challenges of DLT/blockchain technology adoption, such as interdependency of the technology features, the importance of system design, and process time for transactions in developing distributed, decentralized systems compared to centralized systems [15, 16]. It was found that choosing the right technological platform and architecture puts emphasis on system design, value creation [9], and needs considering the organization's operating principles, governing protocol, information storage needs, and willingness to share information [1, 3, 11]. The practical side (e.g., maintaining the systems, issues of scalability and interoperability) and the impact of making technical trade-offs from an ethical point of view have also been mentioned in research [1, 3, 8, 17]. The decision to move from centralized legacy systems towards more distributed and decentralized solutions requires some understanding about balancing between costs and benefits, the technology and community involvement [7, 18]. However, there is an imbalance in understanding disruptive new technology's impacts and characteristics [15, 19].

Current research found that cultural norms, practices, industry standards, and many other formal requirements affect the degree of distribution and decentralization that an organization is willing to adopt [1]. Chong et al. [10] found that there is no one-size-fits-all approach and each business model has its challenges that are not yet answered. Early research in the financial industry has shown that even if blockchain technology-based solutions hold potential in transforming processes across multiple industries [8], they preferably will be a complementary technology that enables alternative data and value transactions [2].

Governance related challenges were emphasized both by practitioners and researchers [1, 20]. The discourse of providing accountability using technical means seems to be shifting more to realizing that some level of institutional engagement and coordination is needed, for example, to resolve conflicts and manage risks and costs [7, 20].

2.2 Related Projects

An investigation of grey literature appointed two main research projects in related problem domains of enabling value tokenization and issuing rule-based benefits without centralized intermediaries. First, the Commonwealth Scientific and Industrial Research Organization's (CSIRO) Data 61 and the Commonwealth Bank of Australia in 2018 developed a proof of concept in a similar problem domain and similar product requirements in an example environment of Australia's National Disability Insurance Scheme (NDIS) [21]. In the trial called "Making Money Smart", NDIS provides funding on the blockchain network to people with disabilities to spend according to pre-set rules on support services. The technical solution was built on a permissioned Ethereum network and focused on payment functionality. The project sought to find whether and in what ways blockchain could improve conditional payments. In addition to the technical prototype, they also included user testing, managers, service providers, and experts [21].

The project demonstrated the potential to deliver economic benefits through efficiency gains and network effects, especially with multiple conditional payment environments. The concept was as seen promising in enhancing public policy programs, empowering users to optimize their budgets, and reducing friction and costs for various stakeholders. However, the report highlighted the need for further research and development on technical performance and confidentiality, and integration with existing systems. Considerations of alternative conditional payment environments, accessibility, and compliance with legislation and regulation were mentioned in the final report [21].

Second, the United Nations World Food Programme (WFP) developed a blockchain-based solution to make beneficiary cash transfers more efficient, secure, and transparent in refugee camps. The program strives to enable more choices and more control for refugees over their cash assistance [22]. The goal of developing the solution was to make direct transactions without a possible insufficient or unreliable financial intermediary. The first pilot for blockchain-related was launched by WPF in 2017 when the organization initiated a proof of concept project in Pakistan for authenticating and registering beneficiary transactions. Next blockchain-based technologies were used to deliver food assistance to Syrian refugees in Jordan. WFP has announced its interests in exploring the technology's possibilities in, e.g., supply chain tracking and digital identity management for refugees [23]. The Building Blocks were built on a private, permissioned blockchain Parity Ethereum by Ethereum Foundation [24]. It was integrated with biometric authentication technology, and it has been currently being used in refugee camps in Jordan. The network started with a single authority but has since grown to include other UN Women [24]. This expansion further has resulted in improved security and accountability through two organizations validating each other's transactions and holds the potential to reduce costs and risks [25].

3 Experience Collection Mechanisms

To gather empirical data and experiences in real-world settings, we co-developed a technical proof of concept for smart contracts using DLT/blockchain technologies in collaboration with a company and its partner organizations. We assessed the existing literature, current industry practices, as well as the needs of the stakeholders even-handed. Observations were gathered from meeting memos, notes, project and version control documentations, code repositories, project management documentations (e.g., Scrum agile development method and Kanban lean management method documents) and other forms of sources available online. The team actively followed national and international discussions, projects, pilots, and, for example, the development of legislation related to blockchain-based technologies. Furthermore, the research team participated in discussions with other companies interested in utilizing the DLT/blockchain technology for their use cases or offering services related to their customer' technologies. Additionally, we collaborated with another research team whose primary goal was studying how blockchain technology can be made trustworthy [19]. This research team offered us a new, ethical perspective to develop blockchain-based systems and a practical tool to implement the idea of an ethical, lawful, and robust system.

In the design and development phase, we created a proof of concept in several iterations. The iterations included several consultative and workshop meetings with the partner company and its partners as checkpoints of the work direction and shared understanding of the objectives. An overview of the events is presented in Table 1.

Table 1. Empirical data collection sources

Events	Quantity/length	External participants
Project meeting with the partner company	10 instances	Partner company representatives, possibly an external expert
Consultative meeting with the partner company	10 days	Developer; partner company representatives
Proof of concept workshop meetings	2 instances	Developer; partner company representatives, project partner representatives
Research conference	5 days	Technically aligned research group representatives (hosted by a research center)
Technical event	1 day	Developer representatives interested in DLT/blockchain technology or using it
Business event	4 days	Business representatives interested in DLT/blockchain technology or using it
Technical training program	2 instances	External technical instructors
Ethical research meeting	8 instances	Collaborating research team
Ethical research interview	2 instances	Collaborating research team representative
Technology-related lecture	3 days	External lecturers (hosted by universities)
Proof of concept technical meeting	2 instances	Project partner technical developers

This paper describes the lessons learned in this study based on active participation and careful documentation of the development process. For these purposes, we used the data collected from various empirical sources and analyzed them iteratively. First, we grouped the relevant information into experiences using post-it notes. Second, we analyzed the notes and grouped the key experiences into categories. We describe the resulting findings in Sect. 4 in the form of Primary empirical observations (PEOs).

4 Findings

In this section, we give an overview of the lessons learned in our work. In the next subsection, we describe the requirements of the proof of concept solution. In the second subsection, we justify our technological choices. In the third subsection, we communicate our key experiences in the form of Primary Empirical Observations (PEOs).

4.1 The Requirements for Proof of Concept

As a case study, we focused on designing and developing a technical prototype Smart Money, a distributed business network for conditional payment guarantees. The concept could be used across various use cases enabling businesses to issue funds in the form of rule-based digital tokens. The network services allow dynamic rule validation and reliable near real-time transaction data. We chose to concentrate on implementing the concept in the domain of social welfare benefits (shown in Fig. 1). It presented us with several challenges, such as a highly regulated environment, a high number of transactions, and a comprehensive and broad end-user base. Thus, we expected to face possible barriers in technical, market, and institutional dimensions. We were primarily interested in the efficiency gains that the technologies enable by removing the need for intermediated data-synchronization and concurrency control. However, we noticed that practitioners faced similar issues in utilizing DLT/blockchain technologies in various use cases.

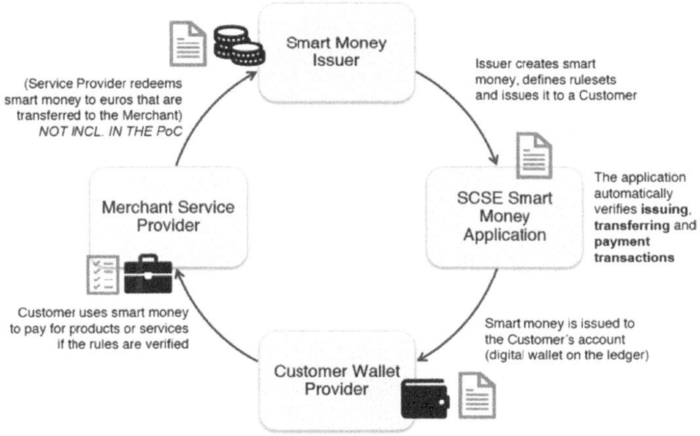

Fig. 1. Smart Money token lifecycle in the proof of concept trial.

The Smart Money blockchain-based solution could improve the current system of social and welfare benefits by reducing administrative burden and costs as well as simplifying and automating processes. It allows an Issuer to create and transfer a token with predefined rulesets to a Customer's digital wallet (shown in Fig. 1) who spends them according to the spending rules on products or services. Merchants accept tokens.

Table 2. Functionalities implemented in the Smart Money proof of concept.

Functionality	Design criteria	Implementation and constraints
Creating Smart Money accounts	Using and interacting with the system should be easy and not require knowledge about the technology. Users connect to the network through their role-based service providers	In the time of the development, Corda did not have an account feature. We chose to use a Corda-based third-party software called Cordite by Cordite Foundation
Creating Token ruleset	Tokens could be used as vouchers or cash; they should be generalized enough for scalable use. The Token rulesets should be easily updatable by the Issuer when laws, regulations or standards change	Updating rules require node hosts to implement changes. One-time-use vouchers are clearer than divisible cash as changing token type rulesets affect every consumer with the same type of tokens. In our scope, the operator's rights are comparable to a centralized system
Issuing Token on an Account	The system should promote human oversight control and intervention if necessary. The Issuer should be permissioned to modify the expiry of the Smart Money Tokens or state them worthless. The origin of the allowance should be traceable but protect the Customers' privacy	The scope does not include updating the transaction after Issuance. The ledger hosts e.g., public service provider credentials, but all confidential data is maintained outside of the ledger. The allowance origin can be tracked to the Issuer without revealing additional Customer data
Transacting a payment	Spending allowance should promote efficiency and simplify the process to the Customers and Merchants. The system should be resilient to misuse and potential attacks and its mechanisms, constraints, and decisions should be transparent and auditable	With limited resources we did not concentrate on exception management. The unwanted use of the system was evaluated to belong to managing participants rights and access rules outside the system

The Customers and Merchants access the network through their Service Providers, who are network nodes alongside with the Issuer. The application enables a fund issuer to define customized spending rules on a token before sending it to a recipient's account. After receiving the token, the recipient can use it to buy products and services if and only if the pre-set rules are met. The rules could include price-caps, lists of approved service providers, and expiration dates, among others. See Table 2 for details related to designing and implemented high-level functionalities. The application was developed with an enterprise-level blockchain platform Corda (release version 4.1) by a software company R3.

Additionally, we considered long-term requirements such as redeeming tokens for payment, digital identity management, keeping track of transactions, validating payments with smart contracts, and token type-specific rules. Furthermore, we implemented ethical requirements into the proof of concept development process through a practical tool that supported raising ethical awareness and discussion. We followed the guidelines for Trustworthy AI by the European Commission [14] that state that a trustworthy system should be lawful, ethical, and robust. The objectives are realized with seven key requirements: 1) human agency and oversight, 2) technical robustness and safety, 3) privacy and data governance, 4) transparency, 5) diversity, non-discrimination and fairness, 6) societal and environmental well-being, and 7) accountability [14].

4.2 Technological Considerations

One of the most critical decisions is related to choosing the best fitting blockchain protocol. Enterprise blockchains differ from traditional permissionless, public blockchain designs, e.g., in areas of identity, privacy, and transaction scalability [7, 26]. Thus, there were multiple discussions concerning the advantages and disadvantages of different alternatives. In Table 3, we describe the three most promising alternatives (Corda, Fabric, and Enterprise Ethereum). Based on various decision criteria presented in the table, the Corda platform was chosen. Corda is an open-source, enterprise-level blockchain that provides a platform for recording and managing contracts between designated parties in a transaction and deals with network sharing, data, business logic, and the current state of shared facts [26].

Table 3. Enterprise Blockchain comparison considering network and transaction features as presented by R3 in Q3/2019 [27].

Feature	Corda by R3	Fabric by IBM	Enterprise Ethereum by several companies
Real-world identity	Legally valid and unique	Certificate-based (not assured)	No inherent notion
Scalability	Scalable as not every node handling all transactions	Limited by channels architecture (increases with participants)	Low due to complex zero-knowledge proof privacy calculations
Method to guarantee uniqueness	Pools of known notaries	An ordering service	Validation nodes (most of the time)
Privacy	Only participants to a transaction have access to the data	Channels architecture allow private transactions	Private deployment of Ethereum has a viable privacy model
Conclusiveness	The completed transaction cannot be reversed	The completed transaction cannot be reversed	Small possibility completed transaction can be reverser

We chose the Corda platform for different reasons. First, Corda's consensus mechanism requires transaction validity and uniqueness [26, 28]. Second, the platform is mature related to different issues, such as data privacy, identity, emphasis on legal agreements, regulator/public sector collaboration, and interoperability/integration and is actively developed [29]. Third, the Corda platform also has higher scalability than some of the other enterprise-level blockchains (e.g., Fabric and enterprise Ethereum) as each node in the network does not handle all transactions [28]. Finally, in the Corda platform, each business network defines its membership criteria, and only those who participate in a transaction have access to its data, which further enhances the platform's privacy [26].

However, despite Corda's advantages over other alternatives, performance, confidentiality, and system integration raised concerns among practitioners and partners in our use case study. First, there is a concern related to the adequacy of the open-source version of Corda. Open Source Corda has some limitations related to its scalability and capacity of handling massive amounts of transactions [28] after the solution is taken into real use. It indeed needs to be noted that any larger-scale trials should be run on Enterprise Corda. Second, transaction privacy between Corda nodes is secured, but this confidentiality does not apply to the account level. Finally, some concerns were raised related to integrability to legacy systems.

4.3 Lessons Learned

Designing a blockchain-based solution requires many different activities. First, it requires developing a technical solution. Second, besides providing an architecture, the providers should promote the adoption and build a whole ecosystem with its actors and interactions among them. Third, the ecosystem resides in a legal and regulatory context where ethical concerns should be considered as well. In what follows, we describe our key experiences in the form of Primary empirical observations (PEOs) related to these three aspects, as shown in Table 4.

Key Experiences from the Technical Development

PEO 1. [Developer Community]. The leading enterprise blockchain protocols have attracted an active, considerably stable, and frequently pushing developer community.

We made our technological choice based on several objective decision criteria (see Subsect. 4.2); however, one very important success criteria is the developer community's activity behind the platform. The enterprise blockchain Corda platform built and maintained by R3 differs from the other leading enterprise protocols in having been purpose-built and not originating from a traditional technology organization. Partly due to the active developers, by the end of year 2019, Corda was one of the leading enterprise blockchain protocols having the highest total activity and total pushes compared to Linux Foundation's Hyperledger projects Fabric, Sawtooth and Besu, as well as to Quorum (a fork of Ethereum) and MultiChain (a fork of Bitcoin, Coin Sciences).

PEO 2. [Immaturity of the Technology]. Despite high interest across industries, blockchain technology is still in its maturing phase.

Table 4. Key experiences in the form of Primary empirical observations (PEOs).

Activity	Key experience
Technical development	
PEO 1 Developer Community	The leading enterprise blockchain protocols have attracted an active, considerably stable, and frequently pushing developer community
PEO 2 Immaturity of the Technology	Despite high interest across industries, blockchain technology is still in its maturing phase
PEO 3 Interoperability	Compatibility with existing IT systems and interoperability between blockchain networks are critical aspects of incorporating blockchain technology into existing systems
PEO 4 Technological Trade-offs	Many of the DLT/blockchain technology attributes are interdependent; thus, all blockchain technology features cannot be integrated as such, but there is a need to make trade-offs and choose the essential features
Building an ecosystem	
PEO 5 Governance	When developing decentralized systems, a key issue that needs special attention is governance: actors, incentives, access, and control rules
PEO 6 Business Goals	One of the key challenges of blockchain technology adoption is complying with different business requirements in decentralized settings
PEO 7 Technology Acceptance	There is an increasing interest and higher trust in the potential of DLT/blockchain technology in redesigning already existing services of various industries
PEO 8 Information Asymmetry	There is information asymmetry related to DLT/blockchain technology
Ethical and legal considerations	
PEO 9 Ethical Considerations	Blockchain-based solutions should be designed and developed with ethical considerations in mind; however, blockchain technology's ethical aspects are still underdeveloped and need further research
PEO 10 Legal Aspects	Legal predictability is a prerequisite for larger scale blockchain deployment. Lack of legal recognition is one of the most important non-technical limitation of block-chain-related technologies

Even though blockchain technology has gained much interest across industries, its adoption is still on an experimental stage, and the platforms themselves are under development. We faced different challenges related to upgrades from the Corda platform version 3 to 4 and lack of some technological features introduced to the platform in later releases during our proof of concept development. Not having the needed features, we ended up using third-party application components, which raised questions about safety, reliability, and maintainability of the system.

PEO 3. [Interoperability]. Compatibility with existing IT systems and interoperability between blockchain networks are critical aspects of blockchain adoption.

The Corda platform offers integrability with legacy systems and functional information flow between different applications on the same platform and between different blockchain platforms. However, these features (e.g., database support, hardware security module, and technology enabling secure deployment inside corporate data centers) are not yet available open-source but are additional features of Corda Enterprise. As a rising number of organizations is adopting Corda commercially, the platform faces novel requirements. R3, in line with other technology providers, displays willingness to promote simplicity, flexibility, and connectivity of their platform to encourage adoption.

PEO 4. [Technological Trade-offs]. Many of the DLT/blockchain technology attributes are interdependent; thus, all blockchain technology features cannot be integrated as such, but there is a need to make trade-offs and choose the essential features.

Blockchain protocols vary significantly in their configurations related to, e.g., the level of permission, data access, transaction consensus, modularity, scalability, interoperability, centralization, and anonymity. The technology level makes use of various technologies such as distributed ledgers, identification, and cryptography. Many of the attributes enabling each of these features are interdependent, and bending conditions in one of the dimensions could be disadvantageous to another area. Thus, designing a blockchain-based distributed system leads to making technological trade-offs such as sacrificing the system's decentralization or integrity for better scalability.

Building an Ecosystem

PEO 5. [Governance]. When developing decentralized systems, a key issue that needs special attention is governance: actors, incentives, access, and control rules.

Developing a distributed system compared to a centralized requires considering additional questions, e.g. who should have access to the information within the system and how open the system management should be. Managing stakeholders and their rights is even more emphasized in permissioned enterprise blockchain platforms compared to public networks in which every participant is equal in their restrictions and rights. Furthermore, communicating the advantages of the blockchain solution and providing incentives to the stakeholders is a crucial task in system design and development.

PEO 6. [Business Goals]. One of the key challenges of blockchain technology adoption is complying with different business requirements in decentralized settings.

Centralized enterprise legacy systems naturally emphasize security and privacy, whereas distributed and decentralized solutions gain an advantage in sharing services and resources among multiple participants. Privately operated DLT/blockchain technology solutions might be an appealing alternative compared to more open or public blockchain protocols that still fulfill the enterprise business requirements. However, private blockchains do not fully undertake the traditional blockchain technology's ideology and its most distinctive features, such as decentralization and censorship-resistance. Consequently, private blockchains are distributed ledgers that function like closed, secure, cryptography-based databases, and therefore, they introduce new challenges besides their benefits.

PEO 7. [Technology Acceptance]. There is an increasing interest and higher trust in the potential of DLT/blockchain technology in redesigning already existing services of various industries.

DLT/blockchain technology managed to gain traction by its success in re-implementing financial services and enabling both secure transactions and innovation in the financial services industry. As enterprise blockchains have already reached some level of stability, there seems to be a keen commercial interest in transforming processes across various industries beyond the initial fintech applications and currency markets. There are, however, not yet many commercial applications that would offer lessons learned or best practices to encourage wider adoption.

PEO 8. [Information Asymmetry]. There is information asymmetry related to DLT/blockchain technology.

The current state of knowledge related to DLT/blockchain technology is still significantly unequal between those who provide blockchain-related services and those who use these systems. Even though technology providers are reporting an increase in understanding among customers, the research team encountered different concerns related to, among others, the potential benefits of distributed systems as compared to centralized legacy systems, data privacy, and the viability of the business and technology aspects. Moreover, a few technology company representatives emphasized that blockchain technology knowledge and interest are very scattered and mostly concentrated in their financial units.

Ethical and Legal Considerations

PEO 9. [Ethical Considerations]. Blockchain-based solutions should be designed and developed with ethical considerations in mind; however, blockchain technology's ethical aspects are still underdeveloped and need further research.

One of the key conditions for making blockchain-based solutions viable is related to the ethical aspects, such as transparency, accountability, responsibility, and fairness, among others. However, researchers and practitioners concurred that currently, the ethical questions related to blockchain technology are generally unthought and unstructured. Besides privacy and some domain-specific concerns (e.g., medical, finance, insurance), also other important ethical issues (e.g., the ethical impact of technological choices or accessibility), were thought to be distant.

PEO 10. [Legal Aspects]. Legal predictability is a prerequisite for larger-scale blockchain deployment. Lack of legal recognition is a major barrier in adopting blockchain-related technologies.

Blockchain adoption is ready to take a leap from proofs-of-concept to commercial implementations; however, the required laws, regulations, policies, and standards are still under development. There are currently different initiatives to overcome these obstacles in different parts of the world where different actors (e.g., authorities, enterprises, developer communities) are working to promote legal certainty. The current immaturity in laws, regulations, and standards and the uncertainty thereof leads to putting the project on hold until regulatory concerns are cleared.

5 Discussion

The findings of this paper emphasize the need for additional research on the barriers to blockchain adoption. Many of the barriers described in our lessons learned were recured among practitioners in various domains and were to some extent identified in the extant literature but did not yet have comprehensive, comprehensively agreed solutions. Thus, even though the number of academic publications on different aspects of blockchain technology rose significantly [8, 9], our experiences show that further research is needed to bridge the gap between researchers and practitioners.

We categorized our key experiences in three dimensions that should be considered when utilizing blockchain-related technologies: 1) technical development, 2) building an ecosystem, and 3) ethical and legal considerations. Related to the technical challenges of DLT/blockchain technology adoption (PEO 4), we are in line with recent work that identified the interdependency of DLT/blockchain technology features as a barrier and accentuated the importance of system design in developing distributed, decentralized systems compared to centralized systems [15, 16, 18]. Our results contribute to these findings by finding that the lack of conscious design and development choices could diminish transparency, fairness, safety, and auditability (PEO 9). Our findings further revealed that pragmatic use cases are also needed in blockchain initiatives as a means to provide guidelines, usability, and technical competencies (PEO 7). In the design and development phase of our proof of concept solution, we had concerns about scalability and system maintenance (PEO 2). Furthermore, we found that the developer community behind the chosen technology platform is of key importance (PEO 1). We lacked some of the chosen platform features, which raised security concerns if the prototype would be developed further (PEO 2). Besides, we had interoperability issues that we could not anticipate in advance (PEO 3). Finally, we also had to make technical trade-offs from an ethical perspective (PEO 4).

Our lessons-learned revealed that one of the biggest challenges is related to building an ecosystem around blockchain technology. Even though there are an increasing interest and higher trust in the potential of the technology (PEO 7), there is also information asymmetry between the different stakeholders (PEO 8). However, this uncertainty can be mitigated through negotiations and education. In line with earlier research (e.g. [1–3, 20]), one of the key issues is related to governance: establishing incentives, accountability, access, and control rules among stakeholders (PEO 5). Achieving business goals in decentralized settings need careful strategy and actions (PEO 6). The unsolved governance issues found in our research highlight the need for additional research in this area.

Related to the reluctance of truly utilizing the distributed nature of DLT/blockchain technology in automating and digitalizing legacy systems, we found that rethinking pre-existing business practices and implementing novel technical approaches are challenging (PEO 6). However, at the same time, expectations for the technologies' performance are increasing (PEO 7). We highlight the importance of ecosystem thinking: understanding how different stakeholders can jointly create and capture value as well as convincing these stakeholders about this value is crucial in building meaningful DLT/blockchain technology-based business applications (PEO 5). We concur with Chong et al. [10] that there is no one-size-fits-all approach and each blockchain-inspired business model has its own challenges that are not yet answered.

During our research, it became clear that creating effective and fair governance, regulation, and management requires a thorough understanding of the technology PEO 4, PEO 8, PEO 9, in line with [1, 11, 20]). We recognized the immaturity of legal and regulatory context needed for mass adoption (PEO 10). We also found that ethical issues in the development and use of DLT/blockchain technology are not appropriately addressed in earlier research and need additional work (PEO 9).

6 Conclusions

This study presents the findings of a research process during which we designed and developed a proof of concept of a blockchain-based solution for conditional payments using smart contracts and DLT/blockchain technology. These observations can be used to guide decisions on future research topics and discussions in industry practices in different ways. First, our experiences related to the proof of concept requirements and the decision criteria in choosing a suitable blockchain platform could be used by practitioners. Second, our key experiences on the viability of the business solution could be used by both researchers and practitioners for further work.

Our study identified key adoption barriers from the lessons learned that are presented in this experience report. The barriers are divided into three activities that have utter importance in utilizing blockchain-related technologies. First, despite the high interest in the DLT/blockchain technology, the adoption of blockchain is still in its experimental stage, and the platforms keep maturing; thus, further development of technological components is of key importance. Second, the cost and risk of blockchain adoption and implementation quickly can be very high; thus, ecosystem thinking is needed to promote blockchain adoption and enable viable and pragmatic solutions. Third, the immature legal and regulatory context and the unstructured ethical discussions related to DLT/blockchain technology need to be addressed before the blockchain deployment can leap from proof of concepts to commercial implementations. As businesses are eager to move from experimenting with the technology towards commercial deployment of DLT/blockchain technology, we expect these topics described above to gain closer attention.

Despite the growing body of knowledge by academics and practitioners, there are still notable challenges and knowledge gaps related to the development and use of DLT/blockchain technology-related solutions. Some of the adoption barriers, such as legal predictability, require national and international collaboration and cannot solely be addressed by researchers or industry practitioners. Even if research shows that distributed and decentralized solutions gain an advantage over centralized systems in sharing services and resources among multiple participants [18], it is not yet happening in practice. Companies experimenting with the DLT/blockchain technology are currently building solutions for individual use cases instead of establishing blockchain-based infrastructures. As the situation stands, the future deployment and the significance of these technologies can only be speculated until further adoption.

This research has some limitations. The findings are based on the development of one technical proof of concept and limited discussions with practitioners, and thus, further research is needed to make these observations more generalizable. Further-more, additional work is required in the research areas discussed in this paper, such as technological immaturity, ecosystem governance, redesigning business processes and models as well as legal uncertainty and ethical issues.

References

1. Trump, B.D., Florin, M.V., Matthews, H.S., Sicker, D., Linkov, I.: Governing the use of blockchain and distributed ledger technologies: not one-size-fits-all. IEEE Eng. Manag. Rev. **46**, 56–62 (2018). https://doi.org/10.1109/EMR.2018.2868305
2. Zachariadis, M., Hileman, G., Scott, S.V.: Governance and control in distributed ledgers: understanding the challenges facing blockchain technology in financial services. Inf. Organ. **29**, 105–117 (2019). https://doi.org/10.1016/j.infoandorg.2019.03.001
3. Chang, V., Baudier, P., Zhang, H., Xu, Q., Zhang, J., Arami, M.: How blockchain can impact financial services – the overview, challenges and recommendations from expert interviewees. Technol. Forecast. Soc. Change **158**, 120166 (2020). https://doi.org/10.1016/j.techfore.2020.120166
4. Buterin, V.: A next-generation smart contract and decentralized application platform. Etherum White Pap. 1–36 (2014)
5. Gopie, N.: What are smart contracts on blockchain? - Blockchain Pulse: IBM Blockchain Blog. https://www.ibm.com/blogs/blockchain/2018/07/what-are-smart-contracts-on-blockchain/
6. Antonopoulos, A.M., Wood, G.: GitHub - ethereumbook/ethereumbook: Mastering Ethereum. https://github.com/ethereumbook/ethereumbook
7. Benos, E., Garratt, R., Gurrola-Perez, P.: The economics of distributed ledger technology for securities settlement. Ledger **4** (2019). https://doi.org/10.5195/ledger.2019.144
8. Rossi, M., Mueller-Bloch, C., Thatcher, J.B., Beck, R.: Blockchain research in information systems: current trends and an inclusive future research agenda. J. Assoc. Inf. Syst. **20**, 1388–1403 (2019). https://doi.org/10.17705/1jais.00571
9. Risius, Marten, Spohrer, Kai: A blockchain research framework. Bus. Inf. Syst. Eng. **59**(6), 385–409 (2017). https://doi.org/10.1007/s12599-017-0506-0
10. Chong, A.Y.L., Lim, E.T.K., Hua, X., Zheng, S., Tan, C.W.: Business on chain: a comparative case study of five blockchain-inspired business models. J. Assoc. Inf. Syst. **20**, 1308–1337 (2019). https://doi.org/10.17705/1jais.00568
11. Hughes, L., Dwivedi, Y.K., Misra, S.K., Rana, N.P., Raghavan, V., Akella, V.: Blockchain research, practice and policy: applications, benefits, limitations, emerging research themes and research agenda. Int. J. Inf. Manag. **49**, 114–129 (2019). https://doi.org/10.1016/j.ijinfomgt.2019.02.005
12. Deloitte: 5 Blockchain Trends for 2020 (2020)
13. Budman, M., Hurley, B., Khan, A., Gangopadhyay, N.: Deloitte's 2019 Global Blockchain Survey (2019)
14. High-Level Independent Group on Artificial Intelligence (AI HLEG): Ethics Guidelines for Trustworthy AI. Eur. Comm. 1–39 (2019)
15. Lapointe, C., Fishbane, L.: The blockchain ethical design framework. Innov. Technol. Gov. Glob. **12**, 50–71 (2019). https://doi.org/10.1162/inov_a_00275

16. Janssen, M., Weerakkody, V., Ismagilova, E., Sivarajah, U., Irani, Z.: A framework for analysing blockchain technology adoption: integrating institutional, market and technical factors. Int. J. Inf. Manag. **50**, 302–309 (2020). https://doi.org/10.1016/j.ijinfomgt.2019.08.012
17. Wang, Y., Singgih, M., Wang, J., Rit, M.: Making sense of blockchain technology: how will it transform supply chains? Int. J. Prod. Econ. **211**, 221–236 (2019). https://doi.org/10.1016/j.ijpe.2019.02.002
18. Pereira, J., Tavalaei, M.M., Ozalp, H.: Blockchain-based platforms: decentralized infrastructures and its boundary conditions. Technol. Forecast. Soc. Change **146**, 94–102 (2019). https://doi.org/10.1016/j.techfore.2019.04.030
19. Vakkuri, V., Kolehmainen, T., Kultanen, J., Abrahamsson, P.: Trustworthy Blockchain: Considering Ethics in Blockchain Systems and Their Development (2019)
20. Beck, R., Müller-Bloch, C., King, J.L.: Governance in the blockchain economy: a framework and research agenda. J. Assoc. Inf. Syst. **19**, 1020–1034 (2018). https://doi.org/10.17705/1jais.00518
21. Royal, D., et al.: Making money smart: empowering NDIS participants with Blockchain technologies (2018)
22. WFP Innovation: Building Blocks: Blockchain for Zero Hunger. https://innovation.wfp.org/project/building-blocks
23. Juskalian, R.: Inside the Jordan refugee camp that runs on blockchain | MIT Technology Review. https://www.technologyreview.com/2018/04/12/143410/inside-the-jordan-refugee-camp-that-runs-on-blockchain/
24. Dhameja, G.: UN World Food Programme uses Parity Ethereum to aid 100,000 refugees | Parity Technologies. https://www.parity.io/un-world-food-programme-uses-parity-ethereum-to-aid-100-000-refugees/
25. UN Women: Press release: UN Women and WFP harness innovation for women's economic empowerment in crisis situations. https://www.unwomen.org/en/news/stories/2018/9/press-release-un-women-and-wfp-harness-innovation-for-economic-empowerment-in-crisis
26. Brown, R.G.: The Corda Platform: An Introduction. Corda Platform White Paper, pp. 1–21 (2018)
27. R3: Blockchain Quick Facts For Business (2019)
28. Hearn, M., Brown, R.G.: Corda: A distributed ledger. Whitepaper, pp. 1–73 (2019)
29. Chainstack: Enterprise Blockchain Protocols: Evolution Index 2020. Chainstack, pp. 1–18 (2020)

Communication of Changes in Continuous Software Development

Telcio Elui Cardoso(✉), Alan R. Santos, Rafael Chanin, and Afonso Sales

School of Technology, PUCRS, Porto Alegre, RS 90619-900, Brazil
telcio.cardoso@edu.pucrs.br, alan.ricardo@acad.pucrs.br, {rafael.chanin,afonso.sales}@pucrs.br

Abstract. The industry competition has changed the way software is managed, developed, and delivered over the years. Some of the approaches that emerged to continuously deliver software to users are Continuous Delivery (CDE) and Continuous Deployment (CD). CDE is the ability to get software functionalities, of any kind, into the hands of users, in small batches, and short cycles. In CD, every change that passes all stages of the production pipeline is released to customers without human intervention. The agility proposed by the Continuous Delivery and Continuous Deployment approaches may introduce some challenges to the software development life-cycle. Some of these challenges are related to the Software Configuration Management process and the communication of software changes to relevant stakeholders such as operations teams. In order to better understand which communication practices are used to communicate software changes in environments where Continuous Delivery or Continuous Deployment were adopted, a systematic literature review and an empirical study with global companies were performed, which allowed us to consolidate a collection of communication practices for communicating software changes that could benefit companies that already adopted or are planning to implement continuous software delivery practices.

Keywords: Software engineering · Software development · Continuous integration · Continuous delivery · Continuous deployment · Continuous release · DevOps

1 Introduction

The growing demand for faster time to market cycles has shaped the way software products were managed, developed and delivered to users over the years. In order to support the faster pace required by the market, *Continuous Software Development* (ConSD) practices such as *Continuous Delivery* and *Continuous Deployment* have emerged in the recent years. A software release may introduce changes or new functionalities to an existing application, which may

E. Klotins and K. Wnuk (Eds.): ICSOB 2020, LNBIP 407, pp. 86–101, 2021.
https://doi.org/10.1007/978-3-030-67292-8_7

require specific communication to help Customer Support Services teams to better understand the changes introduced. Therefore, understanding how the speed of software changes imposed by ConSD practices impact the communication of software changes is extremely important to ensure Customer Support Services teams will be able to support end-users properly.

In order to understand this phenomena, this study performed a Systematic Literature Review (SLR), followed by an empirical study with seven global companies which then had the results triangulated and consolidated in a set of communication practices.

2 Methodology

In order to understand the challenges related to communication in continuous delivery and continuous deployment environments, a systematic literature review (SLR) has been performed, following Kitchenham [17] guidelines. Moreover, in order to get an in-depth understanding about the communication practices in use in the software industry and complement the systematic literature review results, we performed an empirical study with seven participants from seven different companies.

3 Literature Review

According to Kitchenham and Charters [4] a systematic review protocol is a plan that describes the conduct of a proposed systematic literature review. In the following paragraphs we describe the elements that compose the systematic review protocol of this research.

Research questions are used to drive a systematic review process. Based on these questions, a systematic search is performed to identify relevant information, such as papers and journals, which could contribute to the goal of this study. Following, the questions we have defined in our research are presented:

- **RQ1**: How do ConSD practices impact the communication of software changes?
- **RQ2**: How do software changes are communicated to customer support services teams in environments where ConSD practices were adopted?

A good way to create a search string is to structure them in terms of population, intervention, comparison, and outcome [17]. The search string used in this study is presented in Table 1. Additionally, Table 2 describes the inclusion and exclusion criteria applied to our research.

3.1 Data Extraction

Following a systematic literature review protocol, the research questions were used to search for relevant information on the ACM, IEEE, Scopus online

Table 1. Search string

Type	String
Population	(Software engineering OR software development AND)
Intervention	(Continuous deployment OR continuous delivery OR continuous integration OR continuous release OR devops)

Table 2. Exclusion/Inclusion criteria

Type	Description
Exclusion	Event keynotes, summaries, extended abstracts
Exclusion	Papers with less than 4 pages
Exclusion	Language different than English
Inclusion	Papers published between 2010 and 2019
Inclusion	Papers where CI, CDE or CD practices were mentioned

databases. Our initial search results returned 5,348 studies, which were filtered resulting on 102 full papers read. After reading carefully 102 papers, 39 papers were selected based on their relevance. The results of our systematic literature review process are presented in Sect. 3.2.

3.2 Results

In the following paragraphs, this study answers the research questions initially formulated as part of the research protocol and provides details about the challenges and practices identified.

(RQ1) How do ConSD practices impact the communication of software changes?

In the study conducted by Klepper *et al.* [18] the authors argue that many releases can overwhelm users, especially if they do not understand the difference between versions being released. The authors still argue that release notes can help in such situations, however, creating high quality release notes, manually, requires expressive amount of time and effort.

Shahin *et al.* [36] argue that a better visualisation of the CDE process would make a huge difference in the capability of the organisations to release faster and often. In one of the studies described by Shahin *et al.* [35], the authors argue that the status of a project should be visible and transparent to all team members. Shahin *et al.* [35] also argue that coordination and collaboration are challenges for continuous practices. According to their study, as more frequent software is deployed, more communication and coordination with operations teams is required. Their study also describes issues related to merge conflicts caused by the lack of awareness around software changes.

Brandtner *et al.* [5] argue that one of the main issues related to CI environments is the fact that relevant information about the health and quality of the software is spread across several tools and multiple views.

Stahl *et al.* [42] argue that traceability is a key challenge in achieving CI and CDE and describe an industry developed framework named Eiffel, designed to provide real time traceability for ConSD environments. The authors argue that agile methodologies, CI and CDE might be challenging for traceability due to the need of overhead reduction and traceability requirements. Stahl *et al.* [41] argue that even though the fundamental aspects of traceability remain the same regardless of CI and CDE, the nature of faster releases, increased frequencies have increased the amount of data generated in these processes, created new challenges in practice. Palihawadana *et al.* [28] argue that traceability links can be used by DevOps teams to evaluate software changes and their impact, however, also argue that maintaining traceability in agile based environments has become a challenge due to the lack of proper management tools and poor documentation.

Lwakatare *et al.* [25] highlighted studies which described the negative impact on project releases, from time to quality, due the lack of poor communication and lack of early involvement of operations teams in the software development process.

Yaman *et al.* [46] argue that one of the challenges related to communication in CD environments might be the excess of transparency that may lead to customers interference in developers' work.

Olsson *et al.* [27] argue that some of the challenges in such environments are the communication and coordination with suppliers, difficulties of getting an overview of the status of the project and the lack of transparency, including information available to users and other stakeholders who might need them.

Alyahya *et al.* [2] describes some challenges that affect the development progress and highlight the difficulties related to communication in distributed teams in order to maintain an awareness about development progress if they rely just on ad-hoc communication of changes. Alyahya *et al.* [3] argue that it is difficult to keep team members from different sites aware about each one's work.

Diel *et al.* [10] argue that some of the challenges faced in such environments are the lack of training on applications changes and no previous notice of software releases.

Downs *et al.* [11] argue that software teams working in agile projects produce a great deal of information on a daily basis, however, these information are misapplied, communicated ineffectively or ignored, which has impact in the results of these projects. In the study conducted by Shahin *et al.* [35], several papers described the lack of team awareness and transparency among team members as a challenge that may break down transition towards continuous practices. Table 3 has been created to group challenges categories and sumarize the challenges around software changes, previously described. Additionally, Table 4 categorizes papers and their respective communication challenge category.

Table 3. Communication challenges categories

Category	Description
Discovery	Information regarding software changes are not available, are not easily accessible or are not properly communicated
Coordination	Software changes require activities coordination between different teams such as software development and operations teams
Traceability	Tracing software changes from an end-to-end perspective considering the amount of data generated by CI and CDE environments
Training	Training teams to be up-to-date regarding software changes represent a challenge in in high frequency changing environments

Table 4. Papers per category

Challenges	Studies
Discovery	[2,3,5,8,10,11,18,25,27,32,35,36,46]
Coordination	[35]
Traceability	[28,41–43]
Training	[10]

(RQ2) In environments where Continuous Delivery practices were adopted, how software changes are communicated to customer support services team?

In the studies [25,31], the usage of shared Kanban boards has been described as a practice to communicate software changes. The usage of shared Dashboards has been described as a practice in the studies [11,16,29,34,38]. The usage of Ambient Surfaces and Project Radiators have been described by the studies [31, 33,44] as practices to ensure daily progress on projects is completely transparent and available for all stakeholders. Punjabi *et al.* [29], also argue that *user stories* can be maintained and assigned in such a system and could be integrated with source control and CI server to obtain issues addressed in a commit or build.

Centralizing and exchanging changes information through Tracking Systems has been described by the studies [1,2,12–14,19,32,33,39,40,43]. Downs *et al.* [11] and Kim *et al.* [16] mention the usage of issue tracking information along with dashboards and information radiators in order to provide project status. Punjabi and Bajaj [29] describe the usage of bug/issue/task tracking features along with visual boards that support agile development.

In the study conducted by Krusche *et al.* [19], the authors relate the usage of release notes, collected automatically by the CI server and linked to issues in tracking systems to provide visibility about the changes included in a given software release. Klepper *et al.* [18] propose a solution that uses a semi-automatic approach to release notes generation to reduce workload for the development team and release manager while still allowing them to provide properly targeted content depending on the context and recipients of a release. Still according to the authors, the information that is already produced during the development process is used to prepare release notes content. Kula *et al.* [20] relate the impact of missing release notes on rapid-releases with are delayed in such cases.

In the study performed by Neely *et al.* [26], the authors described some process changes required to implement CDE, which included the replacement of big meetings by crisp emails along with internal wikis and blogs in order to share knowledge about new features with other teams such as sales and support teams. Younas *et al.* [47] describe the usage of email, among other tools for collaboration in agile development. Brandtner *et al.* [6] describe the usage of email as a notification channel for CI-Tools. Krusche *et al.* [19] describe the usage of email to send release notes to users with details about solved issues, which can be also checked through an issue tracking system.

Wiedemann *et al.* [45] argue that traces are essential for application management, therefore, everything must be logged. In one of the studies evaluated by Shahin *et al.* [35], the authors suggest the practice of recording changes to a change log and making it visible to customers in order to enable them to track features changed. According to Shahin *et al.* [38], *et al.* [37], organizations practicing CD need to appropriately record, aggregate and analyse logs and metrics as an integral part of their CD environment in order to hypothesise and run experiments for examining different functionalities of a system. Shahin *et al.* [38] still argue that readability of logs for all stakeholders should be taken into consideration due to the fact that developers use to build the logging mechanism into the source code and there is a chance that such logs might become too technical for IT operations teams, such as support people, and may not be efficiently used to their needs. Lai *et al.* [21] describes the logging of relevant information such as programmer and change reasons information in the check-in step of CI processes in order to share this information with relevant stakeholders.

Senapathi *et al.* [34] describe the usage of Yammer to share software releases information with others stakeholders and to promote discussion on completed tasks and lessons learned and Atlassian Confluence to share release plans and software documentation. Schwarzer *et al.* [33] describe the usage of Atlassian Confluence along with ambient surfaces to share build summaries, reports and errors as well as software architects announcements. Neely *et al.* [26] describe the usage of wikis and blogs, replacing big meetings, in order to share information about new features. Heesch *et al.* [43] relate the usage of Atlassian Confluence along with Atlassian Jira to share application design definitions with team members. Heesch *et al.* [43] argue that apart from supporting the realisation of software artefacts, the information available in the tools also serve documentation needs, allowing the visualisation of tasks history. Claps *et al.* [8] describe Atlassian's case, a well established software company, where Confluence and blogs are used for software documentation and customer feature discovery purposes. Leite *et al.* [22] describe the usage of the GitLab tool as a wiki system for knowledge sharing between developers and operators.

In the study performed by Leite *et al.* [22], the authors mention the usage of ChatOps (Chat and Operations) tools in DevOps environments as a model that connects people, tools, processes, and automation through conversation-driven interactions. Lwakatare *et al.* [25] mention the HipChat tool usage for interaction between developers and operators, particularly when setting-up new environments. In the study performed by Luz *et al.* [24], the continuous use of instant messaging tools like Slack and HipChat was cited as the most appropriate option for communication between developers and operators in DevOps environments. In the study performed by Downs *et al.* [11], Instant Messaging conversation was the primary form of communication within the team, and for a wide range of purposes, including on-going status updates and team collaboration. Table 5 summarizes the main communication practices adopted by ConSD teams in order to ensure software changes are visible by other teams in the software development life cycle process.

Table 5. Communication practices

Practices	Studies
Sharing information through visual boards	[5,6,11,15,16,23,25,31,33,34,38,44]
Exchanging information through tracking systems	[1,2,11–14,16,19,22,29,32–34,39,40,43]
Communicating changes through release notes	[18–20]
Communicating changes through Email	[6,19,26,47]
Leveraging Logs to share information	[21,32,35,37,38,45]
Communicating changes through collaborative workspaces	[8,22,26,33,34,43]
Exchanging information through instant messaging	[11,14,22,24,25,30,34]

Based on these results, we performed an empirical study in the industry, which would complement the SLR results. The empirical study is presented in details in Sect. 4.

4 Empirical Study

In order to get an in-depth understanding about the communication practices in use in the ConSD industry and complement the SLR results, we performed an empirical study with seven participants from seven different companies. In the following paragraphs we provide details regarding the methods used to perform this research, from data collection and criteria to select the participants, to the data analysis method applied and finally the results obtained.

4.1 Data Collection and Analysis

Following Creswell's [9] recommendation, a questionnaire has been created to support the empirical study. In order to answer the research questions, we collected information from seven different companies. The interviewees and their companies were anonymised due to non-disclosure agreements, where we use aliases from Company A to Company G. The participants and their companies are briefly described in Table 6.

Table 6. Companies, practices, roles and experience

Company	Employees	Approach	Role	Yrs role
Company A	3,500	CDE	Product Manager	2
Company B	6,000	CD	Performance Engineer	6
Company C	50,000	CDE	Software Architect	3
Company D	2,000	CDE	Platform Engineer	1.3
Company E	7,000	CD	Project Manager	3
Company F	500	CDE	Software Developer	9
Company G	2,000	CDE	Support Engineer	9

4.2 Results

At Company A, software development teams and customer support services teams work apart from each other. The communication between software development teams and customer support services teams, in general, occurs through instant messaging tools or through their issue tracking systems. The *Service Enablement Team* (SET) is a specific team that makes a bridge between software development teams, customer support services teams and customers, mainly responsible for ensuring major software changes will be properly managed in order to avoid any impact on customers and customer support services teams. The SET team organizes bi-weekly meetings with customer support services teams where the main upcoming product changes are communicated, specially the bigger ones. Bigger software changes are communicated to customers through blog posts and built-in modal product banners. Developers and support teams use to interact using hidden messages through their issue tracking systems in order to follow-up changes required to fix bugs or features requested by customers. Even having daily deploys of product changes to production small changes are not communicated to customer support services teams on a daily basis, which represent some challenges to the support teams who sometimes receive customers complaints about changes in the products that are not reflected to the public documentation and were not communicated to them. Company A uses Atlassian Confluence to support the communication of major changes and releases in their products to customer support services teams.

At Company B, software changes, in general, are not communicated to customer support services teams and end-users. Whenever further information is required regarding a software change, instant messaging, memo pages and emails are the main channels to share information regarding software changes between development and customer support services teams. The usage of a change log database has been described in order to record several types of change logs, which can be accessed and tracked by the customer support services teams by using tools developed by internal teams specifically for this purpose.

At Company C, the communication of software changes, between software development and customer support services teams, occurs mainly through tickets in their issue tracking system, email messages and formal meetings. Formal meetings with key people in the customer support services teams are performed once a month to share details about the major changes being released to production, being these key people in support responsible for sharing details about the changes with their support teams. At Company C, customer support services teams have access to the development teams summarize Boards, therefore, they can also have visibility about the upcoming software changes being developed or about to be released. Release notes are used to share changes details and are available to software development teams and customer support services teams. End-users are communicated about software changes through a *"What's New"* web page, that is built into the product.

At Company D, most of the communication around software changes is performed through instant messaging and email channels. Projects use to structure their information using internal wiki pages which are then open to other teams that can track information about software changes and projects status. Issue tracking systems are also used to communicate the progress and communicate the status of software changes, specially bug fixes and feature requests.

At Company E, formal communication of software changes is mainly restricted to a showcase meeting, organised by the Product Owner. In this meeting, which use to occur every 15 days, the status of new features and bug fixes, among other project relevant information use to be shared with relevant stakeholders, such as customer support services teams and other software development teams. Additionally, the communication between different teams around software changes use to occur through instant messaging tools and tickets created at their tracking system where comments are added in order to provide details and status of such software changes.

At Company F, communication of software changes uses to be performed by Product Owners who share details about the changes with account managers and customers. There are no specific criteria to define which software changes will be communicated to the customers and is under the Product Owner the responsibility to decide which changes should be communicated and which one should not. Product Owners use to communicate software changes to customers through email and face-to-face meetings. The communication channel and frequency of these communication varies based on the requests being released.

At Company G, the communication of software changes to customer support services agents is facilitated by the fact that their software development teams include the customer support role in the team structure. End-users do not use to be notified about software changes, mainly because such changes use to have a minimum impact on the way customers use their software. Additionally, teams use to share information about software changes through instant messaging channels and CI tools are also used as source of information to get status and further technical details about software changes. The company is working to implement an issue tracking system in order to better support the flow of requests between teams.

5 Threats to Validity

Even though we have followed a SLR protocol, some threats to validity might be identified: (i) the research strategy is not correct; and (ii) the research bias regarding some of the studies selected. Such threats to validity were minimised by having this research protocol as well as the results of this work, reviewed by other two researchers. Regarding our empirical research, even though we have followed a protocol to conduct the interviews, the number of participants of this empirical study might represent a threat to the validity. Interviewing additional participants from other companies or even within the same companies, would have been useful to complement the results of our study.

6 Discussion

This section presents the main results of this research which were obtained by triangulating the SLR and the empirical study results. The data triangulation results are discussed and presented as a set of good practices.

> **Good Practice 1** - *Increasing awareness and transparency around software changes by sharing information through kanban boards, dashboards and information radiators with relevant stakeholders.*

Challenges related to the communication and visualization of project status have been reported in the SLR research by the studies [6,11,27,32,35,38,42]. Shahin *et al.* [38] argues, based on the studies evaluated as part of their research, that a better visualisation of the end-to-end software development life-cycle would allow software teams to release faster and often. In this sense, the usage of shared electronic Kanban Boards between different teams allows a visual tracking of software changes and has been reported as a common practice between the interviewees in the companies A, C, E and F as well as by the studies [25,31]. Team members can navigate in the content of User Stories, in order to better understand details of each change such as feature details, planning release dates, stakeholders affected and developers responsible for such features. Such level of transparency improves communication and provides autonomy to teams, which contributes to organisations in several aspects, from risk reduction to customer satisfaction. The implementation of this practice should take into consideration that, in case of customers adoption, the level of transparency may have negative implications, once customers may interfere in the development process frequently, as stated by Yaman *et al.* [46], reducing the release speed.

The traceability of changes could take advantage of shared Dashboards, once, as electronic Kanban Boards, they provide a visual mechanism to keep other stakeholders aware about progress and status of software changes, with the advantage of allowing layout and content modelling according to information needed and the target audience.

The usage of Information Radiators has been reported in the studies [16, 31, 33, 44] as an effective practice to increase transparency and awareness around project status and software changes for all stakeholders. Along with Dashboards, can be a practice for those teams which work at the same physical, once rely on infrastructure aspects to be used.

Good Practice 2 - *Using tracking systems to provide information around software changes to relevant stakeholders, from bug fixes to feature requests.*

The usage of tracking systems has been reported by the studies as well as by the companies A, B, C, D, E and G. Tracking systems were described in the literature and in the industry as tools to centralize information from different sources and track the software development progress, usually represented by bug-fixes and customers' requests. Such systems allow real-time interaction between different stakeholders and use to provide lower level granularity information, mainly focusing on operational information. The information exchanged between software development teams, operations teams, users, among other stakeholders, occurs through text comments in the tickets or through notifications, which might be triggered automatically every time there is a change in the status. Tracking Systems might be also integrated to other CI tools in order to support the deploy process.

Good Practice 3 - *Logging software changes to a central log database and sharing these information with relevant stakeholders.*

The practice of logging software changes to a central change log repository and sharing this information with relevant stakeholders has been cited in the studies [32, 35, 37, 38] and by the companies B and D. At Company B, the interviewee has described the usage of a change log database in order to record software changes performed at the company, which can be used by Customer Support Services teams to track software changes. Such information might be used for traceability purposes as well as to report issues related to the deployed functionalities. The practice of logging software changes may complement the information provided by Tracking Systems. Additionally, a central source of changes logs could be integrated with other tools to improve the communication of changes, such as Kanban Boards and Dashboards as well as be used to generate automatic notifications and release notes.

Good Practice 4 - *Automating the release notes generation process in order to reduce manual efforts.*

The usage of Release Notes have been reported by the studies [7,18–20] as well as by the companies C and G. As frequent as software development teams release changes to users, less is the usage of release notes as a mechanism to communicate changes, once they require manual intervention to be created. Therefore, the usage of Release Notes is a recommended practice, however, due to the fact that its creation requires manual effort, its usage might not be recommended to development teams where a high volume of software changes and deploys are performed on a daily basis. The usage of some level of automation to generate automatic release notes as described in the literature by Krusche *et al.* [19] and Klepper *et al.* [18] might represent an alternative to reduce the effort necessary to create release notes.

Good Practice 5 - *Using email channels to share details about software changes with relevant stakeholders.*

The usage of Email, sometimes as channel and in others as communication practice, is still recommended in ConSD environments, however, as the practice of Release Notes, its usage is directly related to the frequency of software releases deployed in production environments. As the time passes and companies move from CDE to CD practices, the communication of software changes through emails tend to be replaced or complemented by other practices such as the usage of shared virtual boards and tracking systems. Its usage has been described in the studies [6,19,26,47] as well by the companies B, C, D and F. One of the main advantages of email over other synchronous communication practices such as status meetings, is the fact that interested stakeholders can consume relevant information about software changes whenever they understand is necessary, what is also something Neely *et al.* [26] described in their study, where the replacement of big meetings by crisp emails in order to communicate users about new software features has been reported.

Good Practice 6 - *Using instant messaging rooms to share projects status and software changes information.*

The usage of instant messaging as a communication channel for communicating software changes has been reported in the studies [11,14,22,24,25,30,34] as well by the companies A, B, E and F. Instant Messaging practices are usually used by software development and operations teams in order to exchange additional details around software changes which could not be found in other sources. Companies such as Company A also use instant messaging channels to broadcast communication around software changes, what has been also reported by Downs *et al.* [11]. Such practice may replace the usage of emails to communicate software changes, once allow the centralisation of information in specific chat rooms.

Good Practice 7 - *Using wiki pages, blogs and collaborative portals to share software changes information.*

The practice of sharing information related to software changes through wiki pages, blogs and collaborative portals is described in the literature by the studies [8,22,26,33,34,43] as well as by the companies A, B and D. The information shared through such portals are usually available in a higher granularity of details. The advantage of this practice over other practices such as the usage of dashboards is the fact that such portals usually include collaboration features in a central space, which might be useful for several reasons. Such portals might also be integrated with Information Radiators and use information stored in change log databases in order to share relevant information regarding software changes with relevant stakeholders.

7 Conclusion

This study has assessed the challenges and impacts of ConSD practices on the communication of software changes and consolidated a set of good practices that aim to contribute to improve the communication of software changes in such environments. Initially, a SLR explored the challenges and practices related to communication of software changes between development and operations teams in ConSD environments. Additionally, an empirical study has been performed with professionals from seven global companies, which helped us to understand additional industry practices.

The overall results of this study indicate that challenges and practices related to the communication of software changes in ConSD environments vary according to a set of factors, including frequency of software changes and deploy, teams' structure and product design. As higher is the frequency of changes released, higher is the need for automatic and asynchronous communication practices to communicate software changes such as the usage of shared kanban boards and tracking systems. In the opposite side, less frequent releases allow the usage of synchronous or manual communication practices, such as structured meetings, release notes and emails. Product design is also an important factor in the process of communicating software changes. As complex is the product design, higher is the need to communicate software changes that affect its usability, including public product support documentation.

Finally, creating mechanisms to foster teams' autonomy and transparency around the communication of software changes should be a goal for those companies who want to deliver better products and services in the pace required by ConSD environments.

References

1. Aghajani, E., et al.: Software documentation issues unveiled. In: Proceedings of the 41st International Conference on Software Engineering, ICSE 2019, pp. 1199–1210. IEEE Press (2019)
2. Alyahya, S., Ivins, W.K., Gray, W.A.: Co-ordination support for managing progress of distributed agile projects. In: IEEE Sixth International Conference on Global Software Engineering Workshop, pp. 31–34 (2011)

3. Alyahya, S., Ivins, W.K., Gray, W.A.: A holistic approach to developing a progress tracking system for distributed agile teams. In: IEEE/ACIS 11th International Conference on Computer and Information Science, pp. 503–512 (2012)
4. Ba, K., Charters, S.: Guidelines for performing systematic literature reviews in software engineering, vol. 2, January 2007
5. Brandtner, M., Giger, E., Gall, H.: Supporting continuous integration by mashing-up software quality information. In: Software Evolution Week - IEEE Conference on Software Maintenance, Reengineering, and Reverse Engineering (CSMR-WCRE), pp. 184–193 (2014)
6. Brandtner, M., Giger, E., Gall, H.: SQA-mashup: a mashup framework for continuous integration. Inf. Softw. Technol. **65**, 97–113 (2015)
7. Callanan, M., Spillane, A.: DevOps: making it easy to do the right thing. IEEE Software **33**(3), 53–59 (2016)
8. Claps, G.G., Svensson, R.B., Aurum, A.: On the journey to continuous deployment: technical and social challenges along the way. Inf. Softw. Technol. **57**, 21–31 (2015)
9. Creswell, J.: Research Design: Qualitative, Quantitative, and Mixed Methods Approaches. SAGE Publications, New York (2009)
10. Diel, E., Marczak, S., Cruzes, D.S.: Communication challenges and strategies in distributed DevOps. In: IEEE 11th International Conference on Global Software Engineering (ICGSE), pp. 24–28 (2016)
11. Downs, J., Hosking, J., Plimmer, B.: Status communication in agile software teams: a case study. In: 2010 Fifth International Conference on Software Engineering Advances, pp. 82–87 (2010)
12. Feitelson, D.G., Frachtenberg, E., Beck, K.L.: Development and deployment at Facebook. IEEE Internet Comput. **17**(4), 8–17 (2013)
13. Gupta, R.K., Venkatachalapathy, M., Jeberla, F.K.: Challenges in adopting continuous delivery and devops in a globally distributed product team: a case study of a healthcare organization. In: ACM/IEEE 14th International Conference on Global Software Engineering (ICGSE), pp. 30–34 (2019)
14. Itkonen, J., Udd, R., Lassenius, C., Lehtonen, T.: Perceived benefits of adopting continuous delivery practices. In: Proceedings of the 10th ACM/IEEE International Symposium on Empirical Software Engineering and Measurement, ESEM 2016. Association for Computing Machinery, New York (2016)
15. Jurca, G., Hellmann, T.D., Maurer, F.: Agile User-Centered Design, pp. 109–123. Wiley, New York (2017). Chap. 6
16. Kim, E., Ryoo, S.: Agile adoption story from NHN. In: IEEE 36th Annual Computer Software and Applications Conference, pp. 476–481 (2012)
17. Kitchenham, B.: Procedures for performing systematic reviews, vol. 33. Keele University, Keele, UK, August 2004
18. Klepper, S., Krusche, S., Brügge, B.: Semi-automatic generation of audience-specific release notes. In: IEEE/ACM International Workshop on Continuous Software Evolution and Delivery (CSED), pp. 19–22 (2016)
19. Krusche, S., Alperowitz, L., Bruegge, B., Wagner, M.O.: Rugby: an agile process model based on continuous delivery. In: Proceedings of the 1st International Workshop on Rapid Continuous Software Engineering, RCoSE 2014, pp. 42–50. Association for Computing Machinery, New York (2014)
20. Kula, E., Rastogi, A., Huijgens, H., Deursen, A.v., Gousios, G.: Releasing fast and slow: an exploratory case study at ING. In: Proceedings of the 2019 27th ACM Joint Meeting on European Software Engineering Conference and Symposium on the Foundations of Software Engineering, ESEC/FSE 2019, pp. 785–795. Association for Computing Machinery, New York (2019)

21. Lai, S., Leu, F.: Applying continuous integration for reducing web applications development risks. In: 10th International Conference on Broadband and Wireless Computing, Communication and Applications (BWCCA), pp. 386–391 (2015)
22. Leite, L., Rocha, C., Kon, F., Milojicic, D., Meirelles, P.: A survey of DevOps concepts and challenges. ACM Comput. Surv. **52**(6) (2019)
23. Liechti, O., Pasquier, J., Reis, R.: Beyond dashboards: on the many facets of metrics and feedback in agile organizations. In: IEEE/ACM 10th International Workshop on Cooperative and Human Aspects of Software Engineering (CHASE), pp. 16–22 (2017)
24. Luz, W.P., Pinto, G., Bonifácio, R.: Adopting DevOps in the real world: a theory, a model, and a case study. J. Syst. Softw. **157**, 110384 (2019)
25. Lwakatare, L.E., et al.: Devops in practice: a multiple case study of five companies. Inf. Softw. Technol. **114**, 217–230 (2019)
26. Neely, S., Stolt, S.: Continuous delivery? easy! just change everything (well, maybe it is not that easy). In: 2013 Agile Conference, pp. 121–128 (2013)
27. Olsson, H.H., Alahyari, H., Bosch, J.: Climbing the "stairway to heaven" - a mulitiple-case study exploring barriers in the transition from agile development towards continuous deployment of software. In: 38th Euromicro Conference on Software Engineering and Advanced Applications, pp. 392–399 (2012)
28. Palihawadana, S., Wijeweera, C.H., Sanjitha, M.G.T.N., Liyanage, V.K., Perera, I., Meedeniya, D.A.: Tool support for traceability management of software artefacts with DevOps practices. In: Moratuwa Engineering Research Conference (MERCon), pp. 129–134 (2017)
29. Punjabi, R., Bajaj, R.: User stories to user reality: a DevOps approach for the cloud. In: IEEE International Conference on Recent Trends in Electronics, Information Communication Technology (RTEICT), pp. 658–662 (2016)
30. Rahman, A.A.U., Helms, E., Williams, L., Parnin, C.: Synthesizing continuous deployment practices used in software development. In: Proceedings of the 2015 Agile Conference, AGILE 2015, pp. 1–10. IEEE Computer Society, USA (2015)
31. Rodríguez, P., et al.: Continuous deployment of software intensive products and services: a systematic mapping study. J. Syst. Softw. **123**, 263–291 (2017)
32. Savor, T., Douglas, M., Gentili, M., Williams, L., Beck, K., Stumm, M.: Continuous deployment at Facebook and OANDA. In: IEEE/ACM 38th International Conference on Software Engineering Companion (ICSE-C), pp. 21–30 (2016)
33. Schwarzer, J., Draheim, S., von Luck, K., Wang, Q., Casaseca, P., Grecos, C.: Ambient surfaces: interactive displays in the informative workspace of co-located scrum teams. In: Proceedings of the 9th Nordic Conference on Human-Computer Interaction, NordiCHI 2016. Association for Computing Machinery, New York (2016)
34. Senapathi, M., Buchan, J., Osman, H.: Devops capabilities, practices, and challenges: insights from a case study. In: Proceedings of the 22nd International Conference on Evaluation and Assessment in Software Engineering 2018, EASE 2018, pp. 57–67. Association for Computing Machinery, New York (2018)
35. Shahin, M., Ali Babar, M., Zhu, L.: Continuous integration, delivery and deployment: a systematic review on approaches, tools, challenges and practices. IEEE Access **5**, 3909–3943 (2017)
36. Shahin, M., Babar, M.A., Zahedi, M., Zhu, L.: Beyond continuous delivery: an empirical investigation of continuous deployment challenges. In: ACM/IEEE International Symposium on Empirical Software Engineering and Measurement (ESEM), pp. 111–120 (2017)

37. Shahin, M., Babar, M.A., Zhu, L.: The intersection of continuous deployment and architecting process: Practitioners' perspectives. In: Proceedings of the 10th ACM/IEEE International Symposium on Empirical Software Engineering and Measurement, ESEM 2016. Association for Computing Machinery, New York (2016)
38. Shahin, M., Zahedi, M., Babar, M.A., Zhu, L.: An empirical study of architecting for continuous delivery and deployment. Empirical Softw. Eng. **24**(3), 1061–1108 (2019)
39. Siqueira, R., Camarinha, D., Wen, M., Meirelles, P., Kon, F.: Continuous delivery: building trust in a large-scale, complex government organization. IEEE Software **35**(2), 38–43 (2018)
40. Stettina, C.J., Heijstek, W.: Necessary and neglected? An empirical study of internal documentation in agile software development teams. In: Proceedings of the 29th ACM International Conference on Design of Communication, SIGDOC 2011, pp. 159–166. Association for Computing Machinery, New York (2011)
41. Ståhl, D., Hallén, K., Bosch, J.: Achieving traceability in large scale continuous integration and delivery deployment, usage and validation of the eiffel framework. Empirical Softw. Eng. **22**(3), 967–995 (2017). https://doi.org/10.1007/s10664-016-9457-1
42. Ståhl, D., Hallén, K., Bosch, J.: Continuous integration and delivery traceability in industry: needs and practices. In: 42th Euromicro Conference on Software Engineering and Advanced Applications (SEAA), pp. 68–72 (2016)
43. Van Heesch, U., Theunissen, T., Zimmermann, O., Zdun, U.: Software specification and documentation in continuous software development: a focus group report. In: Proceedings of the 22nd European Conference on Pattern Languages of Programs, EuroPLoP 2017. Association for Computing Machinery, New York (2017)
44. Virtanen, A., Kuusinen, K., Leppnen, M., Luoto, A., Kilamo, T., Mikkonen, T.: On continuous deployment maturity in customer projects. In: Proceedings of the Symposium on Applied Computing, SAC 2017, pp. 1205–1212. Association for Computing Machinery, New York (2017)
45. Wiedemann, A., Forsgren, N., Wiesche, M., Gewald, H., Krcmar, H.: Research for practice: the DevOps phenomenon. Commun. ACM **62**(8), 44–49 (2019)
46. Yaman, S.G.: Customer involvement in continuous deployment: a systematic literature review. In: Daneva, M., Pastor, O. (eds.) REFSQ 2016. LNCS, vol. 9619, pp. 249–265. Springer, Cham (2016). https://doi.org/10.1007/978-3-319-30282-9_18
47. Younas, M., Jawawi, D.N., Ghani, I., Fries, T., Kazmi, R.: Agile development in the cloud computing environment: a systematic review. Inf. Softw. Technol. **103**, 142–158 (2018)

Startups Transitioning from Early to Growth Phase - A Pilot Study of Technical Debt Perception

Orges Cico[1](✉), Renata Souza[2], Letizia Jaccheri[1], Anh Nguyen Duc[3], and Ivan Machado[2]

[1] Norwegian University of Science and Technology, Trondheim, Norway
{orges.cico,letizia.jaccheri}@ntnu.no
[2] Universidade Federal da Bahia, Salvador, Brazil
{renatamss,ivan.machado}@ufba.br
[3] University of South-Eastern Norway, Notodden, Norway
anh.nguyen.duc@usn.no

Abstract. Context: Software startups are software-intensive early phase companies with high growth rates. Previous researchers regarded startups' time to market as short and decisive in establishing the product/service success. This led to shortcuts in software engineering decisions. Researchers in previous investigations documented a high accumulation of technical debt (TD) in early startup phases. However, we found little evidence in the literature concerning TD when startups transition to the growth phase. Aim: Our goal was to evaluate how the transition from early to growth phases affects TD perception in software startups. Methodology: We conducted a pilot study guided by semi-structured interviews from multiple software startup cases. Results: We identified the four following dimensions: (1) managing, (2) accepting, (3) avoiding, and (4) ignoring TD. Contribution: Our study will allow practitioners to address TD in growth-phase software startups. Future researchers can benefit from our findings by conducting exploratory studies and providing educated recommendations.

Keywords: Software startups · Technical debt · Multiple case study

1 Introduction

A startup is commonly defined as a newly established company with small teams, limited resources, and an aim to rapidly scale the business models [3,12]. In the early stage, the primary goal is to meet a marketplace need by developing a viable business model for products, services, processes, or platforms. The failure rate of startups is commonly high. However, successful startups have had a major effect on the industry. This is particularly true for startups developing software-intensive products. These have shown higher rates of scaling [7], making them stand out.

E. Klotins and K. Wnuk (Eds.): ICSOB 2020, LNBIP 407, pp. 102–117, 2021.
https://doi.org/10.1007/978-3-030-67292-8_8

Facing Technical Debt[1] (TD) is becoming even more of an urgent need for many software startups [4,10,28]. Empirical evidence on how TD is perceived from software startups when transitioning from early to growth phases is still meager [1,4,18,19,26]. There is a need for empirical evidence [29]. Software startups are known to accumulate TD via their early stage prototyping and product development. This requires companies to pay the debt eventually, causing initial growth to hinder productivity [13]. TD affects startups' quality and productivity when they transition to the growth phase with stable resources [17]. There is minimal consideration of TD perception during the startup transition compared with previous efforts studying TD at different startup phases. We aimed at understanding the TD perception when startups transition from early to growth phases. First, we formulated the following research question (RQ):

RQ: *How does transitioning from early to growth phases affect TD perception in software startups?*

We designed semi-structured interviews and used purposive sampling to select the interviewees [27]. We conducted interviews with seven chief executive officers (CEOs) and chief technical officers (CTOs) from six software startups. We focused on startups that were transitioning in the growth phase. We observed that TD is deliberately embraced if product/service delivery deadlines and good enough quality are met. This was consistent with previous research. However, we found that TD in the early phase is characterized by accepting and ignoring. In the growth phase, startups are more prone to manage and avoid TD.

The findings of our study allow practitioners to consolidate their perception of TD, learn how to utilize TD to their advantage, and understand when to vary product feature development by inflating and deflating TD introduction in their software practices. Researchers can benefit from our findings by gaining better insights into TD perception in transition phases, conducting exploratory studies, and providing educated recommendations.

The remainder of the paper is structured as follows. Section 2 presents background and related work. The study's design and methodology are discussed in Sect. 3. Section 4 presents the obtained results and key findings. Section 5 discusses the findings, lessons learned, and validity threats. Finally, Sect. 6 provides conclusions for this study and suggests future work.

2 Background and Related Work

2.1 Software Startups Life-Cycle Phases

Startups have high failure rates. However, successful startups have had a major effect on the industry [7]. Typically, startups operate and evolve in an ecosystem with connections to various stakeholders, from types of investors to incubators,

[1] Metaphoric concept of TD has been first introduced by Ward Cunningham [9] in 1992. Read more on Sect. 2 about its relation to software startups.

accelerators, and third-party vendors. Startups typically undergo the following phases: (1) Generation based on a product or service idea with a clear mission and vision; (2) Startup based on team commitment, with the initial product commonly validated through iterations and testing the initial idea; (3) Growth based on scaling with a focus on key performance indicators; and (4) Establishment with increasing growth and market potential [8].

Startup transitions are marked by the methodological evolution from ad hoc or customized development practices [23] to more principled software engineering approaches. A lean startup methodology is popular at the early and validation stages [13,29]. This involves shortening the product development cycle through iterative product releases, market experimentation, and validation. Teams that adopt a lean startup strategy develop a continuously changing MVP to identify product/service potentials utilizing limited resources. If software startups desire to transition toward the growth phase, they must be established in the market by creating valuable products. The growth phase inherits many technological features, benefits, and drawbacks (including TD) from its successful MVP predecessor. Here, a professionalized product/service fulfils a specific market need.

2.2 Technical Debt

Brown et al.'s [6] provides a precise definition of TD:

> *"Developers sometimes accept compromises in a system in one dimension (e.g., modularity) to meet urgent demand in some other dimension (e.g., a deadline), and ... such compromises incur a "debt" : on which "interest" has to be paid and which the "principal" should be repaid at some point for the long-term health of the project."*

More recently, Avgeriou et al. [2] stated: "The term technical debt refers to delayed tasks and immature artifacts that constitute a 'debt' because they incur extra costs in the future in the form of increased cost of change during evolution and maintenance." In early 2011, Seaman and Guo [25] reported issues associated with TD. She proposed a TD management framework and a research plan for validation. Kruchten [20] presented TD from a theory and practice standpoint. This author raised the need for more tools to manage TD. Guo et al. [15] provided a practical evaluation of how TD might affect real software projects throughout their lifecycle. The authors evaluated TD's effects and emphasized what research methodologies can be used to investigate TD management.

A systematic mapping of TD and its management was provided by Zengyang Li [21]. This author consolidated the TD term usage and identified a need for more empirical studies with high-quality evidence from industry practices in managing TD. Martini et al. [22] studied TD tracking and awareness in large organizations. They argued for the need to introduce tools and approaches for TD tracking and awareness in organizations at an early stage. They also proposed implementing a strategic adoption model, facilitating TD management throughout the product lifecycle. Holvitie et al. [16] addressed the TD perception from practitioners' perspectives in an agile software development context.

They argued that practitioners and agile stakeholders are implicitly aware of the TD concept. They claimed that TD instances reside mainly in the implementation phase of the software development lifecycle. The authors argued that TD management can be achieved without introducing new and disruptive methods. A more recent study by Apa et al. [1] presented TD perception and management from the perspectives of startups' practitioners in Uruguay. The authors found that TD prevention is one of the most frequent activities in software startups.

2.3 Growth Phase Software Startups and Technical Debt

Not until 2013–2016 was the need for TD research in the software startup context reported [10,29]. Based on the open questions and product roadmap recommendation that needs to be stated by Abrahamsson et al. [29], many researchers started conducting empirical investigations about TD in the software startup area. Their primary concern was how TD is introduced in different software engineering knowledge areas (code, design and architecture, environment, knowledge distribution and documentation, and testing) in a software startup context [28]. According to Gralha et al. [14], "Improved ability to handle technical debt results in a higher ability to prioritize requirements with greatest customer impact." This provides a solid theory about dimensions (requirement artifacts, product quality, knowledge management, TD, requirements-related roles) that determine product requirement practices in startups. Garkavtsev et al. [11] empirically evaluated how programming language choices may affect the level of TD introduced in small teams and startups. Moreover, studies reporting empirical evidence on when TD is commonly revealed from startups in an industrial setting [9] facilitate research decisions on which startup phases require more attention in managing TD. Besker et al. [4] also reported empirical evidence on how the taking on or embracing of TD is deemed to be an essential option for software startups. The authors analyzed how TD is accumulated and refactored at different stages of startup development to provide sufficient software quality. Moreover, Klotins et al. [18,19] provided vivid arguments about the TD prevalence in software startups and keeping TD under control.

3 Methodology

We aimed to understand the perception of TD in software startups in the growth phase. Therefore, the RQ (How does the transitioning from early to growth phase impact TD perception in software startups?) guided our investigation. To gather and interpret evidence for answering our RQ, we devised a qualitative approach. The instrument was based on semi-structured interviews with seven CEOs/CTOs from the six software startups. Our methodology is based on Runeson and Höst's [24] guidelines for conducting and reporting case study research in software engineering and the EU General Data Protection Regulation (EUGDPR.org) rules.

3.1 Case Selection

We primarily collected data from a tech event in the United States involving more than 100 startups (about 70% of the samples). The remaining data were collected from Norway. We selected the sample population using the purposive sampling technique. Purposive sampling is a form of non-probability sampling in which researchers rely on their judgment when choosing members of the population to participate in their study [27]. We used the following criteria for sample selection:

1. The startup was in series A financing. The company had acquired VCs and offered ownership to outside investors;
2. The startup was up to 5 years old;
3. The startup had entered the growth phase at the latest in the last two years;
4. The startup had a self-owned or independent headquarters;
5. The startup had had positive return incomes during the last two years;
6. The startup had a core development team larger than five participants;
7. The startup had established revenues or investment to provide market-rate compensation to participants.

3.2 Case Demographics

We collected data from the startups' online resources after initial contact (email or face to face) and later from CEOs and CTOs. From more than 100 startups in the tech event in the United States, we identified 12 as potential candidates. However, only five agreed to an interview. We then looked into startups from Norway, asking three for an interview. Of these, two agreed to participate. Demographics of the six startups are reported in Table 1. Notably, all the interviewees are co-founders of the startups, with active roles in product lifecycle development.

Table 1. Software startups' sample demographics.

SCN	Role	Country	P/S	E	PC	CDTS
Startup 1	CTO / CEO	USA	SW product	2008	2017	8
Startup 2	CEO	USA	SW/HW product	2016	2017	5
Startup 3	CEO	USA	SW product	2015	2016	7
Startup 4	CTO	USA	SW/HW product	2012	2017	14
Startup 5	CTO	Norway	SW product	2017	2018	6
Startup 6	CEO	Norway	SW product	2012	2012	5

Legend: **SCN:** Startup Case Number, **P/S:** Product/Service, **E:** Establishment (in years), **PC:** Product Commercialization, **CDTS:** Core Development Team Size.

We summarize each startup's context and present lifecycle phase in Table 2. We established the growth phase based on the following: (1) the startup's customer base and (2) the stability in the market during the last year (cf. Sect. 2).

Table 2. Startups' contexts.

SCN	HTS	SDP	SP	NC
Startup 1	Genomic search engine	Agile/Scrum	Growth Phase	100+
Startup 2	Solves mechanist skilled workers shortage by automating physical component design industry.	Prototyping	Transitioning to Growth Phase. MVP limitations.	5+
Startup 3	GPU-accelerated software for rapid secondary analysis of next-generation sequencing data.	Agile/XP	Transitioning to Growth Phase	5+
Startup 4	Wind turbine inspection through drone technology.	Agile/FDD	Growth Phase	80+
Startup 5	Optimal wind farm layout services.	Agile/Scrum	Growth Phase	20+
Startup 6	Real estate business intelligence.	Agile/Scrum	Growth Phase	50+

Legend: **SCN**: Startup Case Number, **HTS**: High Tech Solution, **SDP**: Software Development Practices **SP**: Startup Phase, **NC**: Number of Customers.

3.3 Interview Design

We performed a pilot study on multiple startup cases, based on an interview template for data collection. Writing the interview questions beforehand allowed us to focus our interview questions in connection to the research question.

The interview process took place in three parts (Table 3). In the first part, the interview questions primarily addressed demographic information about the startup (duration: 10–15 min). The second part focused more on a broad context of the software and technological aspects of the startup (20–30 min). The third part concentrated the perception of TD for each case (30–40 min). Dividing the interview into various parts helped us guide the startups in expressing their standpoints without generating bias due to our expectations.

The approach followed does not compromise the data gathered because we planned a semi-structured interview from the start. Thus, we had little control over the chosen samples. All authors collaboratively planned the interviews. Only one author executed them. The results were peer-reviewed by the other authors.

3.4 Data Collection

Based on recommendations from Runeson [24], we collected data from semi-structured, face-to-face interviews to answer our RQ. We interviewed eight CTOs/CEOs from seven startups in two countries, all having a high-tech product focus. Each interview lasted around 80 min. Questions related to startup software practices represented 75% of the interview time. We recorded all interviews for later transcription.

The interviews aimed to understand the TD perception from startup founders, commonly represented by both CEOs and CTOs (Table 1). All the CEOs/CTOs interviewed had an active role in the software development, testing, and release cycles. During the first part of the interview, we asked to what extent they participated in all the cycles. Both CEOs and CTOs have a higher interest in a smooth transition from MVPs to product/services while transitioning in the growth phase.

Table 3. Interview parts and questions.

Interview Part	Questions
Part 1 Startup Demographics	***Q1:*** *What is the startup core product/service?* ***Q2:*** *When was your startup established?* ***Q3:*** *Where is your startup located?* ***Q4:*** *What is your role?* ***Q5:*** *What type of ecosystem are you presently working in?* ***Q6:*** *How many employees do you have at the moment?* ***Q7:*** *What is your team composition?* ***Q8:*** *Do you proactively participate in the product life-cycles such as production, testing, and release? If yes, to what extent?*
Part 2 Software Engineering Practices	***Q1:*** *What software development practices, tools are you using?* ***Q2:*** *Briefly describe how?* ***Q3:*** *What are the most important quality attributes (UX, performance, security, reusability) for your current products?* ***Q4:*** *What testing practices do you adopt in validating and verifying the quality of your product/service?* ***Q5:*** *How much have you invested in testing activities?* ***Q6:*** *How do you document your product at different phases of development and testing?* ***Q7:*** *How are your documents updated?* ***Q8:*** *How do you keep track of changes?*
Part 3 Technical Debt Perceptions	***Q1:*** *How much aware are you about TD within your Startup?* ***Q2:*** *What is your perception of TD?* ***Q3:*** *How do you cope with TD? Do you ignore TD? Do you accept and manage TD? Do you avoid TD?* ***Q5:*** *How did you cope with TD in the early phases?* ***Q6:*** *How are you coping with TD now that you are at the growth phase?* ***Q7:*** *Do you have a lot of feature creep?* ***Q8:*** *Do you throw away a lot of code during the development/maintenance of your product/service?* ***Q9:*** *Have there been cases that you had to through the entire product code away?*

3.5 Data Analysis

First, we carefully collected data to obtain significant evidence that would help us answer our research question. We then used the thematic analysis approach [5] and thematic coding tool NVivo 12 This consisted of identifying recurring patterns and themes within the interview data. The steps to conducting the systematic analysis consisted of the following:

1. **Reading the transcripts.** This step initially involved quick browsing and correction of the automatically transcribed data from the audio recordings. Later, we reviewed the transcribed data more carefully by reading judiciously, line by line;
2. **Coding.** During this step, we focused on choosing and labeling relevant words, phrases, or sentences and even larger text fragments or sections related to TD phenomena.
3. **Creating themes.** After gathering all the codes, we decided on the most relevant ones and created different categories or themes.
4. **Labeling and connecting themes.** We decided on which themes were more relevant and defined appropriate names and relationships for them.

5. **Drawing the results summary.** After deciding on the themes' importance and hierarchy, we generated a summary of the results (cf. Sect. 4) and discussed them in relation to previous studies (cf. Sect. 5).

4 Results

We identified several factors that influenced how the CEOs and CTOs of the startups perceived TD while transitioning to the growth phase (Figure 1). Thus, we identified four primary categories—Managing TD (Sect. 4.1), Avoiding TD (Sect. 4.2), Accepting TD (Sect. 4.3), and Ignoring TD (Sect. 4.4), each helping to answer our RQ.

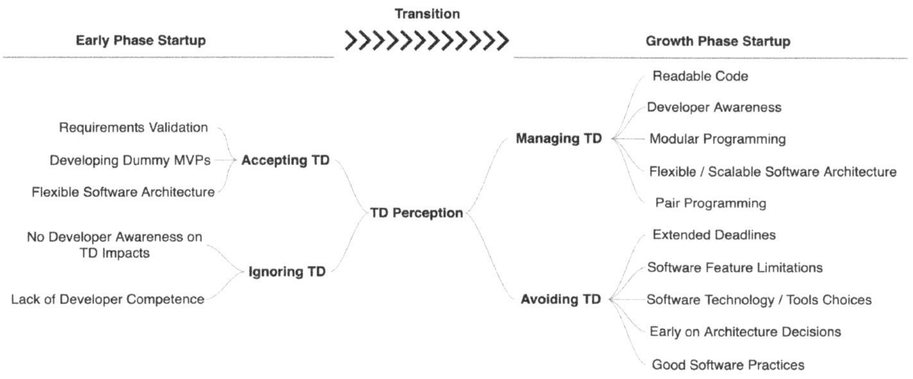

Fig. 1. Themes summary.

We observed that startups at an early phase are more oriented toward accepting or ignoring TD. The overall perception is that introducing TD is not bad at an early stage. Paying the software debt later is seen as a more viable option. Primary reasons for accepting TD are related to requirement validation either through dummy MVPs or flexible architectures. However, ignoring TD is connected with a lack of developer awareness or competence. In contrast, startups undertake a more mature approach in the growth phase by managing or even avoiding TD. Managing TD comprises the adoption of good programming practices combined with modularized and flexible software architectures. TD avoidance is accompanied by slowing the development pace and extending deadlines, limiting feature number, adopting software engineering tools and proper software architectures, and deciding on practices earlier in the product lifecycle. In the growth phase, the overall perception is that the earlier TD is managed the better.

4.1 Managing TD

Managing TD includes recognizing, analyzing, monitoring, and measuring it. In our cases, TD management was reported as the most common option when a startup is in the growth phase. The CEOs from two startups (Cases 3, 5) emphasized that increased awareness helped them have better control over the TD. This was common even in large contingents of development teams adopting a pair programming approach to software development. Developers deliberately introducing TD to certain modules would raise a flagship to make other team members aware of the situation:

> *"... We sort the story cards and set aside team time to address TD. Everybody on the team tends to know what the state of the code is in the project and where the challenges or things to be solved are. If someone says, "Hey, we're going to change this part of the code," someone else might raise their hand and say, "Hey, we really need to improve that code...." **[Case 3]***

In Case 5, the TD trade-off was accepted whenever deadlines had to be met. However, team members were aware of the situation and admitted that TD issues had to be dealt with later on:

> *"... We accept TD can happen, take responsibility for it, and this is all about trade-offs we need to make in achieving deadlines. Our team is highly deadline-driven, but fully committed to handling TD..." **[Case 5]***

Likewise, Case 3 reported that managing and isolating code issues modules with low coupling helped control TD. The same case emphasized the possibility of mitigating TD whenever there are backend software architectures, which can be easily modified and scaled.

We found a recurring pattern, including readable code and code refactoring, from all cases, and this can be part of managing TD. Readable code allows the developers to quickly unfold whenever TD is introduced to the software system without requiring extensive documentation. The readable coding approach was considered of immediate relevance for all our cases under investigation. Examples of reports from some cases are as follows:

> *"...See, that's OK. It's time to refactor. That's because we have made the shortcut. Two, three times earlier before..." **[Case 5]***
>
> *"... We all agree in our team that the code should be highly readable and peer-reviewed if we want to manage technical debt..." **[Case 6]***

4.2 Avoiding TD

We define TD avoidance as a proactive strategy to identify all potential software cycles (production–test–release) where TD can occur and to take measures for preventing it. In comparison with TD management, which focuses more on action taken after TD may have occurred, TD avoidance takes measures beforehand. We found that avoiding TD is primarily perceived as positive when sacrificing software features seems a good option. Case 3 reported:

"...We can develop anything but not everything within the given time limitations...". ***[Case 3]***

Another case reported that avoiding TD is strongly connected with missed deadlines:

"...We always use best approaches, although we accept that we cannot achieve perfect software without exceeding deadlines..." ***[Case 1]***

In other reports, we find that architecture, programming language, and technology flexibility helped the software startups take precautions to avoid TD. One case reported the following:

"...We don't want to be locked up in one specific programming language or one set of libraries courses to the point that they are running a lot to make that work... We want to make the system a lot more modular with some things that are running now... So, the flexibility built into our infrastructure in the understanding of how to remove a system or reengineer it quickly if we need to helped us avoid TD..." ***[Case 2]***

The cases commonly accepted that there has to be a trade-off and it was hard to circumvent scenarios introducing TD. Highly competent senior developers were perceived as a particular case that can elegantly fulfill the requirements while introducing marginal levels of TD. One case revealed,

"...There's a subset of senior-level developers that I call the highly creative senior-level developers. You don't even have to tell them what to build. You just tell them why you're building it, and they help you figure out what to build. And so that kind of gets to your question about TD because they're the ones who have the experience and the creativity, not just the technical knowledge of how to build something efficiently or quickly or in a well-tested manner..." ***[Case 1]***

Another case at a later stage of startup development stated:

"...But now that we are getting bigger, we are trying to use good software techniques and like to make sure that everything is robust. We are trying to make all the code follow all the different guidelines to avoid technical debt..." ***[Case 3]***

4.3 Accepting TD

We defined TD acceptance as the presence of TD in any software cycle (production–test–release) but without any further action taken to properly detect and correct software code or architecture. The TD acceptance was primarily present in the early startup phase. At this stage, the CEO/CTO considered acting along with TD to be beneficial. One case reported the following about requirement validation:

"...We could define better our requirements when developing dummy MVPs that can be thrown away due to the large amount of TD introduced..." ***[Case 2]***

Another case reported the following on product-market validation and TD:

"...Technical debt isn't bad. Because if you have no technical debt it maybe you spent way too much time and money building in before you really got out and started verifying..." ***[Case 3]***

Another case reported that they can accept TD at the early startup phase if it does not hamper the overall product outcome:

"...You also don't want to do something that built the startup into a corner too much...So it's all about finding like the right amount of technical debt that gets us to the point of being able to you know to develop the initial product..." ***[Case 6]***

Acceptance of TD is sometimes associated with a shortening of the time to market in the startup's early phase. In one case, the CEO stated the following in relation to this phase:

"...We took lots of shortcuts. Mmhmm. So it was all about shortcuts to get to the first prototype sooner. Okay. So at that point, we didn't care about robust engineering..." ***[Case 4]***

4.4 Ignoring TD

We defined TD ignorance as the lack of software engineering rigor in any software cycle (production–test–release). We found that this category was strongly associated with a lack of TD awareness from the team from Case 3. Planning to throw away prototypes can also lead to ignoring TD for those modules. An example was made earlier with dummy MVPs from Case 2. However, to differentiate from the previous example, when a startup decides to ignore TD, this is a deliberate long-lasting decision that may or may not affect the product during its operational lifetime. Still, the reason for doing this is the lack of team competence, which cannot be compensated for:

"...They connect us with the one company in Germany that writes automation for almost every industry. Now, I think we did integration in about nine months times with our competitors for the MVP prototypes stage, nothing in production. We fly to Germany to speed with them and get something in production running with customers in about 10 days..." ***[Case 2]***

Nevertheless, ignoring TD may still be part of trade-offs in startups in the early phase, when software is not in the production stage. Case 4 elegantly reported this scenario:

"...And we were pretty convinced that we could just do this...When we finally realized, after taking several shortcuts, oh, crap, this is really hard. We can't do this, or it's going to take two years if done appropriately. The failed prototype allowed us to learn about factors towards achieving our goal..." ***[Case 4]***

Thus, despite not being fully aware of the TD, even when they became aware, ignoring it at this phase proved to be efficient. Looking for competence elsewhere and joint ventures seemed to be successful options. Another case reported the total lack of software practices, resulting in the startup ignoring TD occurrence in the early development phase:

> *"...I feel like everything you ask me and goes under, uh, technical debt. We did no documentation, no testing and uh, in some cases, uh, sort of down to the shortcuts. At early times we should have used better interfacing and stuff like that..."* ***[Case 5]***

5 Discussions

5.1 Early Versus Growth Phase Startup Technical Debt Perceptions

This study focuses on highlighting perceptions about TD in software startups transitioning to the growth phase. Although we have a limited number of participants, the study's qualitative nature permitted us to obtain legitimate results that focus on deeply understanding the TD perceptions. Although the study focuses on a particular niche context, startups transitioning to the growth phase, our results unfold unnoted differences from previous sources. Thus, we can offer practitioners and researchers unique insights. Nevertheless, the study has limitations. We mention these in Sect. 5.2. Previous studies have focused on covering and addressing several startup lifecycle phases by unfolding the TD challenges and benefits [1,4]. We focus more on investigating how TD perception evolves when startups transition from early to growth phases. We argue that our investigation is of interest because of the following: (1) It is understudied in previous research [4,11,14,18,19], and (2) it is during such a transition that startup disruptions occur, and successfully overcoming TD thresholds is significant for the startups' success [4]. Our findings permit us to emphasize three additional perceptions, which we devise as three separate dimensions, namely TD acceptance, ignorance, and avoidance. While TD management is widely accepted and defined [2], we argue that it is not the only dimension that startups have at their disposal. Furthermore, as Avgeriou et al. [2] stated, there are no standard practices in place for managing TD. Reasons for this may vary, but we argue that the research community has yet to reach maturity in TD in general and for software startups in particular. We also recently observed that all the other dimensions are encapsulated in TD management. However, we argue that treating TD management so broadly may be harmful for standardizing future TD practices [1]. For instance, avoidance/prevention versus management assumes separate connotations in other scientific fields. For example, in project management, the terms management versus prevention of the crisis depict separate concepts. While the former deals with handling situations after a crisis has occurred, the latter invests resources in avoiding the occurrence of the crisis. Accumulated TD can lead to a software development crisis with high risks of slowing down new features or even making the software product redundant or maintainable.

Key recommendations:

1. Different TD mindsets should be applied depending on the startup development phase. Accumulating TD at early phases may be beneficial, in a similar way to managing or avoiding TD at the startup growth phase.
2. Sacrificing software features is a valuable practice in avoiding TD and meeting deadlines when under market pressure.
3. When in early phase, startups should accept TD and make it work to their advantage. It is recommended to build as many dummy MVPs as possible until the product requirements and market viability are certain.
4. Early investment in networking and expertise from other practitioners allows startups to refrain from ignoring TD in case of lack of competence or unawareness.

Researchers can benefit from our study in the following ways: (1) by having better insights on how startups perceive TD in the transition from early to growth phases, (2) by collecting similar data that could help in surveying the startup transition, and (3) by providing guidelines/recommendations for how to adopt TD approaches for early and growth phase startups. Practitioners can benefit from our study in the following ways: (1) Consolidating their perception of TD. Four dimensions can be identified (managing, avoiding, accepting, and ignoring). In previous research, only TD management was well defined and prioritized. Consolidation can help startups choose among the best options considering their startup development phase; (2) Learning to utilize TD efficiently and not always holding negative perceptions related to TD; (3) Understanding when to limit or increase the features of their products to limit the overall TD.

5.2 Threats to Validity

As often reported in qualitative research [24], the main threats to validity related to the following:

1. **External Validity.** This is related to the sample size and limited context under consideration. We upheld this validity by choosing software startups after transitioning to the growth phase. We also decided to investigate startups in different geolocations. We admit that ours is a pilot study. A larger sample size is required to generalize the results. To mitigate this threat to validity, we plan to recruit further samples and interview other roles in the startups (follow-up questionnaires).
2. **Internal Validity.** Internal threats to validity in qualitative studies are related to data extraction and analysis. We tried to mitigate this by carefully coding and categorizing the transcriptions and gradually shrinking to the most significant data.
3. **Construct validity** in our cases is related to previous knowledge about TD. The maturity level of the startups proved that they were all familiar with the concept. Furthermore, our instrument is like previous research instruments in investigating TD [4,10,11,14,29], although applied with a different investigation scope and lenses. Consequently, we argue that this threat to validity is almost non-existent.

6 Conclusions and Future Work

We focused on understanding how software startups perceive TD in the early phase and later transition to the growth phase. After interviewing six different software startups and seven co-founders in either the CEO or CTO role, we identified two perceptions in the early phase as follows: 1) accepting TD and 2) ignoring TD. Another two were identified in the growth phase as follows: 1) managing TD and 2) avoiding TD. Reasons for such a discrepancy between the early and growth phases vary. However, it will be worthwhile for both researchers and practitioners to investigate and validate our claims. We do not know if early phase startups should have a similar approach toward managing and avoiding TD or whether accepting and ignoring TD is legitimate from their infantile development phase. Our findings spark an intriguing debate on the startup transition between phases and TD approaches. Moreover, we argued that startups in the early phase need to make deliberate educated decisions on using TD to their advantage. In contrast, in the growth phase, the amount of TD should be limited as much as possible. We can only improve startup awareness by providing options to cope with TD at different startup phases. In the future, we plan to collect further data by surveying and interviewing a larger sample. The triangulation will allow us to generalize our findings and provide a clear roadmap and guidelines to be exploited by the research and practitioner community actively participating in software startups.

References

1. Apa, C., Jeronimo, H., Nascimento, L.M., Vallespir, D., Travassos, G.H.: The perception and management of technical debt in software startups. In: Nguyen-Duc, A., Münch, J., Prikladnicki, R., Wang, X., Abrahamsson, P. (eds.) Fundamentals of Software Startups, pp. 61–78. Springer, Cham (2020). https://doi.org/10.1007/978-3-030-35983-6_4
2. Avgeriou, P., Kruchten, P., Ozkaya, I., Seaman, C.: Managing technical debt in software engineering (Dagstuhl seminar 16162). In: Dagstuhl Reports, vol. 6. Schloss Dagstuhl-Leibniz-Zentrum fuer Informatik (2016)
3. Berg, V., Birkeland, J., Nguyen-Duc, A., Pappas, I., Jaccheri, L.: A systematic mapping study. J. Syst. Softw. Softw. Startup Eng. (2018)
4. Besker, T., Martini, A., Lokuge, R.E., Blincoe, K., Bosch, J.: Embracing technical debt, from a startup company perspective. In: IEEE International Conference on Software Maintenance and Evolution (ICSME), pp. 415–425. IEEE (2018)
5. Braun, V., Clarke, V.: Using thematic analysis in psychology. Qual. Res. Psychol. **3**(2), 77–101 (2006)
6. Brown, N., et al.: Managing technical debt in software-reliant systems. In: Proceedings of the FSE/SDP Workshop on Future of Software Engineering Research, pp. 47–52. ACM (2010)
7. Cannice, M.V.: Confidence among silicon valley venture capitalists Q3 2017–Q4 2018: trends, insights, and tells. Journal Private Equity **22**(3), 18–24 (2019)
8. Crowne, M.: Why software product startups fail and what to do about it. Evolution of software product development in startup companies. In: IEEE International Engineering Management Conference, vol. 1, pp. 338–343. IEEE (2002)

9. Cunningham, W.: The WyCash portfolio management system, experience report. In: Proceedings on Object-Oriented Programming Systems, Languages, and Applications (OOPSLA 1992) (1992)
10. Devos, N., Durieux, D., Ponsard, C.: Managing technical debt in it start-ups–an industrial survey. In: International Conference on Software and System Engineering and their Applications (ICSSEA) (2013)
11. Garkavtsev, M., Lamonova, N., Gostev, A.: Chosing a programming language for a new project from a code quality perspective. In: IEEE Second International Conference on Data Stream Mining & Processing (DSMP), pp. 75–78. IEEE (2018)
12. Giardino, C., Wang, X., Abrahamsson, P.: Why early-stage software startups fail: a behavioral framework. In: Lassenius, C., Smolander, K. (eds.) ICSOB 2014. LNBIP, vol. 182, pp. 27–41. Springer, Cham (2014). https://doi.org/10.1007/978-3-319-08738-2_3
13. Giardino, C., Paternoster, N., Unterkalmsteiner, M., Gorschek, T., Abrahamsson, P.: Software development in startup companies: the greenfield startup model. IEEE Trans. Softw. Eng. **42**(6), 585–604 (2016)
14. Gralha, C., Damian, D., Wasserman, A.IT., Goulão, M., Araújo, J.: The evolution of requirements practices in software startups. In: Proceedings of the 40th International Conference on Soft- ware Engineering, pp. 823–833. ACM (2018)
15. Guo, Y., et al.: Tracking technical debt. an exploratory case study. In: 27th IEEE International Conference on Software Maintenance (ICSM), pp. 528–531. IEEE (2011)
16. Holvitie, J., et al.: Technical debt and agile software development practices and processes. An industry practitioner survey. Inf. Softw. Technol. **96**, 141–160 (2018)
17. Jabangwe, R., et al.: An exploratory study of software evolution and quality: before, during and after a transfer. In: 2012 IEEE Seventh Inter- national Conference on Global Software Engineering, pp. 41–50. IEEE (2012)
18. Klotins, E., et al.: Exploration of technical debt in start-ups. In: IEEE/ACM 40th International Conference on Software Engineering: Software Engineering in Practice Track (ICSE-SEIP), pp. 75–84. IEEE (2018)
19. Klotins, E., et al.: A progression model of software engineering goals, challenges, and practices in start-ups. IEEE Trans. Softw. Eng. (2019)
20. Kruchten, P., Nord, R.L., Ozkaya, I.: Technical debt: from metaphor to theory and practice. IEEE Software **29**(6), 18–21 (2012)
21. Li, Z., Avgeriou, P., Liang, P.: A systematic mapping study on technical debt and its management. J. Syst. Softw. **101**, 193–220 (2015)
22. Martini, A., Besker, T., Bosch, J.: Technical debt tracking: current state of practice: a survey and multiple case study in 15 large organizations. Sci. Comput. Programm. **163**, 42–61 (2018)
23. Nguyen-Duc, A., Wang, X., Abrahamsson, P.: What influences the speed of prototyping? An empirical investigation of twenty software startups. In: Baumeister, H., Lichter, H., Riebisch, M. (eds.) XP 2017. LNBIP, vol. 283, pp. 20–36. Springer, Cham (2017). https://doi.org/10.1007/978-3-319-57633-6_2
24. Runeson, P., Höst, M.: Guidelines for conducting and reporting case study research in software engineering. Empirical Softw. Eng. **14**(2), 131 (2009)
25. Seaman, C., Guo, Y.: Measuring and monitoring technical debt. In: Advances in Computers, vol. 82, pp. 25–46. Elsevier (2011)
26. Silva, V.M., Jeronimo Jr., H., Travassos, G.H.: A taste of the software industry perception of technical debt and its management in Brazil. J. Softw. Eng. Res. Develop. **7**, 1 (2019)

27. Suri, H., et al.: Purposeful sampling in qualitative research synthesis. Qual. Res. J. **11**(2), 63 (2011)
28. Tom, E., Aurum, A.K., Vidgen, R.: An exploration of technical debt. J. Syst. Softw. **86**(6), 1498–1516 (2013)
29. Unterkalmsteiner, M., et al.: Software startups-a research agenda. e-Informatica Softw. Eng. J. **10**(1) (2016)

How to Conduct Customer Interviews? A Workshop Format for Teaching Customer Interview Skills

Neslihan Özal[1] and Jürgen Münch[2](✉)

[1] CGI Deutschland B.V. & Co. KG, Leinfelder Straße 60, 70771 Leinfelden-Echterdingen, Germany
neslihan.oezal@cgi.com

[2] Reutlingen University, Alteburgstraße 150, 72768 Reutlingen, Germany
juergen.muench@reutlingen-university.de

Abstract. Context: A fast way to test business ideas and to explore customer problems and needs is to talk to them. Customer interviews help to understand what solutions customers will pay for before investing valuable resources to develop solutions. Customer interviews are a good way to gain qualitative insights. However, conducting interviews can be a difficult procedure and requires specific skills. The current ways of teaching interview skills have significant deficiencies. They especially lack guidance and opportunities to practice. **Objective:** The goal of this work is to develop and validate a workshop format to teach interview skills for conducting good customer interviews in a practical manner. **Method:** The research method is based on design science research which serves as a framework. A game-based workshop format was designed to teach interview skills. The approach consists of a half-day, hands-on workshop and is based on an analysis of necessary interview skills. The approach has been validated in several workshops and improved based on learnings from those workshops. **Results:** Results of the validation show that participants could significantly improve their interview skills while enjoying the game-based exercises. The game-based learning approach supports learning and practicing customer interview skills with playful and interactive elements that encourage greater motivation among participants to conduct interviews.

Keywords: Business agility · Customer development · Customer interviews · Educational games · Game-based learning · Product management · Lean startup

1 Introduction

Along with digitization and the fast pace of change over the last years, customers' lives, behaviors, product and service expectations have profoundly changed [1]. Big companies that once dominated the markets over decades often missed these changes, failed to innovate and thus disappeared from the markets [2]. In modern days, traditional product development approaches are insufficient to build successful products. The entrepreneur

E. Klotins and K. Wnuk (Eds.): ICSOB 2020, LNBIP 407, pp. 118–133, 2021.
https://doi.org/10.1007/978-3-030-67292-8_9

Steve Blank once said, "There are no facts inside the building so get the heck outside." [3]. Blank developed the "*Customer Development Methodology*" that helps agile product teams to discover customers by getting out of the building, talking to them and gaining a deeper understanding of who they are, what needs and problems they have and their regular life behavior patterns. The Customer Development Methodology consists of a continuous learning process by validating assumptions about a product idea. It influenced the rise of the Lean Startup approach [4] that is nowadays a wide-spread product development approach. Both, Customer Development and Lean Startup strongly propose talking to customers to validate business model assumptions and backlog items.

Customer interviews are a fast and cheap way to validate assumptions and learn more about customers to test a market or a product idea, before investing time and money to develop wrong things [5]. These interviews support avoiding easy mistakes and building unnecessary features. Even though customer interviews are fundamental within these methodologies, many product teams face different challenges in practice. Some teams fear to talk to strangers, some simply do not know how to talk to their customers, some ask bad questions that provide bad data, others do not really understand the customers' problem, or customers do not tell the truth since they want to be friendly [6, 7]. Consequently, talking to customers can also lead to false conclusions and therefore building wrong products or features. Getting out of the building and conducting interviews can be a difficult procedure. It is not a common practice and there is a lack of guidance on how to talk to customers. The current ways of teaching interview skills lack opportunities to practice and are not efficient. For this purpose, the approach presented in this paper deals with the question of whether or not interview skills can be taught in a more practical and efficient way.

This paper is structured as follows: After the introduction, Sect. 2 presents related approaches for teaching interview skills as well as selected educational games. Section 3 describes the research method, followed by details of the execution. In Sect. 4, a game-based workshop format for teaching interview skills is presented. The validation of the workshop format is described in Sect. 5. Section 6 presents limitations and Sect. 7 closes with a summary and an outlook.

2 Related Work

In the following section, relevant literature for conducting customer interviews is sketched, related approaches for teaching interview skills are classified and exemplified, and an overview of selected educational games is given. An overview of the relevant literature can be found in Özal [8].

2.1 Conducting Customer Interviews

In this article, we focus on conducting customer interviews as part of modern product management and user research to understand customer problems and needs under conditions of high uncertainty. This is typically the case in dynamic markets where technologies, customer behaviors or other factors change rapidly and are difficult to predict.

The focus is not on eliciting solution requirements but on understanding and testing potential customer problems.

Several well-known books have been published that provide guidance on conducting such kind of interviews: Maurya [9] offers a roadmap and practical set of guidelines that support entrepreneurs from framing the idea to product-market fit. Maurya proposes using Problem and Solution Interviews to validate assumptions. For this, he presents both a Problem and a Solution Interview Script including examples that illustrate these scripts. Constable [10] focusses on defining assumptions, finding potential customers by using creative approaches, asking correct questions to understand the customers, learning about the assumptions and risks as well as analyzing the insights. Fitzpatrick [6] provides a widely-cited, practical how-to handbook. He focuses, for instance, on asking good questions and integrates practical exercises, such as presenting good or bad questions. Fitzpatrick provides a cheatsheet in which he summarizes the most important facts and advice.

In the academic area of requirements engineering, several studies have been published on how to teach interview skills for the elicitation of requirements. Here, the focus is traditionally on more predictable contexts with few uncertainties. Diesto and Juristo have compiled a literature review of elicitation techniques [11]. Ferrari et al. [12], for instance, have specifically studied how to teach elicitation interviews as part of requirements engineering activities.

2.2 Approaches for Teaching Interview Skills

Games. In the realm of games, approaches for teaching interview skills are rare. However, Jobs To Be Done (JTBD) Cards, conceptualized by Jonathan Briggs, provide a deck of 50 cards to practice interview skills [13]. The JTBD cards are conceptualized to support asking the right questions to uncover customers' problems, needs, motivations and the context in which they occur. Like the approach presented in this paper, JTBD cards focus on revealing core problems or motivations. Moreover, the cards provide good questions, hints, and categories that are considered in the approach presented in this paper. Also, the use of cards as a haptic element for teaching and learning is incorporated in the approach presented here as well as the roles for conducting interviews. However, the difference to the approach presented in this paper is that the workshop format will not only consist of cards but also include further interactive elements.

Blog Posts. There are several blog posts reporting about conducting interviews in the context of Customer Development. Some blog posts provide an overview with different resources to read for mastering customer interviews, while others report on their personal experience and lessons learned [14, 15]. Many blog posts define Customer Development and customer interviews and their importance for Lean Product Development. Justin Wilcox provides both, a comprehensive theory and a practical guide in his blog named "*Customer Development Lab*" [16]. Wilcox provides a broad knowledge base regarding Customer Development. However, the focus of the approach presented in this paper lies in teaching interview skills rather than teaching the whole Customer Development Process. Thus, only the practice part for customer interviews is considered for the approach presented in this paper.

Online Courses. Another way interview skills are taught is through online courses. Several online learning platforms like Udemy, Coursera, and OpenClassrooms provide courses for studying the techniques of customer interviews, some of which are fee-based and some are free. Steve Blank himself adapted his "*Lean LaunchPad*" course for Udacity for free, with which he teaches the Customer Development Methodology at Colleges and Universities [17]. Also, Rob Fitzpatrick, the author of *The Mom Test*, launched a course on Udemy in which he explains and gives practical insights for conducting customer interviews [18]. However, most courses provide little practical guidance and more theoretical background.

YouTube Videos. YouTube videos represent another way to teach customer interview skills. LIFFFT Inc published a series of 6 videos about customer interviews [19]. In these videos, they discuss the importance of customer interviews and present techniques for getting people to talk. Moreover, they present some rules to consider while interviewing customers. Furthermore, Fitzroy Academy, an online school for entrepreneurs provides a series of 4 videos, focusing on Customer Discovery interviews [20]. The lecturers present the content by using a conversational question-answer approach. Additionally, the lecturers talk about further techniques for facilitating the interview. They apply these techniques by illustrating a real example throughout all videos. In general, the content for conducting customer interviews is repeated in all the videos mentioned above and was incorporated in the concept of the approach presented in this paper.

2.3 Educational Games

The Berkeley Method of Entrepreneurship [21], developed by the University of California at Berkeley, is a game-based approach for teaching entrepreneurship skills. In essence, different games are intended to trigger certain behaviors and mindsets of the participants. After completing the games, they reflect and compare their own behavior and mindsets with those of prosperous entrepreneurs. The results of the evaluation give insight to the participants' willingness to become entrepreneurs or to work on skills which they should improve in order to attain the mindset of an entrepreneur.

Playing Lean [22] is a board game with the aim to teach the Lean Startup method. The game is designed for ninety minutes and includes different cards that represent experiments as well as provide insight into Lean Startup. The players take on different social media roles which are Facebook, Friendster, Myspace and Twitter. In general, the players must conduct experiments to learn about their customers and win the highest market share. As soon as they find out what their customers need, they start to build the product and at the same time, they start with marketing activities to get the customers into the sales funnel and sell the product to them. Playing Lean puts the idea of experimentation in the foreground.

Lego for Scrum [23] presents a playful way of teaching product development skills using the SCRUM framework and further agile practices. The game is designed for 100–120 min and constructed for 20–150 participants who are divided into groups. The facilitator gets the role of the Product Owner and communicates the task of building a city as a product with predefined features (such as shop, school, river, bridge, hospital).

All teams will be working to build one single product. The main components of the product are Lego bricks. Playing Lego for Scrum puts the idea of agile thinking in the foreground.

Job Interview Challenge [24] offers a board game which teaches certain job interview skills. The game is designed for 3–6 players. In summary, a fictitious job applicant looks for advice from the players on how to successfully master a job interview. During the game, the players learn eight interview skills, such as matching strengths to the job, supporting position with facts or using body language. Additionally, seven types of questions are provided to ask in an interview, such as direct questions for information, follow-up questions or stress questions. Also, exemplary answers to the interviewers' questions are presented, which the job applicant can then use. Moreover, other job interview topics are illuminated, such as the preparation or the contacting process. The game focuses on job interview skills.

The Wish Game [25] provides a classroom exercise for one semester to teach entrepreneurship skills. The game starts by asking the students to write down three wishes. Then, the facilitator gathers the wishes in a hat and pulls out one of them. The class works as a team and tries to fulfill that wish. The team begins by interviewing the student whose wish was pulled since often the wish written on the paper is not what the students really want. Therefore, they are trying to find out the core motivation for the wish by conducting interviews. After understanding the wish, the students start to plan how to fulfill the wish within one week. The student who mostly supported to fulfill the wish, will get his wish fulfilled next. Otherwise, the facilitator pulls out another wish from the hat. During the semester, the students learn to develop and to evaluate ideas, interviewing customers, iteratively prototyping under time constraints, using limited resources as well as presentation and reflection.

In contrast to the mentioned educational games above, the approach presented here puts the idea of conducting customer interviews and teaching interview skills in the foreground.

3 Research Approach

The goal of the approach presented in this paper is to teach interview skills that are required for conducting good problem interviews in a short time. This means, that by using these skills, customers' needs, problems and the context in which they occur to build products or services they really want and need can be identified and understood. To help reduce the lack of opportunities to practice, this approach considers interactive elements for practicing interview skills. The required skills for conducting good customer interviews, which are described in detail in Özal [8], are the foundation for the workshop and its elements. In this context, the following research question was defined.

- **RQ: How can workshop participants be motivated to learn interview skills in a more interactive way?**

In order to answer this question, a Design Science Research (DSR) approach was chosen. Considering the flexible structure in DSR that enables a learning process through iterations, it can be seen as a suitable approach for the execution of the work. The research method of this work refers to Peffers et al. [26]. The DSR process includes six activities. The customization of this process is described as follows:

1. Problem Identification and Motivation. Interviews are a fast and cheap way to validate business model assumptions especially in the early stages of a business idea. However, talking to customers in a wrong way can lead to false conclusions. As a result, it is essential to prepare the interview, ask the right questions and finally know how to make sense of the answers to keep learning. The current ways of teaching interview skills for conducting interviews have significant deficiencies.

2. Objectives of a Solution. The objective is to develop a format to teach relevant customer interview skills in a practical manner. This includes understanding and identifying the customers' problems, as well as the context in which they occur in order to develop products or services they really want and need.

3. Design and Development. Design and development cover the research question. Design: First, it is determined which functionalities the artifact should have. After a wide literature review and further research, the following skill set resulted in order to conduct good customer interviews [8]: 1. Understanding Customer Development and the Importance of Interviews, 2. Asking Good Questions, 3. Understanding Ground Rules, 4. Creating an Interview Guideline, 5. Asking for a Commitment.

The development of the artifact describes the game-based approach. It includes the following elements in order to teach customer interview skills: 1. Introduction, 2. Good or Bad Question Game, 3. Ground Rules, 4. Interview Guideline with Suitable Questions 5. Good or Bad Meeting Game.

4. Demonstration. In order to demonstrate that the game-based workshop format solves the problem, it was applied and validated in four workshops with different participants from varied backgrounds: undergraduate students, graduate students, consultants, and employees of a product and service development unit.

5. Evaluation. The evaluation is based on observation, the analysis of the game results, as well as the feedback gained with an online survey. For the latter, a survey was created with Google Forms and integrated via QR-Code into the presentation so it can be scanned easily by participants' mobile devices. The feedback was used to assess the value of each step of the workshop and for improving subsequent workshops. Section 5 describes the validation by explaining the execution and the lessons learned. The workshop has been iterated four times.

6. Communication. The communication is carried out through the underlying article.

4 The Game-Based Approach

In order to develop the artifact, research was conducted on interactive and effective ways of learning. Educational games are a common practice for teaching entrepreneurship skills [27]. People receive information most effectively when they are actively engaged in the learning process and do the tasks themselves [28]. Based on this information, a game-based workshop format was conceptualized in order to teach interview skills more interactively. The workshop is based on the required skills for conducting good customer interviews, which are discussed in Özal [8]. To motivate participants and create a more interactive workshop, playful and diversified elements were integrated into the format. In the following sections, each step of the workshop is described more thoroughly.

Step 1: Introduction. In order to teach the skill of understanding the importance of the Customer Development Process before getting out of the building and conducting customer interviews, the workshop starts with an introduction in the form of a presentation. The goal of the presentation is to familiarize the participants' understanding with Customer Development and the importance of conducting interviews. Introductory slides were created.

Step 2: Good or Bad Question Game. After the introduction, the workshop continues by teaching the skill of asking good questions through a board game. The board game is divided into two parts and is constructed as follows:

Part 1: Good or Bad Question Board Game. The "Good or Bad Question Game" aims at assessing the participants' current knowledge about asking good questions in an interview. Required materials are a board game, 13 "Good or Bad Question" cards and clear instructions presented on one slide for clarification (see Fig. 1). At the beginning, the workshop participants are shown a slide with clear instructions and they get a five-minute explanation of the game and the rules. The participants start by shuffling the cards and placing them in the middle of the board with the question mark turned upwards. Then, they get fifteen minutes to play the game. One person alternately pulls a card and reads the question aloud to the group. The participants then discuss whether the question is a good or bad question. Depending on the groups' decision, the card is put to the left (bad question) or right (good question) side of the board. In total, the game covers thirteen questions to ask in an interview, eight of them are good and five are bad. At the end, the facilitator takes a picture of the board of each group to document the results. The game is played in groups of between 2–6 participants.

Fig. 1. Game board and "good or bad question" game cards

Part 2: Resolving the Good or Bad Question Game. When the game is over, the results are explained. The goal of the resolving part is to enhance the participants' understanding of good and bad questions in an interview. The facilitator starts by explaining the rules of the resolving part. For each wrong assignment, the group must remove the card from the board so that in the end only the right assignments are on the board. For each right assignment, they get 1 point. The maximum number of reachable points is 13 since there are 13 questions. Then, the facilitator continues by showing the resolving slides and explanations of the answers and how to ask them in a better way if they are a bad question.

Step 3: Ground Rules. There are some ground rules to be considered for conducting good interviews. To teach these ground rules, a card-based approach was created. The goal of "Ground Rules" is to teach the interview ground rules in an interactive and creative way. The Ground Rules support the participants in asking good questions. The required materials are clear instructions presented on one slide for clarification and 6 cards for teaching the Ground Rules (see Fig. 2). Flip chart paper and pens with different colors are provided to support the participants' presentations. The workshop participants are given a five-minute explanation of the exercise by showing instructions on a slide. Then, depending on the group size, each participant or one group member pulls a rule card. Afterwards, they read both sides of the card. Group members discuss the rule and individual participants can ask questions if they have any. After coming to a common understanding, the participants are asked to prepare a presentation of the Ground Rules in any way, by using flip chart paper and pens. For this task, the participants are given ten minutes. When they have finished their task, the results are placed on the wall, so they are visible during the course. Then, a five-minute presentation and explanation of the rules follow. After the presentation, the results are documented by taking a photograph. Depending on the group size, the Ground Rules can be prepared by one participant or by the group. Considering there are 6 Ground Rules and more than 6 workshop participants, rules can be prepared twice and presented together.

Step 4: Interview Guideline with Suitable Questions. The next part of the workshop is about teaching participants to follow a rough structure during the interview. For this, an "Interview Guideline" was created and serves as a basis. Since puzzles are a creative approach for teaching certain skills in the entrepreneurship context [23], a puzzle with an Interview Guideline was created. The exercise is divided into two parts and is structured as follows:

Part 1: Interview Guideline Puzzle. The goal of the exercise is to familiarize the workshop participants with the Interview Guideline to be roughly followed during an interview. The required materials are an "Interview Guideline Puzzle" (see Fig. 2) and clear instructions presented on one slide for clarification. The workshop participants are given a five-minute explanation of the task. Depending on the group size, each group or participant receives puzzle pieces. The workshop participants get the task of putting the puzzle pieces together to reveal the interview guideline. After completing the exercise, the participants explore the content of the puzzle. Then, the facilitator explains the guideline, the steps, and the corresponding questions. The puzzle can be put together individually or in groups.

Part 2: Practicing Through Role-Playing Game. After finishing the puzzle, the facilitator gives a brief instruction for the next exercise. The groups are asked to prepare an interview guideline for a random subject with possible questions for each step. Then, each participant receives an "Interview Guideline Template" to fill in suitable questions. For this task, the groups are given fifteen minutes. In the next step, the facilitator explains the next task, which is to practice the prepared guideline and the questions. The participants are given four role cards. They can choose between the "Interview Master", "Customer", "Note Taker" and "Observer". On the front side of the card, the role is displayed and on the back side the role and the task are described. Depending on the group size, the Observer can be represented through multiple participants. Then, the participants are given fifteen minutes to practice. Once the interview is over, the workshop participants give feedback to the facilitator and reflect on their experiences. The preparation of the "Interview Guideline", as well as the practicing part, are done in groups of between 3–6 participants.

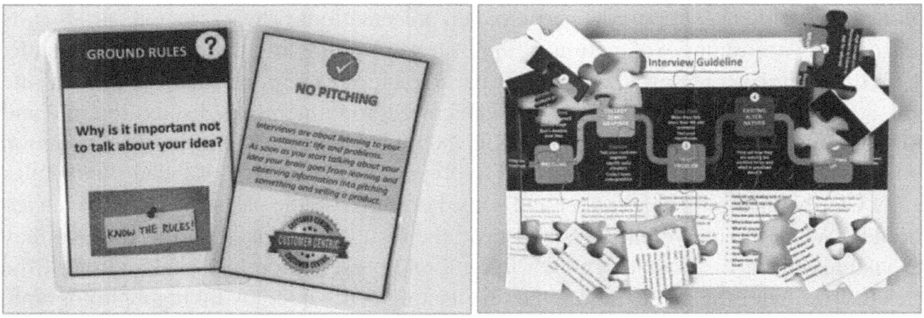

Fig. 2. Ground rule cards and puzzle

Step 5: Good or Bad Meeting Game. Bad data can lead to false conclusions and building products nobody wants. In order to teach this skill, a card-based game, the "Good or Bad Meeting Game", was created in which participants first practice and then play the game. The goal of this game is to allow the workshop participants to experience the feeling of an interview meeting going "good" or "bad". Bad meetings include bad data. In this context, the workshop participants learn to recognize bad data and how to transform those bad meetings into good ones by asking for a commitment. The required materials are slides for explaining the consequences of bad data and how to avoid it, the definition of commitments, and clear instructions presented on slides for clarification. For the practicing part, eight "Good or Bad Meeting Game" cards were created. On the front side of each card, a comment or a question is shown. On the back side, the answer is shown with an explanation of the comment and a recommendation. Half of the cards are "Good Meetings" and the other half are "Bad Meetings" and "Lives", provided to the participants at the beginning of the game in the form of mushrooms (Nintendo item). Before starting the exercise, the workshop participants receive an explanation of the consequences of bad data, and get advice on how to avoid them by asking for a commitment.

For this, a brief description of commitments is given. The introduction and the instructions are shown on slides. Then, each participant receives eight cards and gets 10 min to learn the explanation on the back side of each card. After the given time, the facilitator takes the cards away. Next, the groups are asked to send a representative to the front. All representatives stand in a row and receive two "Lives" in the form of mushroom cards. Then, the facilitator gives a brief instruction of the game. The representatives are treated like the "princess" in the Super Mario Bros. game powered by Nintendo, who is waiting to be rescued. Therefore, they are not allowed to speak nor make gestures during the game. Afterwards, the game starts and the facilitator reads a card, asking the first representative's group whether the comment contains a commitment and belongs to a good or bad meeting. The group members must give an answer within five seconds. If the statement is from a bad meeting, the group then explains why and makes a recommendation about how to ask for a commitment. If it is a good meeting, the group explains the commitment. When the group answers incorrectly, the representative loses one life. When both lives are lost, they are out of the game. The game is over when the facilitator has read all the cards twice. The winner is the representative who still has the most lives. The game is played in groups with 3–6 participants. However, in the practicing part the participants learn individually.

5 Validation

For the validation 55 people participated in the workshops, divided into 14 groups. In total 4 workshops were completed with graduate and undergraduate students as well as with professionals. The workshop participants had similar backgrounds and were not mixed. In the first workshop, there were undergraduates studying Business Informatics Studies, whereas in the second workshop there were employees of a consulting company. The third workshop was conducted with employees of an utilities company and the fourth workshop with students pursuing a masters degree in Services Computing Studies. The findings are based on observation, pictures, the evaluation of the board game results, as well as the survey results. The majority of the participants used the opportunity to provide feedback since 47 surveys were submitted. In summary, nearly all participants responded positively regarding the game-based exercises. This finding is also evident in the feedback form where 95.7% of the participants indicated that they enjoyed the whole workshop (see Fig. 3). Moreover, Fig. 3 shows that more than half of all participants rated their interview skills before the workshop between "*satisfactory*" to "*poor*", while a smaller number said they had "*very good*" or "*good*" interview skills. After the workshop, nearly all of the participants rated that they could improve their interview skills.

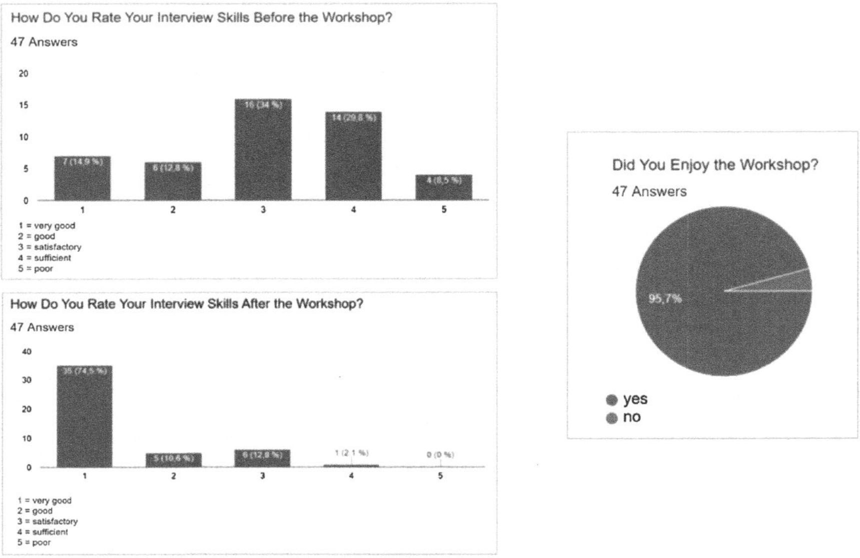

Fig. 3. Self-evaluation – interview skills before and after the workshop; overall summary

In the following, the findings are described.

Step 1 – Introduction. In the first two workshops, the authors tried to give an overview of the context by briefly outlining related topics. However, this approach revealed to be very confusing. A reason could be that if participants are not familiar with Lean Startup principles or agile approaches, a long presentation is not the best way to familiarize the participants with customer interviews. Therefore, the introduction section was significantly shortened. Instead of giving a brief introduction to several connected topics, the focus now lies more on interviews and starting the exercises sooner to have more time for practice. For this, a short introduction about the importance of conducting interviews in order to validate business model assumptions is given and the challenges within this topic are briefly explained. The presentation part was reduced to ten minutes, including answering questions. This modification was sufficient in the next two workshops and led to no further confusion for the participants.

Step 2 – Good or Bad Question Game. Starting with a self-evaluation exercise, the Good or Bad Question Game had a big effect on the participants' learning. Some questions were clear and assigned correctly by all groups, e.g., "*Do you think it's a good idea?*", "*How are you dealing with it now?*" and "*What else have you tried to solve the problem?*". Some questions were assigned incorrectly, such as "*Where does the budget come from (B2B)?*", or "*What would your dream product do?*". These questions especially had a big learning impact on the participants since they were convinced of their assignment and did not expect them to be wrong. A significant learning impact was caused by the question "*Is there anything else I should have asked?*". Nearly all groups assumed that this question would put the interviewer in a bad position, although this question gives them the opportunity to uncover unknowns. Through all workshops, small changes were made regarding the wording of the questions in order to improve the participants' understanding. The board game was evaluated as "*very helpful*" by 66% of the participants. Furthermore, 74.5% of the participants determined the resolving part as "*very helpful*" which also got the best evaluation result. This finding could be linked to the fact that learning by trying and failing has a bigger impact on participants than just giving them the answers and the explanation. Concurrently, if they assigned questions incorrectly, they automatically participated in the discussion to better understand their mistakes. Moreover, they were more engaged and focused on the resolving part since they were in competition mode and wanted to collect the points for the sweets reward the facilitator had promised them.

Step 3 – Ground Rules. In the subsequent Ground Rules section, two changes were made during all workshops which included visualizing the Ground Rule titles better and providing further support for formulating "why-questions". In total 55.3% of the participants determined the exercise as "*very helpful*" and 36.2% as "*helpful*". The participants were given the freedom to express themselves and individually decide how to explain the rule. This could be the reason for the survey comments that they liked learning the rule through freely and creatively visualizing the explanation.

Step 4 – Interview Guideline In the Interview Guideline, minor extensions were made regarding warm-up questions and building empathy towards the interviewee which were helpful for the practicing part. The puzzle for revealing the Interview Guideline was fun for each participant but not very helpful for everyone. The exercise was assessed as "*very helpful*" by 46.8% of the participants, whereas only 17% determined it to be "*sufficient*". However, the revealed Interview Guideline with helpful questions for each step was invaluable for the participants. The feedback underlines this insight since 56.5% found the preparation of an interview guideline for a topic as "*very helpful*" and 37% as "*helpful*". A reason for this could be that the Interview Guideline makes the application more accessible through the helpful questions provided. In practice, they might find it difficult to formulate the right questions to ask. Also, practicing the prepared guideline in a role-play was assessed as "*very helpful*" by 53.3% and "*helpful*" by 42.2%. In the conception phase, fifteen minutes were scheduled for practicing the prepared interview guideline. After the workshops it was determined this schedule was insufficient, thus the participants needed more time for the practicing part. Most of them were in the "Deep Dive" phase after fifteen minutes, where they tried to find out the core motivations and problems. Perhaps, some participants needed a lot of time at the beginning of an interview to try building empathy by asking warm-up questions and afterwards had difficulties getting back on point.

Step 5 – Good or Bad Meeting Game. For the last exercise, the Good or Bad Meeting Game, one change was required during all workshops. Since the participants had difficulties remembering the definition of a "commitment", the explanation slide with the definition and examples for commitments was continuously shown during the practice part. The exercise was determined as "*very helpful*" by 44.4% of the participants and as "*helpful*" by 40%. This finding could be attributed to the fact that this exercise was gamified the most. The treating of the representatives as "princesses", to be rescued by the group, the time pressure to give an answer, as well as the illustration of the cards, might have increased the enjoyment and ability to learn the main principle behind the exercise, which was to recognize bad data and ask for a commitment.

6 Limitations

In this section, the results of the presented approach are critically discussed with respect to internal and external threats to validity.

Internal Validity: Regarding internal validity, it must be considered whether the study is conducted properly. For this, the following questions critically examine the study. Are the subjects representative? The workshops were conducted with several participants from various backgrounds. Undergraduate and graduate students, as well as professionals participated in the validation of the workshop format. Is prior knowledge required to participate in the workshop? For the workshop, no prior knowledge is required since the participants get a brief introduction to the topic which was designed for both participants with or without prior knowledge. In the workshops, all of the participants had similar knowledge levels. Half of them had little prior knowledge and the other half had no prior knowledge. Are the overall results correct? For the overall results, the participants were asked to rate their interview skills before and after the workshop through Google Forms. They were given enough time to complete the survey at the end of the workshop. It cannot be guaranteed that every participant was honest, but the survey results showed that nearly every participant felt their interview skills had improved after the workshop. Regarding the board game results, photographs were taken before and after the resolving part to better compare the groups' assignments and to prevent cheating during the resolving part. Are the chosen interview skills the right ones to conduct successful interviews? One author completed a literature review in the context of conducting customer interviews, analyzed widely cited content, identified patterns, categorized them and as a result defined the key skills [8]. Other skills could also be defined. Further research would be necessary to evaluate whether the chosen skills are the right ones. *Construct Validity:* Regarding construct validity, it must be considered whether the validation measures what it claims. It should be mentioned that the study does not provide findings on whether the participants could conduct the interviews better. However, they gained a better understanding of how to conduct interviews successfully. *External Validity:* With regard to external validity, the question must be asked if the results are applicable to other workshops. The workshop format is designed for conducting customer interviews in order to learn about customers' needs and problems to validate a product idea. Therefore, it is not appropriate to be used in any other kind of interviews such as a job interview. Since there is no prior knowledge required to participate, the workshop format can be conducted with all kinds of groups who are interested in learning customer interview skills in the context of validating a product idea.

7 Summary and Outlook

In general, the key finding is that the game-based workshop format was successful in teaching the interview skills required for good customer interviews. The format provides a how-to practice to encourage participants to get and conduct customer interviews. Almost all workshop participants enjoyed the workshop while learning and practicing the interview skills. It was observed that most of them were unfamiliar with interview skills in general and surprised by the impact of good and bad questions, not only while conducting customer interviews but also in other areas of life. Considering the experiences during the workshops, the outlook can be summarized as follows: In order to get familiar with the learned interview skills, there is a need to investigate whether to incorporate another part into the workshop in which participants get out of the building and conduct interviews with real customers. On the one hand, this would validate the suitability of the defined interview skills, and on the other hand, participants would gain experience. Regarding the exercises to learn and practice the interview skills, opportunities other than visual and haptic elements could be integrated into the workshop. This could include an auditive exercise such as audio, in which participants listen to an interview example and evaluate it, or they first listen to a bad interview, recognize the mistakes and afterwards listen to the good version and learn how to perform it more effectively. The credibility of the interviews would highlight the challenges in real customer interviews and support countering them. Moreover, there are other games that can be investigated as to whether or not they can be adopted for teaching certain interview skills. Conducting customer interviews can support product teams to better understand their customers, figure out current customer behavior and avoid the mistake of building unnecessary features. However, conducting customer interviews on its own cannot guarantee that reliable information will be gained for making decisions in agile product development. Further experiments can be used to support the validation of gained insights [24]. This could be an important aspect to consider for future research.

Acknowledgements. We thank the participants of the study for their time and contributions. All feedback collected gave us great insights and motivates us to continue our research and to refine the approach.

References

1. Sacolick, I.: Driving Digital. The Leader's Guide to Business Transformation Through Technology. AMACOM, New York (2017)
2. Aaslaid, K., Valuer (ed.): 50 Examples of Corporations That Failed to Innovate (2018). https://valuer.ai/blog/50-examples-of-corporations-that-failed-to-innovate-and-missed-their-chance/. Accessed 20 Aug 2020
3. Blank, S.: The Four Steps to the Epiphany. Successful Strategies for Products That Win, 2nd edn. Steve Blank, Askews and Holts, Pasadena (2013)
4. Ries, E.: The Lean Startup. How Constant Innovation Creates Radically Successful Businesses: Portfolio Penguin (2011)
5. Maurya, A.: Scaling Lean. Mastering the Key Metrics for Startup Growth. Portfolio/Penguin, New York (2016)

6. Fitzpatrick, R.: The Mom Test. How to Talk to Customers and Learn If Your Business Is a Good Idea When Everyone Is Lying to You. Foundercentric, New York (2014)
7. Gutbrod, M., Münch, J., Tichy, M.: How Do Software Startups Approach Experimentation? Empirical Results from a Qualitative Interview Study, pp. 1–8 (2017)
8. Özal, N.: Teaching customer interview skills through game-based learning. Technical report, Reutlingen University, Department of Business Informatics (2019)
9. Maurya, A.: Running Lean. Iterate from Plan A to a Plan that Works, 2nd edn. O'Reilly, Beijing (2012)
10. Constable, G.: Talking to Humans. Success Starts With Understanding Your Customers. The Author, New York (2014)
11. Dieste O., Juristo, N.: Systematic review and aggregation of empirical studies on elicitation techniques. IEEE Trans. Softw. Eng. **37**(2), 283–304 (2011). https://doi.org/10.1109/TSE.2010.33
12. Ferrari, A., Spoletini, P., Bano, M., et al.: SAPEER and REVERSESAPEER: teaching requirements elicitation interviews with role-playing and role reversal. Requir. Eng. **25**, 417–438 (2020)
13. Briggs, J.: JTBD Cards. Learning to Interview Customers, 2nd edn. Crimson Sunbird LLP, Singapore, Singapore (2016)
14. Turnbull, A., Groove (ed.): Customer Development for Startups: What I Learned Talking to 500 Customers in 4 Weeks (2014). https://www.groovehq.com/blog/customer-development. Accessed 20 Aug 2020
15. Woodpecker: 65 Customer Interviews: How We Made That Happen & What We've Learned (2017). https://blog.woodpecker.co/news/65-customer-interviews/. Accessed 4 Feb 2020
16. Wilcox, J.: Customer Development Labs. HOW to do Lean Startup (2017). https://customerdevlabs.com/. Accessed 4 Feb 2020
17. The Lean Launchpad, Blank, S., Mullaney, K. (contributors), Udacity (ed.): How to Build a Startup (2012). https://www.udacity.com/course/how-to-build-a-startup--ep245. Accessed 20 Aug 2020
18. Fitzpatrick, R., Udemy (ed.): Practical Customer Development. The Mom Test with Rob Fitzpatrick (2017). https://www.udemy.com/practical-customer-development/. Accessed 20 Aug 2020
19. LIFFFT, YouTube (ed.): Customer Interviews (2013). https://www.youtube.com/user/LIFFFTInc/feed. Accessed 20 Aug 2020
20. Fitzroy Academy, YouTube (ed.): Customer Discovery Interviews (2017). https://www.youtube.com/watch?v=bbkudRVMT3k. Accessed 20 Aug 2020
21. Sidhu, I., Singer, K., Johnsson, C., Suoranta, M.: Introducing the Berkeley method of entrepreneurship - a game-based teaching approach. In: 122nd ASEE Annual Conference & Exposition, pp. 1–8 (2015)
22. Playing Lean: Playing Lean 2: The next release (2018). https://www.youtube.com/watch?v=WQniEuQXW3U. Accessed 20 Aug 2020
23. Krivitsky, A.: #Lego4Scrum: SCRUM Simulation with Lego (2017). https://www.lego4scrum.com/. Accessed 20 Aug 2020
24. Franklin Learning Systems: Interview Challenge (2017). https://www.creativetherapystore.com/products/interview-challenge. Accessed 20 Aug 2020
25. Wilcox, J., TeachingEntrepreneurship (ed.): Wish Game: Entrepreneurship Through Giving Back (2018). https://www.teachingentrepreneurship.org/category/curriculum/. Accessed 20 Aug 2020
26. Peffers, K., Tuunanen, T., Rothenberger, M.A., Chatterjee, S.: A design science research methodology for information systems research. J. Manage. Inf. Syst. **24**(3), 45–77 (2007). https://doi.org/10.2753/mis0742-1222240302

27. Hart, J.D.: Classroom Exercises For Entrepreneurship. A Cross-Disciplinary Approach (Elgar Guides to Teaching). Edward Elgar, Cheltenham (2018)
28. Neck, H.M., Greene, P.G., Brush, C.G.: Teaching Entrepreneurship. A Practice-Based Approach. Edward Elgar, Cheltenham (2014)

Towards Ethical Guidelines of Location-Based Games: Challenges in the Urban Gaming World

Sonja M. Hyrynsalmi[1](✉), Minna M. Rantanen[2], and Sami Hyrynsalmi[1]

[1] Department of Software Engineering, LUT University, Lahti, Finland
{sonja.hyrynsalmi,sami.hyrynsalmi}@lut.fi
[2] Turku School of Economics, University of Turku, Turku, Finland
minna.m.rantanen@utu.fi

Abstract. Location-based games—urban games which are played in real life locations—are growing their share in the mobile gaming markets. While these kinds of games have been present since the growing popularity of so-called feature phones, they gained remarkable momentum through the popularity of Niantic Inc.'s *Pokémon Go*, *Ingress* and later *Harry Potter: Wizards Unite*. As modern location-based games are gathering hundred of millions dollars monthly revenue, also related social, economical, and even juridical questions have raised; however, the ethical questions embodied into the location-based games or augmented reality games have not been completely unveiled. As the mobile game industry is growing its importance in the software industry, also business ethics questions should be taken into account during the design and development of game products and services. This paper seeks to understand the relevant ethical concerns of location-based games by using the viewpoints of individual, community and business.

Keywords: Location-based games · Business ethics · Mobile gaming · Pervasive games · Ethical guidelines

1 Introduction

Location-based games (LBGs) have been increasing their popularity over the past few years among mobile games. In this paper, a LBG refers to games which *"– – use networked digital technologies to experiment with stranger's behavior and interaction in shared public spaces through a game format. They also use a combination of ad hoc, readily available technologies, and specialized equipment to interweave and blend the physical environment and player's actions in it with the virtual game world. And they require players to communicate, work together, and move about to complete the goals of the game."* [15, p. 3].

The most popular games in this gaming genre are for example augmented reality (AR) game *Pokémon Go*, alternate reality game *Ingress* and for the newest addition *Harry Potter: Wizards Unite* game. All of these three games are

E. Klotins and K. Wnuk (Eds.): ICSOB 2020, LNBIP 407, pp. 134–142, 2021.
https://doi.org/10.1007/978-3-030-67292-8_10

from the same gaming company *Niantic Inc.*, which is the leading location-based game company. For example, it has been estimated that *Pokémon Go* alone has already surpassed 3,6 billion USD lifetime revenue and the game generated 445,3 million USD in the first half of the year 2020[1].

1.1 Related Work

Ethical analysis of rising topics in games are not rare. For instance, ethical questions of gamification and gamified solutions [7,10], cheating in online games [11,27] as well as a new kind of monetization models (for example, the new 'loot boxes') of games [6,11] have been discussed previously. However, in more specific context of LBGs, there are remarkably less work done. Furthermore, often the viewpoint is fully philosophical with a little practical guidelines given.

Mukhra et al. [17] lists various questions related to Pokémon Go game, yet they mainly raise up the problems without deep analysis of ethical consequences or offering solutions. In addition, their focus is purely on a single game. From another point of view, Neely [18] was inspired by the same game and studies the ethical questions regarding augmenting a privately owned physical space with third-party's property. Neely raises up questions regarding, e.g.., augmenting a private daycare with sexually explicit material. However, also her focus is tightly on a question at hand—augmented reality—and little consideration on the location-based games is presented.

1.2 Motivation, Objectives and Structure

The game mechanism of location-based games require that players share their location to interact in the game. This means, that players also move in real life locations to proceed in the game. This, however, can create conflicts and challenges with surrounding neighbourhoods and urban areas, when there can be a surprisingly large number of people using the physical space in a different way than it has been meant and how others are using it [9]. Furthermore, for instance *Pokémon Go* was criticised shortly after the launch as there were more playable content in richer neighbourhoods[2].

However, at the same time location-based games are renewing how people use their urban areas and explore new areas and location during the game play. They also offer a possibility for players to create new social interactions and be a part of new communities, which born around these games. These communities bring people internationally together and can play important role in gamers' life.

[1] Sam Desatoff. "Pokemon Go surpasses $3.6 billion in lifetime revenue". GameDaily.biz. July 6, 2020. https://gamedaily.biz/article/1795/pokemon-go-surpasses-36-billion-in-lifetime-revenue.

[2] Christopher Huffaker. "There are fewer Pokemon Go locations in black neighborhoods, but why?". Miami Herald. July 14, 2016. https://www.miamiherald.com/news/nation-world/national/article89562297.html.

Location-based games can also do good for business, when game places, points of interest, spawn near shops and tourist areas. [3,19].

While these issues are not typically discussed and analysed by the designers and product managers during software and new product development projects, the changing modern economy put emphasis on software producing companies to act ethically and take wider equality questions into account. These observations motivates this paper. *Our objective is to study whether non ethical-savvy persons can perform an ethical concern analysis of location-based games by using an existing analytical framework.* For this purpose, we select a model by Tang et al. [25]. In order to reach the objective, we set the following sub-research question:

SRQ. What are the ethical challenges in location-based games?

As it is common with applied ethics, we use philosophical argumentation to discuss the phenomenon at hand. We use selected references, selected with a literature study, to support our argumentation. The remaining of this paper is structured as follows. In the following, Sect. 2 presents our analytical framework as well as raised ethical considerations. Section 3 emphasise the central finding, points the way for further work, and closes the study.

2 Ethical Considerations

The objective of this paper is to analyse ethical questions related to the LBGs and their quickly rising popularity. In emerging new technologies and their implementations, ethical discussion is always needed. In this paper, we discuss the ethics of location based games, the moral dilemmas and the conflicts which location-based games can create in society, business and individuals own life. The aim of this short paper is to present initial findings from the analysis.

To approach the research objective, we adopt the ethical analysis framework discussed and presented by Tang et al. [25] for the context of blockchains. With small modifications, it suit also in more general analysis of ethical concerns for new technological innovations. Their two dimensional analytical tool has combined micro-, meso- and macro-levels as one dimension and technological, application and business level as another. To adapt the framework in our needs, we replace the technological and application aspects with individual and community aspects, respectively. Thus, we use three different aspects in our analysis (see Fig. 1). Due to the space limitation of this reporting, we refer the interested readers to the original study for more comprehensive description.

On general level, LBGs share the typical ethical concerns with any application of mobile technology. General topics such privacy, accuracy, property and access [16] are always important in these cases. Similarly, issues of transparency, for example in user-agreements, and just treatment of users are something to be considered [23]. Additionally, many ethical issues of games such as addiction [11], dark patterns [5] and doing immoral or violent things in games matter. More unique ethical issues of LBGs raise from their set up in the real world. In following sub-sections we will discuss these issues further.

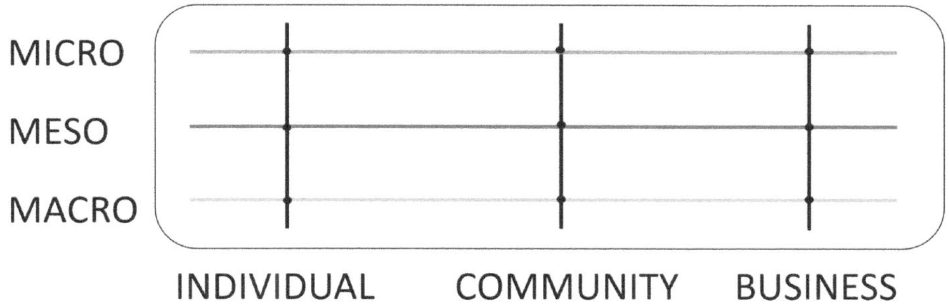

Fig. 1. An analytical framework

2.1 Individual

Games have always been one place to individual express themselves. In the most of the LBGs, individuals can choose what kind of a player type they represent. Playing digital games is more than just stereotype of anti-social nerd. Different kind of dynamics and player types among digital game players can be identified [26]. Ability to choose a player type and style to play provide players some autonomy and supports their free will, thus enhancing their role as moral agents within the game. For example, Sicart [24] argues that there can and should be room for making ethical choices in games.

However, as in LBGs the game is set up in the real world instead of virtual one, moral agency is not limited to the game. The selection of player type in LBGs can then have different implications in individuals life than in fully virtual games. For example, LBGs have unique characteristic of being limited in specific areas. This provides ground for a territorial player behaviour, where players attach to some real-world places in the game and start protecting them. This can lead also in conflicts in both in the game and real-life. [14] Thus, selection of playing style in LBGs can have greater ethical implications than the similar selection in virtual environments.

How individuals choose to play the game is also a matter of physical security and safety. For instance, Pokemon Go has raised questions about security of players, as the game draws the attention while moving around. Playing while walking or even driving a car can put the individuals in risk, which begs to question how LBGs could be safer to the players [2]. Of course, in this case legislation and game design can have some effect, but also rely on choices of individuals. Game companies should try to make their games safe to play, but in case of LBGs there are so many scenarios that cannot be predicted that the players should take responsibility of their own safety.

Individuals can also choose to play against rules and cheat. Cheating is not a new phenomena in the gaming world, but it can have new forms in LBGs. In LBGs unfair advantage can be sough from for example double accounts or location spoofing, manipulating the players location with the help of technology such as GPS or VPN and move player to the totally different location in the game. The motivation for this can be found from catching rare game items from different regions or competing in game progression compared to the other players [20, 29]. Cheating always creates conflicts among players and game companies try to prevent cheating with various rules and techniques, so they can maintain the players satisfaction level among players. If a game company fails preventing cheating in game, it can lead to the playing satisfaction drop and make game more unattractive. Therefore, preventing cheating is important for gaming companies both in the eyes of business and game attraction.

Because location-based games require moving in real-world location, the increase of players physical activity has been one of the most popular topic to research. There has been also enough data to collect, because games such as Ingress and Pokemon Go have gamified elements inside the game to track kilometres walked. Encouraging people to exercise is positive effect of LBGs as it promotes the well-being of the individuals also on physical level [4]. Naturally, gamification of moving can cause addiction and unhealthy competition. Thus, balancing the game elements and considering their consequences is important.

2.2 Community

Social interactions is one of reasons why people play online games, among immersion and collecting achievements [28]. LBGs do not make any exception in that case [3, 19]. As players are individuals, playing location-based games in real-world location exposes players to respect common norms and laws. For example, players can not risk themselves or others by violating traffic laws, or be guilty for jailwalk [21]. In location-based games, points of interests can be located for example in cemeteries or in quiet neighbourhood areas. In these occasions, players has to appreciate the surrounding area and people living or using the locations services and be respectful in their actions. Neglecting the social rules can create tensions and conflicts.

Location-based games creates, as digital games tends to create, social communities. For example in *Pokémon Go*, there are many game elements which encourage and almost force players to interact and collaborate [1]. LBGs then hold great potential for social encounters and even friendships in both online and real environment. This can create communities that expand the social circles of people. As video games have been for long argued to cause social isolation (mainly wrongly though [12]), this could be seen as positive aspect of LBGs.

LBGs can create possibilities for important social connections, but they also create 'us versus them' mentality, social hierarchies when players create their own groups to organise and potential places for internet bullying. In these cases, companies creating location-based games has to justify themselves why and how they use game elements, which almost forces people to interact.

2.3 Business

Because location-based games has so big effect on acting in real life locations, the software companies behind these games has great responsibilities on how their players are encouraged to act in real life locations.

Furthermore, also if there are no points of interest in some areas, is it company's benefit or not? There has been for example been situations were there has not been as much of points of interest in rural areas or in black neighbourhoods [8]. Should companies provide same amount of playing material for all the areas? Favouring some specific areas or points of interest also raises the question about the possibility of manipulation or persuasion through game design. Thus, dark patterns, such as disguised ads [5] could create ethically questionable business models.

The problem is, that in some cases companies use data which is created by players. For example, Niantic uses points of interest, which are almost all created by players [13]. Niantic also uses players as the evaluators of new points of interest places. This creates a possibility that players can try trick more points of interests in their own areas and, for example, areas where there are not so much advanced players suffer. Same with restaurants and the honeypot effect—if there are interesting enough points of interest nearby some business places, some businesses can get unfair advantage from that [9].

Additionally, companies which create location-based games needs data, but to get that data they need players. Players are then both producers and consumers of the data within the game, but that data can be also used to create further business value through secondary use. Value can be created by the game company itself or they can sell the data forward to other companies. Location-based data is sensitive data, but it also holds potential value in larger data economies as well. Data analyses of data sets can, for example, be used to profiling and personalising services. These actions can create a possibility more specific manipulation through LBGs.

It should also discussed, do players really know that data they have collected and provided to their game, can be sold forwards? People are often seen as mere data subjects, although in reality they should be considered as active actors of data economies and their needs should be valued. From this perspective it is paramount that the game companies respect the players as autonomous actors, treat them justly, protect their data. To do so, the companies should be transparent and honest to players [22].

3 Discussion and Conclusion

This short study reported initial findings from using an adapted ethical analysis framework to study ethical considerations related to location-based games. The key findings of this paper are: *(i)* The adapted ethical tool was usable to identify some of the ethical concerns related to the case study object. Furthermore, it was easy-to-use even for non ethical-savvy users. Yet, there are little if any ways to evaluate how comprehensive the analysis has been. Therefore, general guidelines could work better for software producing organisation than ethical analysis tools. *(ii)* Further work is needed to developed more holistic approach analysis approach or ethical guidelines for LBG developing organisations. As pointed out through the analysis and discussion in the paper, there are risks related to augmenting real-world locations that should be taken into account and mitigated during the product development work. *(iii)* Given that organisations rarely involve responsibility or ethics officers, further work should also clarify game development processes and propose how to embedded ethical analysis into the development work itself.

Finally, to conclude the study, this short paper discusses ethical concerns related to location-based games. This paper studied whether an existing approach can be used to identify ethical considers. The used analytical framework helped to identify some of the concerns; however, there were no way to evaluate comprehensiveness of the analysis. Furthermore, general guidelines could serve product development managers better than ethical analysis tools. This short paper calls for further work to develop and test such guidelines for practitioners.

References

1. Aal, K., Hauptmeier, H.: Pokémon GO: collaboration and information on the GO. In: Proceedings of 17th European Conference on Computer-Supported Cooperative Work. European Society for Socially Embedded Technologies (EUSSET) (2019)
2. Adams, A.: The ethics of augmenting reality. In: CEPE/Ethicomp 2017 Electronic Collection, Proceedings of CEPE/Ethicomp 2017, pp. 1–3 (2017)
3. Alha, K., Koskinen, E., Paavilainen, J., Hamari, J.: Why do people play location-based augmented reality games: a study on Pokémon GO. Comput. Hum. Behav. **93**, 114–122 (2019)
4. Baranowski, T., Lyons, E.J.: Scoping review of Pokemon Go: comprehensive assessment of augmented reality for physical activity change. Games Health J. **9**(2), 71–84 (2020)
5. Gray, C.M., Kou, Y., Battles, B., Hoggatt, J., Toombs, A.L.: The dark (patterns) side of UX design. In: Proceedings of the 2018 CHI Conference on Human Factors in Computing Systems, CHI 2018, pp. 1–14. Association for Computing Machinery, New York (2018). https://doi.org/10.1145/3173574.3174108
6. Hyrynsalmi, S., Kimppa, K.K., Smed, J.: The ethics of game experience. In: Bostan, B. (ed.) Game User Experience And Player-Centered Design. ISCEMT, pp. 253–263. Springer, Cham (2020). https://doi.org/10.1007/978-3-030-37643-7_11
7. Hyrynsalmi, S., Smed, J., Kimppa, K.K.: The dark side of gamification: how we should stop worrying and study also the negative impacts of bringing game design elements to everywhere. In: Tuomi, P., Perttula, A. (eds.) Proceedings of the 1st International GamiFIN Conference. CEUR Workshop Proceedings, vol. 1857, pp. 96–109. CEUR-WS, May 2017. http://ceur-ws.org/Vol-1857/gamifin17_p13.pdf
8. Juhász, L., Hochmair, H.H.: Where to catch 'em all? - a geographic analysis of Pokémon Go locations. Geo-Spatial Inf. Sci. **20**(3), 241–251 (2017)

9. Kelly, R.M., Ferdous, H.S., Wouters, N., Vetere, F.: Can mobile augmented reality stimulate a honeypot effect? Observations from Santa's Lil helper. In: Proceedings of the 2019 CHI Conference on Human Factors in Computing Systems, pp. 1–13 (2019)
10. Kim, T.W., Werbach, K.: More than just a game: ethical issues in gamification. Ethics Inf. Technol. **18**(2), 157–173 (2016). https://doi.org/10.1007/s10676-016-9401-5
11. Kimppa, K.K., Heimo, O.I., Harviainen, J.T.: First dose is always freemium. ACM SIGCAS Comput. Soc. **45**(3), 132–137 (2015). https://doi.org/10.1145/2874239.2874258
12. Kowert, R., Kaye, L.K.: Video games are not socially isolating. In: Ferguson, C.J. (ed.) Video Game Influences on Aggression, Cognition, and Attention, pp. 185–195. Springer, Cham (2018). https://doi.org/10.1007/978-3-319-95495-0_15
13. Laato, S., Hyrynsalmi, S.M., Paloheimo, M.: Online multiplayer games for crowdsourcing the development of digital assets. In: Hyrynsalmi, S., Suoranta, M., Nguyen-Duc, A., Tyrväinen, P., Abrahamsson, P. (eds.) ICSOB 2019. LNBIP, vol. 370, pp. 387–401. Springer, Cham (2019). https://doi.org/10.1007/978-3-030-33742-1_31
14. Laato, S., et al.: Do primal instincts explain engagement in location-based games? A hypothesis-forming focus group study on territorial behavior. In: Proceedings of the 4th International GamiFIN Conference. CEUR Workshop Proceedings, vol. 2637, pp. 115–125. CEUR-WS.org (2020)
15. Leorke, D.: Location-Based Gaming. Springer, Singapore (2019). https://doi.org/10.1007/978-981-13-0683-9
16. Mason, R.O.: Four ethical issues of the information age. MIS Q. 5–12 (1986)
17. Mukhra, R., Baryah, N., Krishan, K., Kanchan, T.: "Pokémon Go" and ethical considerations – are Pokémons poking us enough? J. Inf. Ethics **28**, 117–124 (2019)
18. Neely, E.L.: Augmented reality, augmented ethics: who has the right to augment a particular physical space? Ethics Inf. Technol. **21**(1), 11–18 (2018). https://doi.org/10.1007/s10676-018-9484-2
19. Paasovaara, S., Jarusriboonchai, P., Olsson, T.: Understanding collocated social interaction between Pokémon GO players. In: Proceedings of the 16th International Conference on Mobile and Ubiquitous Multimedia, pp. 151–163 (2017)
20. Paay, J., Kjeldskov, J., Internicola, D., Thomasen, M.: Motivations and practices for cheating in Pokémon GO. In: Proceedings of the 20th International Conference on Human-Computer Interaction with Mobile Devices and Services, pp. 1–13 (2018)
21. Pourchon, R., et al.: Is augmented reality leading to more risky behaviors? An experiment with Pokémon Go. In: Nah, F.F.-H., Tan, C.-H. (eds.) HCIBGO 2017. LNCS, vol. 10293, pp. 354–361. Springer, Cham (2017). https://doi.org/10.1007/978-3-319-58481-2_27
22. Rantanen, M.M.: Towards ethical guidelines for fair data economy-thematic analysis of values of Europeans. In: Proceedings of the Third Seminar on Technology Ethics 2019, pp. 27–38. CEUR Workshop Proceedings (2019)
23. Roquilly, C.: Control over virtual worlds by game companies: issues and recommendations. MIS Q. **35**(3), 653–671 (2011). http://www.jstor.org/stable/23042802
24. Sicart, M.: The banality of simulated evil: designing ethical gameplay. Ethics Inf. Technol. **11**(3), 191–202 (2009)
25. Tang, Y., Xiong, J.J., Becerril-Arreola, R., Iyer, L.S.: Ethics of blockchain. Inf. Technol. People **33**(2), 602–632 (2020)

26. Vahlo, J., Kaakinen, J.K., Holm, S.K., Koponen, A.: Digital game dynamics preferences and player types. J. Comput. Mediated Commun. **22**(2), 88–103 (2017)
27. Wu, Y., Chen, V.H.H.: Understanding online game cheating: unpacking the ethical dimension. Int. J. Hum. Comput. Interact. **34**(8), 786–797 (2018)
28. Yee, N.: Motivations for play in online games. CyberPsychol. Behav. **9**(6), 772–775 (2006)
29. Zhao, B., Zhang, S.: Rethinking spatial data quality: Pokémon Go as a case study of location spoofing. Prof. Geogr. **71**(1), 96–108 (2019)

Continuous Experimentation with Product-Led Business Models: A Comparative Case Study

Rasmus Ros(✉)

Lund University, Lund, Sweden
rasmus.ros@cs.lth.se

Abstract. Context. Continuous experimentation is used by many companies to improve their products with users data. In this study, the efficacy of continuous experimentation as used in two different types of business models (*product-led* or *sales-led*). **Method.** Two case companies with a product-led business model and three companies with sales-led business model were compared against each other. 14 interviewees were selected from the cases. **Results.** Having a product-led business model enabled four different drivers to continuous experimentation: 1) development and sales & marketing integration, 2) improved prioritization, 3) decreased feature bloat, and 4) product measurability. **Conclusions.** The takeaway message is that a company must be structured in the right way to obtain benefits from experimentation.

Keywords: Continuous experimentation · Business models · SaaS

1 Introduction

Continuous experimentation is used by high profile service based web companies to improve software products with user data. Experiments on prototypes or finalized features can evaluate the impact of developing a new feature. Cycles of such experiments can lead to constant improvements in product quality and usability [5]. Continuous experimentation has been studied to see whether it is possible to apply in various challenging different software segments [15], such as for automotives where there are technical obstacles to overcome [8], or business-to-business companies where there are organizational obstacles [14] and possibly a lack of access to user data [23].

This study is a comparative case study that aims to see whether there are differences on the applicability of experimentation in the circumstances of standard software companies, i.e. companies that sell their software online with no physical products. Instead, the case companies in this study have differences in their business models that in industry is known as either having a sales-led growth or a product-led growth [1]. Companies with a business model that is product-led tend to have focus more on software development than sales and marketing and acquire their customers through focusing on meeting user needs.

E. Klotins and K. Wnuk (Eds.): ICSOB 2020, LNBIP 407, pp. 143–158, 2021.
https://doi.org/10.1007/978-3-030-67292-8_11

There are prior indications that business models affect experimentation in the continuous experimentation literature, in a seminal paper on controlled experimentation on software, Kohavi et al. [10] mention that experimentation is applicable to software as a service (SaaS) products. The reasoning being that it's easier to define metrics, have enough user data, and implement telemetry. The case companies in this study are all SaaS companies too. However, whether or not being a SaaS company is a sufficient criterion for continuous experimentation has not been answered in the literature on continuous experimentation before. Furthermore, Schermann et al. [17] explains that there is a dichotomy between *business-driven* or *regression-driven*. Business-driven experiments have an impact on company level metrics while regression-driven experiments are done to ensure that quality does not decrease after a release. Schermann et al. states that most companies in their survey only do regression-driven experiments.

The goal of this study is to find whether differences in observed efficacy [5] or applicability [10,17] of experimentation can be explained by differences in business models that are either product-led or sales-led. To this end five case companies and 14 interviewees were selected. Two of them had product-led business models that were suitable for continuous experimentation and three of them had not. The concrete findings include four drivers on continuous experimentation that is enabled by a product-led business model: 1) development and sales & marketing integration through growth teams, 2) improved prioritization with user data, 3) decreased feature bloat, and finally 4) increased product measurability.

The rest of this paper is structured as follows. Section 2 provides background on continuous experimentation, business models, and product-led business models. In Sect. 3 the research method is described and the case companies are described in Sect. 4. Section 5 contain the results. Finally, the paper ends with a discussion in Sect. 6.

2 Background

Companies in many different sectors have adopted continuous experimentation [6,15] where features are evaluated with user feedback. Prototypes of an implementation can be quickly validated with users before implementation. After implementation, the feature can be subjected to a controlled experiment (an A/B test) where a comparison can be made with and without the new feature. Only the features that have a positive impact on a given metric are accepted. The results of an experiment might beget further questions, especially for negative results. Thus, experiments are usually executed in a sequence which is why it's coined continuous experimentation.

2.1 Business Models and Business Model Innovation

The term *business model* is used in industry to refer to how a company collects revenue [21]. In this paper the definition by Zott and Amit [24] from strategic management is used: *'the content, structure, and governance of transactions designed so as to create value through the exploitation of business opportunities'.* This definition is broader and includes company organization and activities performed by employees, etc. Zott and Amit define the *activity system* to structure how a business model is designed with two sets of parameters: 1) *design elements* that discern how the activity system is structured in terms of content, structure, and governance, and 2) *design themes* where the value from the activities are obtained through novelty, lock-in, complementarities, and efficiency. Continuous experimentation can be viewed as a design theme that can be used to increase novelty and efficiency. In this study, the companies (see Sect. 4) have also structured the design elements differently such that it differs on whether experiments are performed and who performs them.

Recently in the business model innovation field, experimentation and prototyping has been studied as a tool to find a combination of a working business model and product to match it [2,19,22]. Successfully implementing changes in an established business model is notoriously hard [3], and the wrong business model will cause good products to fail to reach customers [4]. In this study, business models is used as a lens to view companies since all of the experiments from the interviews are focused on continuous product improvements, rather than on changing the business model itself.

2.2 Product-Led Business Models

A specific type of business model has recently been popularized in industry by the Open View Partners venture capital group[1], under the name of *product-led growth* [1]. According to them, a business model that is product-led relies on the product itself to acquire new end-users rather than direct sales, advertisement, or other sales and marketing activities. A more precise definition of a product-led business model as the term is used in industry has not been found, but in Sect. 3 criteria are defined for categorizing a company as either product-led, or the opposite as sales-led.

The license that a software is sold under is a closely related concept to product-led business models. The *freemium* product license model is used by both product-led companies in this study. A freemium product [12] is available both for free and as a paid premium version. The premium version might for example have more features.

Business-to-business (B2B) companies has been used by researchers in continuous experimentation as an explanation for challenges faced with adopting experimentation [14,23]. A B2B company would face challenges to get access to end-user data from their customers, they might not be able to do software releases with the schedule they wish that causes delays in obtaining results, they may have incentives misaligned due to the metrics in the experiment not having a direct impact on company revenue, and so on. These issues are not faced by companies with a business-to-consumer (B2C) business model. However, the B2B and B2C explanation is not used in this study because it does not explain the

[1] https://openviewpartners.com/product-led-growth/.

data sufficiently, in fact the company that performs the most experimentation is a B2B company with a product-led business model.

3 Research Method

This study follows case study methodology [16]. It is part of a larger ongoing research project with several companies. One prior single-case study has been published in the project [15], on different scenarios that experimentation is used in. Five companies were selected for this study by the criteria of having a product that is offered as software as a service (SaaS) and where what is sold is software. The reasoning being that very complex business models would confound the findings. Some companies that were rejected sold physical products, such as e-commerce, or were business consultants that sold hours.

The initial interviewees were selected by contacting software companies in Sweden that matched the profile. Further companies and interviewees were reached by asking for referrals with an interest in experimentation, i.e. by snowballing. Personal contacts were approached first, when this failed the upper management was involved instead. In total 14 interviewees from the case companies were selected (see Table 2). Each interview took about 45 min on average. The questions included company business model, culture, experimentation process, challenges with experimentation, and so on. The questions on business model were the most relevant for this study. Most of the interviews were done on-site, but two of them were done online due to being in different countries.

The interviews were recorded, transcribed, and then coded with a predefined code structure. The codes were derived by using taxonomies of business model from different sources [18,20,21], company industrial contexts [13], and prior work on continuous experimentation [6,15]. The codes were further improved by comparing the coding results with a colleague. The analysis of the differences between the case companies (see Sect. 5.2) was done qualitatively using constant comparisons [16].

An additional semi-quantitative analysis of the case companies was done to have a comparison baseline in regards to how much experimentation they do and what the focus of their business model is. They were scored from 0–4 on two dimensions: business model (*sales-led* to *product-led*) and experimentation (*none* to *continuous*). Each dimension was scored by the criteria below. The criteria were derived by carefully considering what the crucial differences between the companies were and expressing them precisely. As such, they offer a complimentary view to the main qualitative analysis. Each number below is summed up to give the final score on the two dimensions.

Business model:

- Customers have no *explicit* influence on development prioritization (0.5).
- No direct sales (0.5).
- Less than 25% employees in sales organization (0.5).
- Any product sold as commercial-of-the-shelf (COTS) (0.5).
- Any product with license that is: freemium (1) or trial (0.5).
- User data is *analyzed* for prioritization (0.5) and/or requirements (0.5).

Experimentation:

- Both quantitative (0.5) and/or qualitative (0.5) experimentation is used.
- Advanced techniques (e.g. multi-variate testing) are used (0.5).
- There is sufficient infrastructure for experimentation (0.5).
- Experimentation follows a systematic process (1).
- Many (0.5) or most (1) features are experimented on.

4 Case Companies

The five case companies in this study are (see Table 1): A) a startup with a video sharing site, B) an internationally renowned company with software engineering tools, C) a business intelligence tool with analysis and graphs, D) a company with a customer relations management (CRM) product, and E) a company with a platform for e-commerce algorithms. In this section each case company will be described. The similarities of the case companies are that they all:

- have steady growth in revenue, employees, and users;
- target users that are professionals (as opposed to private individuals);
- offer a product that is sold is software under a SaaS product license;
- all of them claim to work with agile software development;
- have or have had sales organizations working with direct sales (except B).

Table 1. Overview of the five case companies.

Id	Main product	Business model
A	Video sharing	Split into direct sales B2B and a freemium B2C where premium has added functionality
B	Software engineering tools	Freemium B2B where larger companies pay more
C	Business intelligence	Direct sales B2B with very large sales organization
D	Customer relations	Direct sales B2B and integration projects
E	E-Commerce algorithms	Direct sales B2B2C

The interviewees in the study have varying titles and backgrounds. The various titles of the interviewees were standardized to roles to provide additional anonymity. For example, the title Growth Engineer became the Data Scientist role, and the Product Manager roles includes head of research, head of product etc. In Table 2 the roles of the interviewees are stated. It also includes the general seniority level of the interviewees (that they have been in the industry): less than 5 years is junior, and more than 10 years is senior. The names in the *Id* column mirror the case companies.

Table 2. Overview of interviewees at the five case companies.

Id	Seniority	Role
A1	Junior	Data scientist
A2	Mid-level	User experience designer
B1	Senior	Quality assurance engineer
B2	Mid-level	Product owner
B3	Mid-level	Product manager
C1	Senior	Product manager
C2	Senior	User experience researcher
D1	Senior	Product manager
D2	Senior	Product owner
E1	Senior	Data scientist
E2	Mid-level	Product manager
E3	Mid-level	Developer
E4	Senior	Sales manager
E5	Junior	Quality assurance engineer

4.1 Case A: Video Sharing

The first case company has a B2B video sharing platform where users can record and edit videos for marketing purposes. The company has about 200 employees and has been operating for 10 years, about 30 people are in development divided in four teams. Their customers have mainly been other businesses, which they have reached through a fairly big sales organization. They recently added a new product with a vertical market that is targeted at individuals instead; still within a professional capacity. The new product has an entirely separate development organization and no sales persons involvement.

The new product is offered with a freemium model. The free version has limited video uploading capacity and has less features than the premium version. They generate no revenue from the free version, the only revenue stream is to convert free users to paid users or to reactivate inactive users. The conversion rate to paid users is one of their most important metrics. Two people were interviewed from this team (A1 and A2), one of them was working primarily with A/B testing, and the other was a combined user experience designer and user researcher.

4.2 Case B: Software Engineering Tools

Case company B is a large international organization with multiple products, they all focus on supporting the software engineering process. They have existed for roughly two decades and have more than 4000 employees. Each product has its own development organization. They are advocates of both agile and lean software development. Notably, they have no large sales organization and do not use direct sales at all.

The main products are a project and issue tracker product and a team collaboration platform. Two of the three interviewees were at a team that developed a new continuous integration product. During the new development, they stressed experimentation as a way of working. All new features were subject to an experiment to verify that it was really needed. For example, they added buttons that faked the implementation of a feature that would notify the user that the feature is under construction once clicked on. In this way, they avoided implementing features that would not be used otherwise.

4.3 Case C: Business Intelligence

This company offers several advanced business intelligence products for different needs. The products are used to make graphs, tables, and other visualizations from various data sources. Since the company is more than 20 years old the products are in different stages of the life cycle, albeit all of them are still offered. The company is a large enterprise with about 3000 employees. The development teams are split into three countries and are about 500 employees. The sales organization is very large and use primarily direct sales to other businesses.

They have tried many different product licenses, but has recently moved away from on-premise installations to pure SaaS based licenses. In conjunction with this, they have also moved away from bulk sales of thousands of licenses to big corporations to more dynamic license deals. They have also tried various strategies to promote product growth, such as having one of their product be free with the restriction that the created document cannot be shared. There is limited experimentation involving end users. They have a team specialized in user experience research that gathers qualitative feedback on a regular basis. Two people were interviewed from this team (B1 and B2).

4.4 Case D: Customer Relations

The next case company sells a customer relations product to other businesses. The product is highly customizable, so each new customer deployment comes with a long integration project. The integration includes adapting to another company's data model and internal software systems, e.g. human resources. The company is 30 years old and has 200 employees, 35 of which are in software development, divided in three teams. Sales is a large part of the organization, and all sales are done through direct sales. Half of the company is committed to pre-sales and operations that support customers before and after sales due to the complex integration. They have also moved away from on-premise installations to SaaS. No free version or trial of the product is available.

Case C does almost no experimentation on end users. They do have systems in place for measuring performance in terms of query delays, etc., but make no use of any behavioural user data, such as clicks or user sessions. They are aware of experimentation but have no intent of starting it. Their entire development effort is focused on adding feature requests coming from customers, sales, and operations. However, before starting development on a new web based product they did perform some customer interviews to gather requirements, albeit they had no plans to gather any other explicit feedback.

4.5 Case E: E-Commerce Algorithms

The final case offers an e-commerce platform that is sold to e-commerce businesses. The platform consists of various algorithms for ranking products and an administration interface. Note that the algorithms target end-consumers but the administration interface targets managers at the e-commerce companies. The company is fairly small with about 50 employees and was established 20 years ago. They have salespersons working with direct sales as their only source of revenue.

Experimentation is a somewhat frequent activity at the company. Not all features are experimented on, only those that are believed to have an impact on consumers. The administration interface is not subject to any experimentation. The company use only quantitative methods, such as A/B testing.

5 Results

The business models of the case companies are categorized as focusing on *sales-led* or *product-led* business models. As explained in Sect. 2, a sales-led business model relies on direct sales to generate revenue. Companies C, D, and E have sales-led business models. In the alternative of product-led business models, the product is marketed and sold through the web and the product itself, companies A and B have this business model. In Sect. 5.1, the journey that these case companies have taken towards a product-led business model is described. In Sect. 5.2, the impact that the product-led business model has had on experimentation is examined by comparing to a sales-led business model.

5.1 Transition into a Product-Led Business Model

Two companies (A and C) have changed their business model, Case A transitioned into a product-led business model while C transitioned slightly away from a product-led business model. Figure 1 gives an overview of how the case companies transitioned over a five year period in regards to their business model (sales-led or product-led) and their degree of experimentation. All companies in the study have increased their use of user data over time. The scoring criteria are explained in Sect. 3. The figure shows that the companies with product-led business models (A and B) do the most experimentation and the companies that have sales-led business models do less. The two companies with product-led business models had very different journeys to get there, which will be described next.

Figure 1 is divided in four quadrants. In the lower left, the companies are sales-led and do little to no experimentation. This suits companies that do *consulting or bespoke* product development as they have less incentives to perform experimentation. In the lower right, companies rely on the product to acquire new users but do not use any experimentation to make sure their product fits user needs. As such, I believe they have *no business case*, and there were no companies in this quadrant in this study. In the upper left, the companies perform *siloed experimentation*. Either by only being able to experiment on parts of the software or without involving both the software development and sales and marketing departments. In the upper right, the companies are both product-led and perform continuous experimentation. These companies have integrated their marketing and development efforts and perform widespread experimentation (see also Sect. 5.2 for the advantages of this).

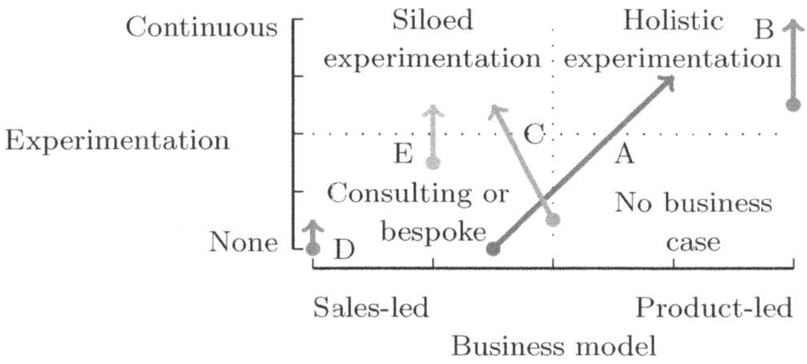

Fig. 1. The transition of the five case companies over a five year period in their degree of experimentation and their business model orientation. All companies have increased their experimentation, but the companies that have a product-led business model have increased more.

Case A: Video Sharing. For Company A the journey to a product-led business model is very recent, which started when they added a product vertical with a freemium version of their product. This initiative was taken by product management and resulted in the creation of an entirely new development unit in the company. Initially, the plan was to reuse as much code as possible to decrease costs. They started with the minimum required functionality and tried to get users to adopt as early as possible. The new product was available for free, with an option to upgrade to a paid premium version. The development team prioritized building and taking features from the old product to the new one that they believed would convert as many users to paid as possible. This was the starting seed to begin experimentation, when they had an straightforward way to measure what features bring value or not. Eventually they created a small dedicated team that worked with evaluating existing and new features.

Experimentation has been central for their new product. All new features undergo multiple prototype evaluations, and are then exposed to real users in a controlled environment. The prototypes are a series of design sketches that test the user experience before implementation. The interviewees describe how they use qualitative methods both to evaluate prototypes and to find issues with the product. This is done through quick sessions where an observant from the company sees how a new user uses the product to solve a pre-defined made up need. These users were recruited either through online services or haphazardly in the vicinity of the office.

They also collect data to ensure that the feature will be used and solves a real user need. For example, by asking users what problems they have or by adding a button in an A/B test that makes it look like the feature is added, but when clicking it, it reveals that the feature is under construction. After implementation they verify that the functionality works as intended with an A/B test that compares the product with or without the feature. As such, both quantitative and qualitative experiments are used at the company.

The company is still not fully product led, since they split in half with a product-led and a sales-led organization. As such, they still use direct sales with a large sales organization, and customers have a large influence on development priorities. While user-data was used for prioritizing incoming feature requests from customers in the old product, now user-data is also used to decide whether features should be part of the new product.

Case B: Software Engineering Tools. In Company B, the business model has been product-led from inception. They have no dedicated sales team and all their products are available with a freemium license. Their experimentation program was started in 2012 and has been growing steadily since then. They started with experimenting by tweaking newly released products to fine tune their performance and usability. In 2020 they have more than hundred employees working with experimentation, both data scientists embedded in the various product development teams, and in a team focused solely on experimentation.

Experimentation was introduced at the case company more than 8 years ago. It started gently as a proof of concept but grew quickly. One of the interviewees was the manager of the team in charge of experimentation, which was eventually called the Growth Team (see Sect. 5.1). Now the team has more than 100 employees and they do the majority of the experimentation for the other development teams. They use both quantitative A/B tests and qualitative user observation studies to find issues with their product.

The score in Fig. 1 for Case B reflect how they have improved their experimentation: using more advanced techniques, experimenting on all new features, and rounding out their experimentation with also using qualitative data. As expressed by Interviewee B3: *"Now I realize that quantitative methods are like scalpels, but if you don't know where the cancer is then there's no point. You have to look at the whole system, you have to zoom back out. And the only way humans can do that is to use qualitative methods to try and find the drop zone."* This insight was reached after many years of experimentation.

Growth Teams. In both cases A and B there has been a need to have some degree of separation from the development organization and experimentation. This has resulted in the creation of a team specialized in experimentation only, called a growth team. The growth teams performed experiments independently of the development teams and handed over the results as needed. In Case A, the growth team was small and would occasionally need to use the resources of the development organization. This added additional delay to experimentation which was avoided if possible. In Case B, the growth team was large, so they had resources to do their own development on the various products in the company. They had also done projects with mixed results to educate software engineers to work with experimentation internally in the product teams. However, the engineers would simply not do much experiments once returned to their teams.

When asked why the growth team was needed as a separate unit, the interviewee from the growth team in Case A said:

> The world that I live in is: build, test, throw out. And theirs is: we have the requirements, we're going to build this thing, and we're going to do these checkups. [...] But you need to test it out and actually measure if it's valuable or not. They assumed that it had already gone through that process. So looping them into a stage earlier in that funnel would take a systematic change which they hadn't gone through as a team. (A1)

In the other company (B) the growth team interviewee responded:

> The standard software engineering approach is 'I've interviewed a bunch of people and done a bunch a of research, I think this might be the problem'. And then they go and build big hard things. Some of those work and some of those don't. It's just a different mindset, and so I find that traditional software teams cannot or do not want to do growth work. (B3)

Sales-Led Business Model Cases. The other case companies that have sales-led business models have also increased their experimentation to various albeit lesser degrees. The experimentation at Case C was only qualitative and increased in scope during the five years. Their main product was offered for free with some restrictions for a long time, but it was recently changed to a trial version instead. Case D and E has not changed their business model during the five years, but have both increased their experimentation. Some of the reasons that these companies do not reach the full level will be given in the next section.

5.2 Product-Led Business Model Drivers

There were many differences between the two product-led companies and the sales-led companies in how they worked with user data and experimentation. The rest of the section contain four identified drivers that impact experimentation: development and sales & marketing integration, improved prioritization, decreased feature bloat, and product measurability.

Development and Sales and Marketing Integration. The most profound difference found in the study between sales-led and product-led business models lies in how the development organization interacts with users. An illustration of this is given in Fig. 2. To the left, the sales-led organization are steered by the sales and marketing department. They act as the intermediaries between development and users, the users come with requests for features to the sales and marketing department that forward it to the development organization. Whenever the development organization needs to make contact with users directly, they have a barrier to go through because the proper communication channels are not set up. I call this the *stakeholder barrier*, because the development organization find it easier to go the first stakeholder they have access to, which is the sales and marketing organization instead. To the right, in Fig. 2, the dynamic between sales and marketing and users may still exist, but the development also interact with users directly.

(a) In a sales-driven business model sales and marketing collect feature requests from users that are delivered to development. Case D is fully sales-driven, while case C and E is mostly sales-driven.

(b) In a product-led business model Sales, Marketing, and Development are integrated and interact with users. Case B is fully product-led and A is mostly product-led.

Fig. 2. The two types of organizations observed in the case companies. This illustration show a simplification, in actuality companies will position themselves between these two extremes.

The interviewees at the companies that have a stakeholder barrier did not express any desire to have more access to users, nor did they acknowledge that there was a need for it. The incentives of the development organization lied with satisfying the requests that come from the users through the sales and marketing organization, so they were content with the situation.

Improved Prioritization. All companies in the study used prioritization techniques to make sure that they are working on the most important things. For example, with the Impact, Confidence and Ease (ICE) scoring method. The companies with a growth team (A and B) both used ICE internally to prioritize experimentation in addition to ordinary software development. As such, there was no difference in how the prioritization as such was done. The difference lies instead with two things: 1) that some features could be aborted earlier when evaluated in an experiment, and 2) that the prioritization could be backed by evidence from data analysis. As expressed by interviewee B1 on why they do experimentation: "*Prioritization. For prioritizing a new product, it will not have all the features. When it exits beta we will have handled the users feedback such that we know what features we should develop.*"

Decreased Feature Bloat. All the sales-led companies (C, D, and E) confirmed that feature requests from users often result in new development added to the product. Sometimes they are added without verifying that it's something other customers would want, for example because it is a paid request by a customer. This can lead to features that perform poorly (because it's not validated in an A/B test) or that the general usability of the product suffers because it's too full with features. This is commonly referred to as *feature bloat* [9]. Interviewees at Case C and D said that this was a problem, and at Case A they mentioned how it used to be a problem before they switched business model:

> A customer will tell them they want something, and they will try to build it [to the B2B product]. We track their usage and their data, and they're not equivalent. I would say our features [on the B2C product] are used by minimum 50–60% of anyone that comes into our platform, their usage numbers are much much lower for that reason. They're not really solving user problems, they're [...] making sure they have a checkbox in a sales process. (A2)

Product Measurability. The indirection caused by the sales-led business model, as seen in Fig. 2, has an effect on how measurable the product is. The companies with a sales-led business model expressed how they used *proxy metrics* because their actual business model was not measurable. For example, Case E has a B2B2C model and the company gets revenue from direct sales to other businesses. However, what they measure is the sales figures of the consumers instead. This has only an indirect effect on their own revenue generation, i.e. by improving the quality of their product Case E might more easily acquire new customers. At Cases C and D they have not even been able to define a metric that they can both measure and is relevant to business.

For the cases with a freemium license (A and B) there is an industry standard for metrics to use who interviewees mentioned, it is called the *pirate metrics* [11]: Acquisition, Activation, Retention, Referral, Revenue (AARRR). In addition, usability metrics are also available, such as clicks or session time. Since the product is free to use, freemium products are more likely to have more users and so have more user data.

One concrete advantage that interviewees from both Case A and B mentioned is that the incentives between the companies and users are aligned, when the product has a subscription based licence. Since the users pay for using the product, the companies are incentivized to improve the product so that users want to use the product more. At Case C they mentioned that they had tried to change their standard licenses from bulk sales to a more dynamic licensing with single orders, such that the developers would be more incentivized to improve usability of the product. They said that it had improved the situation somewhat.

6 Discussion

In this study, I have shown how product-led business models enable continuous experimentation. Four drivers of continuous experimentation were derived by analyzing the difference between companies with product-led business models to companies with sales-led business models: 1) development and sales & marketing integration, 2) improved prioritization, 3) decreased feature bloat, and 4) product measurability. In all the drivers there was a clear division between the two types of business models. Hence, there are strong indications that the business model has an effect on what benefits will be derived from continuous experimentation.

The evidence that continuous experimentation enables product-led growth is clear from other research. Fabijan et al. [5] list the benefits of continuous experimentation, such as improved product portfolio management (similar to the decreased feature bloat in this study). However, not all companies in this case study could derive this benefit due to the fact that they did not perform experiments to validate all features. Other benefits can be had regardless of business model, such as improved product quality (e.g. in computation performance). Regardless, experimentation by itself does not come with all of the benefits. Rather, the right circumstances need to be in place for experimentation to work.

The integration between Sales & Marketing, Development, and Users (see Fig. 1) relates closely to what Fitzgerald and Stol [7] call the upcoming *BizDev* role. That is, business and development integrated in a similar way to development and operations in DevOps. The difference between BizDev and what is observed in this study is that users are also included in the collaboration. However, the advocated BizDev role is already filled at the case companies by the growth teams (see Sect. 5.1).

I have identified the following four threats to the validity of this study. 1) The risk to *reliability* was mitigated by letting another researcher review the study protocol and coding process. 2) In *external validity* the extent to which the results of our case study are transferable beyond our specific cases needs to be assessed by theoretical generalisation and comparing case characteristics. 3) In interview studies there is a risk to *internal validity* that the questions or answers are misunderstood. We mitigated this risk sending summaries to the interviewees. Finally, 4) the *construct validity* cannot be fully guaranteed. There could be alternative explanatory models that also capture the variability in the data.

In future work, I and colleagues plan to address the aforementioned threat to construct validity, by analyzing more case companies and derive a more general theory on drivers and barriers to continuous experimentation. This theory will include more aspects of the collected material, besides whether companies are sales-led or product-led. For example, the product complexity is not assessed in this work. This study will act as a stepping stone towards that goal.

In conclusion, the recommendation for practitioners is that the leverage gained from continuous experimentation will depend on the business model. Adopting a product-led business model alone does not guarantee that a product meet user needs, and meeting user needs is necessary for acquiring users through the product. Conducting experimentation without having a product-led business model may lead to experimenters that, e.g., do not consider doing experiments with business metrics or only do experiments on a small part of the software product. As such, continuous experimentation is enabled by a business model focused on product-led growth, and a product-led business model in turn enables continuous experimentation. For researchers in continuous experimentation, the differences in sales-led or product-led business model may provide a better alternative for analyzing companies in regards to their experimentation rather than whether they are business-to-business companies or not.

Acknowledgements. Thanks to Per Runeson, Elizabeth Bjarnason, and the three anonymous reviewers for valuable feedback. This work was partially supported by the Wallenberg Artificial Intelligence, Autonomous Systems and Software Program (WASP) funded by Knut and Alice Wallenberg Foundation.

References

1. Bartlett, B.: What is product led growth? How to build a software company in the end user era. https://openviewpartners.com/blog/what-is-product-led-growth. Accessed 18 Oct 2020
2. Brunswicker, S., Wrigley, C., Bucolo, S.: Business model experimentation: what is the role of design-led prototyping in developing novel business models? In: Curley, M., Formica, P. (eds.) The Experimental Nature of New Venture Creation. ITKM, pp. 139–151. Springer, Cham (2013). https://doi.org/10.1007/978-3-319-00179-1_13
3. Chesbrough, H.: Business model innovation: it's not just about technology anymore. Strategy Leadersh. **35**, 12–17 (2007)
4. Chesbrough, H., Rosenbloom, R.S.: The role of the business model in capturing value from innovation: evidence from Xerox corporation's technology spin-off companies. Ind. Corp. Change **11**(3), 529–555 (2002)
5. Fabijan, A., Dmitriev, P., Olsson, H.H., Bosch, J.: The benefits of controlled experimentation at scale. In: 2017 43rd Euromicro Conference on Software Engineering and Advanced Applications (SEAA), pp. 18–26. IEEE (2017)
6. Fagerholm, F., Guinea, A.S., Mäenpää, H., Münch, J.: The RIGHT model for continuous experimentation. J. Syst. Softw. **123**, 292–305 (2017). https://doi.org/10.1016/j.jss.2016.03.034
7. Fitzgerald, B., Stol, K.J.: Continuous software engineering: a roadmap and agenda. J. Syst. Softw. **123**, 176–189 (2017)
8. Giaimo, F., Andrade, H., Berger, C.: The automotive take on continuous experimentation: a multiple case study. In: 2019 45th Euromicro Conference on Software Engineering and Advanced Applications (SEAA), pp. 126–130. IEEE (2019)
9. Kaufman, L., Weed, B.: Too much of a good thing? Identifying and resolving bloat in the user interface. ACM SIGCHI Bull. **30**(4), 46–47 (1998)

10. Kohavi, R., et al.: Online experimentation at Microsoft. Data Min. Case Stud. **11**, 39 (2009)
11. McClure, D.: Startup metrics for pirates: AARRR! https://blog.popcornmetrics.com/pirate-metrics-aarrr-a-beginners-guide-for-entrepreneurs-marketers-and-agencies/. Accessed 15 Sept 2020
12. Niculescu, M.F., Wu, D.J.: When should software firms commercialize new products via freemium business models. Under Review (2011)
13. Petersen, K., Wohlin, C.: Context in industrial software engineering research. In: 2009 3rd International Symposium on Empirical Software Engineering and Measurement, pp. 401–404. IEEE (2009). https://doi.org/10.1109/ESEM.2009.5316010
14. Rissanen, O., Münch, J.: Continuous experimentation in the B2B domain: a case study. In: 2015 IEEE/ACM 2nd International Workshop on Rapid Continuous Software Engineering, pp. 12–18. IEEE (2015)
15. Ros, R., Bjarnason, E.: Continuous experimentation scenarios: a case study in e-commerce. In: 2018 44th Euromicro Conference on Software Engineering and Advanced Applications (SEAA), pp. 353–356. IEEE (2018)
16. Runeson, P., Höst, M.: Guidelines for conducting and reporting case study research in software engineering. Empir. Softw. Eng. **14**(2), 131–164 (2009). https://doi.org/10.1007/s10664-008-9102-8
17. Schermann, G., Cito, J., Leitner, P., Zdun, U., Gall, H.C.: We're doing it live: a multi-method empirical study on continuous experimentation. Inf. Softw. Technol. **99**, 41–57 (2018)
18. Schief, M., Pussep, A., Buxmann, P.: The impact of software business model characteristics on firm performance. In: Herzwurm, G., Margaria, T. (eds.) ICSOB 2013. LNBIP, vol. 150, pp. 1–12. Springer, Heidelberg (2013). https://doi.org/10.1007/978-3-642-39336-5_1
19. Sorescu, A.: Data-driven business model innovation. J. Prod. Innov. Manag. **34**(5), 691–696 (2017)
20. Vanhala, E., Kasurinen, J.: The role of business model and its elements in computer game start-ups. In: Lassenius, C., Smolander, K. (eds.) ICSOB 2014. LNBIP, vol. 182, pp. 72–87. Springer, Cham (2014). https://doi.org/10.1007/978-3-319-08738-2_6
21. Vanhala, E., Smolander, K.: What do we know about business models in software companies?–systematic mapping study. IADIS Int. J. WWWInternet **11**(3), 89–102 (2013)
22. Wrigley, C., Straker, K.: Designing innovative business models with a framework that promotes experimentation. Strategy Leadersh. **44**, 11–19 (2016)
23. Yaman, S.G., et al.: Transitioning towards continuous experimentation in a large software product and service development organisation – a case study. In: Abrahamsson, P., Jedlitschka, A., Nguyen Duc, A., Felderer, M., Amasaki, S., Mikkonen, T. (eds.) PROFES 2016. LNCS, vol. 10027, pp. 344–359. Springer, Cham (2016). https://doi.org/10.1007/978-3-319-49094-6_22
24. Zott, C., Amit, R.: Business model design: an activity system perspective. Long Range Plan. **43**(2–3), 216–226 (2010). https://doi.org/10.1016/j.lrp.2009.07.004

A Software Engineering Course that Promotes Entrepreneurship: Insights from a VUCA Perspective

João M. Fernandes(✉) and Paulo Afonso

Dep. Informática and Dep. Produção e Sistemas/Centro ALGORITMI, Universidade do Minho, Braga, Portugal
jmf@di.uminho.pt, psafonso@dps.uminho.pt

Abstract. In a context of higher volatility, uncertainty, complexity, and ambiguity (VUCA), engineering education must promote active learning approaches, where the responsibility of learning is focused on students, enhancing their competencies and ability to be competitive in the market. But, such educational strategies encompass many issues, questions and challenges, both for teachers and students. This article presents and discusses the main changes that have been introduced in a course that promotes entrepreneurship in the field of software engineering. The changes were introduced to address two main aims: (1) to provide opportunities for students to experiment new skills, that prepare them to better behave in a VUCA context, and (2) to make the course more efficiently managed. External elements and personal issues complement the intrinsic motivation related to the course on entrepreneurship.

Keywords: VUCA · Active learning · Problem-based learning · Entrepreneurship · Software engineering

1 Introduction

Volatility, uncertainty, complexity, and ambiguity (VUCA) all describe the conditions under which organizations operate in the world today. As there is no predictability for every issue that may arise, it is necessary to react for any issue that may arise. The VUCA world calls for innovative processes that can be used to cope with in any given situation. If treated right, the VUCA world can be an opportunity for teachers and students to develop effective flexible strategies. VUCA is a way of assessing the changeability of general situations and events that are completely unpredictable.

Higher education institutions are not well prepared for the VUCA world due to rigid structures and lack of agility to embrace change [1]. Indeed, universities face many uncertainties, due to VUCA and the chaotic, vibrant, and rapidly changing educational environment of our days [2]. These external factors demand from professors a constant and quick reshaping of the courses they are responsible for, so that they are more attractive to their students. In this context, higher educational institutions are forced to reshape,

E. Klotins and K. Wnuk (Eds.): ICSOB 2020, LNBIP 407, pp. 159–174, 2021.
https://doi.org/10.1007/978-3-030-67292-8_12

respond to and adapt to a rapidly changing environment as a result of learning, adaption, and development [3].

Entrepreneurship education is a good context for preparing the students for the VUCA side of the world, where adaptability and flexibility are necessary [4]. Entrepreneurship education is among the fastest growing fields of education. The promotion of entrepreneurship in engineering education is getting significant attention (e.g., [5, 6]). Nevertheless, training for entrepreneurship requires approaches that need to be simultaneously efficient and effective [7]. This implies a permanent evolution of good practices and a continuous reshaping of the courses, where those topics are considered. Otherwise, pedagogical practices quickly become inadequate and obsolete.

This manuscript is focused on describing and discussing the evolution of a project-based course (Project in Software Engineering - PSE) since its inception. We analyse with which rationale the changes were introduced, namely to adapt the course to better achieve its objectives or to better satisfy the expectations of the students. In particular, our analysis of the evolution of the course is grounded in the VUCA principles. Thus, the main goal of the research reported in this manuscript is to contribute to the analysis of the evolution of project-based entrepreneurship/engineering courses that can support those VUCA-oriented educational contexts.

This manuscript is structured as follows. Section 2 presents a brief state of the art on similar projects. In Sect. 3, we present the research method. The main ingredients of the PSE course are described in Sect. 4. Section 5 presents the major changes that were introduced in the course to adapt it to different circumstances. Section 6 discusses the impact, limitations, challenges and opportunities of such changes. Section 7 presents the main conclusions and opportunities for further research.

2 State of the Art

In this section, both VUCA and entrepreneurship education in active learning contexts are discussed within the body of the literature.

2.1 VUCA

VUCA is a catchphrase, introduced by the U.S. Army War College to describe an uncertain, complex, and ambiguous, multilateral world, which resulted from the end of the Cold War. The world is currently undergoing a serious transformation and presents many signs of what is described by the concept of VUCA [8]. The increasing rate of changes in the modern world places new demands on people, processes, technologies, etc. According to [9], organizations have been pushed to move from the SPOD world (Steady, Predictable, Ordinary, Definite) to this new paradigm.

There are additional factors that have also increased the turbulence in the global higher education world including: the rise of the digital economy, connectivity, trade liberalization policies around the world, increased global competition and innovation [10]. For example, the covid-19 is a new challenge that calls for rapid adaptation.

Volatility signifies here that the speed, volume, magnitude and dynamics of the changes are all high. The problem is not sufficiently stable, which implies that different conditions may apply in different moments.

Uncertainty means that information that is important to solve the problem is not totally available. Uncertainty is present in volatile environments that are complex and that involve unanticipated interactions.

Complexity is a measure of the difficulty in solving a given problem. Complexity in engineering can be measured by a number of dimensions, most notably technical complexity. Essential complexity is inherent in the problem being solved, and cannot be reduced or eliminated. Intuitively, it is a function of the number of features and the number of relations among them that are needed to decompose the problem.

Ambiguity occurs in situations where there is doubt about the nature of cause-and-effect relationships. It is also related to the fact that the information of the problem is subject to various interpretations. This happens in ill-defined problems, where the information is seldom contradictory, inconsistent or originates from different sources.

Volatility can be managed through agility, uncertainty mitigated gathering new data, complexity asks for abstraction and restructuring, and ambiguity can be reduced through experimentation [11].

If the challenges surrounding us are highly complex, often ill-defined and interdisciplinary in nature, universities should prepare students to tackle these challenges by providing them opportunities to hone skills such as the ability to evaluate new inputs and perspectives, and strengthen autonomy.

Experienced workers, but particularly students, need to learn about and to be competent in several skills to cope with the increasing competitiveness of the companies' world. For example, in [12] the authors identify the dispositions and skills required for the VUCA work environment as following: communications skills, self-management, ability to learn independently and in trans-disciplinary ways, ethics and responsibility, cross-cultural competency, teamwork in real and virtual ways, social intelligence, flexibility, thinking skills and digital skills.

In the context of higher education, volatility refers also to the ease and speed in which teaching and learning best practices change. Additionally, many students are looking for educational environments that are better aligned with their needs, so again educational practices should be modified. The typical one-size-fits-all model of education often does not satisfy the expectations of the students. Teaching is very uncertain for the teachers because they have never been sure about what their students understand, whether the misunderstandings come from inadequate content or incomplete understanding of difficult concepts.

There is still little experience on understanding how VUCA can be addressed in universities. Results of a quasi-experiment developed in [13] highlighted that project-based learning, interdisciplinarity, close collaboration between faculty and external partners, and active mentoring that were integrated in a course, contribute to give to students' skills to be competitive in a VUCA context.

2.2 Entrepreneurship Education in Engineering

Entrepreneurship and consequently innovation are crucial topics offered in many engineering degrees. Universities have been introducing new teaching/learning methodologies such as active learning, which is an educational approach that focuses the responsibility of learning on students. This approach is particularly suitable and relevant in a VUCA context and to prepare people for such an environment.

Among several strategies, approaches and tools, project-based learning (PBL) is an active learning educational approach relatively well known in higher education institutions. Through PBL, students gain knowledge and skills by performing a set of tasks within a concrete project typically based on a real or market situation.

In this context, PBL models have been used as a privileged instrument of the new teaching paradigms. This type of learning consists of a methodology that emphasizes teamwork and the resolution of interdisciplinary problems, the active role of students in the learning process, along with the development of not only technical skills, but also of soft skills [14]. The change from traditional approaches to PBL is not free of challenges and issues that should be considered. Five aspects are highlighted in [15]: (1) critical involvement and input of stakeholders external to the course design team; (2) need to adapt PBL for institutional, discipline and cohort fit; (3) importance of preparing the student cohort to cope with the inherent tensions of PBL; (4) managing their potential demands for additional control; (5) clarification of opportunity and resource costs that arise from implementing PBL.

In engineering, the preference for PBL has been growing, based on the argument that the main competence and activity of the engineer is the development of systems, generally complex [16], and that the focus on design, team action, and decision making creates the most appropriate environment for learning these competences.

PBL approaches are, thus, important to help universities to move from more formal traditional teaching and learning and to redefine their institutional mission to include innovation, entrepreneurship, creativity and marketing.

The education and training of entrepreneurs should include the development of skills and the ability to take risks, to develop high creativity, to build strong motivation to get results, high personal achievement and should highlight a strong sense of commitment. Indeed, the literature highlights the relevance of leadership skills, teamwork and communication, and creativity [17].

Entrepreneurship is important in this context of VUCA that can be promoted using active learning, namely PBL approaches. It is closely linked to the concept of change, i.e. entrepreneurs are agents of change and entrepreneurship is the phenomenon associated with the change process.

The promotion of entrepreneurship in engineering education, more specifically in software engineering is getting significant attention. In particular, it is evident that entrepreneurship requires active educational approaches, so that students learn new skills and reflect on what they have learnt and how they can benefit from and apply those skills. There are some examples.

The multidisciplinary, active, and collaborative approaches used in teaching requirements engineering is described in [18]. The use of game-inspired exercises to address all the relevant topics of software engineering is presented in [19]. In [20], the authors discuss the insights on how providing students the opportunity to explore their entrepreneurial skills has an impact on students towards entrepreneurship.

Indeed, the success or failure of software-based products is highly dependent on a good alignment of technology, market needs and business model in very volatile, uncertain, complex and ambiguous (new) markets and industries. Students must understand that software development processes should meet the needs of all stakeholders (i.e. clients, customers and users) and result in profitable products and services in the actual very competitive globalized and digital-oriented world.

Additionally, learning-by-doing programs, which emphasize practical work in real contexts, require a high degree of student involvement and also significant resources, and, at the end, they can result in a range of different outcomes from case study analysis and business case preparation to the development of startups [21]. Research on the VUCA perspective in the context of entrepreneurship education is still in its infancy and the scarce work on VUCA in engineering education (e.g., [22]) must be complemented with contributions from the study of VUCA in companies (e.g., [23]).

3 Research Method

The research strategy used in this article was essentially qualitative and with descriptive and exploratory nature. The information and data presented were obtained by the researchers as teachers participating in the studied processes, essentially through direct observation, interaction with the students and other interveners in the process (e.g., guests and mentors) and documentary analysis. The research was based on an eminently ethnographic approach, which allows us to understand the behaviour of a group or of a given system based on observable patterns.

The ethnographic approach is particularly appropriate to support the study and understanding of the phenomenon of entrepreneurship within universities and, in particular, the processes and strategies for entrepreneurship training. In a typical case study approach, the action of the researcher is limited to observing and interpreting the phenomenon under study, without influencing it. In this case, researchers assume a participating role by actively intervening in the phenomenon.

The data was collected since 2015 during five consecutive editions of the PSE course. The researchers have been participating actively in the changes made and were able to follow its implementation and routinization over the years. The personal perceptions were complemented with important artefacts of the course, namely the several versions of the course guide provided to all students every year which is updated after each edition, the final reports submitted by students, pitches presentations, feedback provided by mentors and guests, the analysis of marks, peer evaluation, project management information submitted through the project platform (Redmine), final interviews made with all teams on opportunities and expectations for further developments of the project towards possible commercial products or startup creation. Such unstructured data collection approach and subsequent inductive analysis creates conditions for the identification of relevant categories and the development of new perspectives of the phenomenon, new findings and explanations particularly when the context is not well known. The different sources of data, which was collected in different academic years and especially the combined analysis of the two researchers allowed a relevant triangulation of the data collected and analysis made.

4 Entrepreneurship Education in the Software Business

The "Project in Software Engineering" (PSE) course, offered since 2009/2010 to final-year students of the Master Degree in Computer Engineering at University of Minho (Portugal), is a project-based course to teach entrepreneurship in the field of software engineering [5, 24]. This course intends to follow a worldwide trend, linked to the promotion of initiatives, such as prizes and competitions, which promote an entrepreneurial attitude among the population in general and university students in particular. Software is particularly attractive to be exploited from an entrepreneurial point of view, due to its intangible nature that facilitates the development of products or services oriented to the market.

In this course, students combine a technical vision with a business perspective. This combination is still unusual in the training of software engineers. The main aim of PSE is to enable students to acquire a set of skills related to (1) the development (analysis, design, implementation, testing and management) of a software product as a team and (2) the analysis of the business potential of that product. Students are organized in relatively large teams (from 6 to 10 elements) to carry out the project during an academic semester.

Students are evaluated based on three main aspects: (1) the software product that they develop, (2) the respective business model, and (3) the pitch of the product.

In this course, students acquire several skills, which in most cases are not properly explored in their previous academic path, but that are clearly valued by the market. These skills include: leadership, team management, requirements management, interaction with customers/users, product design, software testing, communication and presentation, technical documentation, marketing, business, entrepreneurship [24].

PSE follows the philosophy advocated in [25], which argues that any topic can be achieved more effectively if students were confronted with the whole issue of this topic, instead of isolated parts. Perkins also describes the benefit that results for students when they learn skills and concepts in the context of creating a real-world artefact, using tools and best practices from the professional world. At the same time, students learn the academic subjects required for this level of software engineering.

The analysis made is based on the last five editions, in which 68 teams and 559 students developed a significant range of software products. In the last two editions, ten teams have worked on projects proposed by companies (e.g., Accenture, Bosch, Freeletics, OutSystems), but mostly develop their own product ideas (58 projects). During the period under analysis, the annual teaching staff ranged between four and six teachers and around 80 guests were invited to give feedback to them about the projects. The final presentation has been made outside the university in different places (companies and incubators).

5 The Need of Change, Adaptation and Evolution

A course with these characteristics needs itself to be continuously adapted and changed, according to the surrounding conditions. In the actual world qualified as VUCA, the modern professor needs to rapidly adapt his/her courses according to the reality and the expectations of the society, particularly organizations and students. We analyse the main factors that have induced changes that we, as professors, have introduced in the last five years in the PSE course, basically with two main aims in mind:

- **PSS** (promoting the students' skills): to make it more appealing to the students, by providing them opportunities to experiment important skills.
- **ECM** (easing the course management): to facilitate how the course is managed.

The eight main factors that have induced change in the PSE, as verified throughout its editions, are presented in Table 1. Each one is more associated with a specific set of VUCA dimensions. For example, factor #4, related to the contact with external elements, creates opportunities for students to acquire skills that are useful to deal with volatility, uncertainty and ambiguity. Factor #1 (number of students per team) is related to complexity, as complex projects can only be addressed by a relatively large number of students. The skills are divided in the following major classes: Create (CR), Interact (IN), Plan (PL) Work in a Team (WT), Design and Develop (DD), Communicate (CO), Validate (VA) [5]. These seven classes of skills are to be seen as indicative, as a way to better group the skills, as some overlaps exist among them. For example, when designing and developing (DD) complex software, some form of team work (WT) and planning must be considered.

5.1 Number of Students per Team

Every year, the number of students that attend PSE varies. Since the course is oriented towards team-based projects, the task of the professors is to act as mentors/coaches of the teams, in order to guarantee that the projects progress as smoothly as possible. This variable number of students implies that either the number of teams also varies accordingly, or we have to change the number of students per team, if we want to fix a given number of teams. In both cases, the associated challenges are appreciable.

A high number of elements per team implies a bigger effort in management and typically, when a given threshold is reached, it reduces the capacity of the team to deliver good results. At some point, more elements mean more conflicts and less productivity per element, as indicated by the Law of Diminishing Marginal Returns. According to our experience, the ideal number is between 6 and 9 students.

There are also some challenges for the professors whenever the number of students in each team is high. One of them is the risk that some team members have a reduced (or even null) contribution to the project. Another issue is that all projects are different, so, based again on our experience, it is problematic for a professor to support more than three projects. In this case, if more students are enrolled in the course and the number of professors remains relatively stable, there should be some compromise between the number of teams and the number of students per team. In some cases, this is a difficult equation to solve and there are obviously no definite general answers.

The changes in the number of elements by team is the major one from the perspective of the teachers. The other two are the relevance of own projects and the visits of guests and specialists from the industry.

Table 1. Major factors that have induced changes in the PSE course (in the last five years).

Factor	Description	Skills	Aim	VUCA
1. Number of students per team	Variation in the number of members of each team (in general, between 6 and 9)	WT	ECM	- - C -
2. Project management and leadership	The use of a centralised project management tool is mandatory and each team has a leader	WT PL	ECM, PSS	- - C A
3. Different types of projects	Students can develop their own projects or projects proposed by partner companies of the course	CR DD	PSS	- - - -
4. Contact with external elements	Interaction between students and external elements to receive feedback and suggestions about the business potential of the product idea	IN	PSS	V U - A
5. Going out of the building	Searching for mentorship, getting feedback from the market	IN	PSS	V U - A
6. Accountability of students in the evaluation process	Empowering students in the evaluation process through the implementation of a peer review mechanism	WT	ECM, PSS	- U - A
7. Creation of a business plan	Developing a proper business plan	CR VA	PSS	- - C A
8. Communication with the public	Developing persuasive pitches/presentations	CO VA	PSS	- - C A

5.2 Project Management and Leadership

In a team-based work, free-riding strategies are common, independently of the dimension of the team. Thus, in order to mitigate this problem, the use of a project management tool is mandatory. With this mechanism, the contribution of each student for the project can be controlled. The use of software applications for project management is mandatory, and for uniformity purposes all teams must use the Redmine platform, which is made available by the teaching team.

Online platforms used within PBL courses are powerful tools to improve the attitude of students with respect to continuous work and individual participation in the activities of the team. This is of paramount importance whenever the number of students and the number teams are high.

Leadership is also important in this context because, as other relational skills, it is very important in the VUCA environment as stated in [13]. In this course, the leader must manage the team in a calm but determined way. Furthermore, a balanced team well managed, with people with the proper skills, is a factor that has a very high impact on the success of the projects. Both aspects are highlighted at the beginning of the course and *ad-hoc* seminars on these issues are promoted but it is a process deliberately non-guided by the teaching team, as the grouping of the students in teams. Students must be very pro-active and autonomous in such decisions. Advantages and disadvantages, and also opportunities for improvements, may be explored in further developments to be made in the course.

The composition of the teams is discussed with the professors. It is suggested to choose students with different backgrounds, for the team to include members with different skills. It is also a good approach to not include people on the same team who have conflicts with each other or whose personalities foster some sort of antagonism. In the last edition of the course (2019/20), two students quit their teams as they were not able to cooperate. This was a very extreme situation, which unfortunately implied that those students failed to conclude with success the course. It clearly shows that the composition of the teams is an issue that deserves great attention.

5.3 Different Types of Projects

There has been an increasing number of products developed by the teams and remarkable progress in technical complexity and in the level of sophistication of the solutions, as presented in [5]. The quality of the value propositions underlying the products developed has also improved considerably.

Nevertheless, with big classes (with 100+ students), the expectations of the students are diverse. Thus, since the 2018/19 edition of the course, students are allowed to choose between projects proposed by themselves or by partner companies. The projects proposed by companies are monitored on a weekly basis by their proponents, which provides alignment between what is expected and what is achieved.

These two types of projects allow students to better match the course to their expectations. Many similar skills are required for both types of projects (like, technical development, presentations, team management), but each one also promotes different skills. The projects proposed by the students are more likely to promote creativity and innovation, while the ones proposed by the companies are more oriented towards the correct understanding of the needs of the stakeholders. Students projects require students to put attention in the business model, while company projects are more focused on user experience. Most students prefer to develop their own projects, which represented more than two thirds of the projects in the last editions.

Most teams are quite consistent in developing the project from the beginning, because making considerable changes requires a considerable additional effort. However, some teams hesitate a little in the first weeks about the direction the project can take. Around a quarter of the teams make some changes to their products. The number of radical pivots is very small (at most one per edition, typically), because students have to balance the realism of a business context with the need to approve the course.

5.4 Contact with External Elements

In many universities, the students within their academic activities have very limited or no interaction with people from industry. In engineering, this contact is fundamental, so that students can experience during their academic path the challenges associated with having a more business-oriented approach.

We followed a strategy that promotes the participation of external experts, either from other departments of the university or from companies. The contribution of these elements was reinforced since 2014, by increasing the number of companies that regularly collaborate with the course.

As of the 2014/15 edition, the teams began to be visited, for eight weeks, by several specialists in the software business area (entrepreneurs, engineers, product managers, business angels), who discussed the respective value proposals. On average, 16 guests and business specialists visit the teams in every edition of the course.

The feedback and suggestions provided by these external elements are quite useful in general and expose students to the scrutiny of business experts and specialists, which is a new experience for them. However, sometimes students follow immediately all the suggestions that are provided by the experts, without carefully analyzing the impacts of those suggestions in the project and without the necessary critical spirit and self confidence in the potential of the project whatever others' opinions. This is not a reasonable approach, since often those suggestions, even if relevant, imply significant or even drastic changes, which may put in risk the success of the project. Every year, there are one or two teams that are not able to deal with the different comments and suggestions made by the visitors and change the business idea repeatedly. These teams begin the development of the software product very late and typically cannot reach a very sophisticated product at the end of the semester.

5.5 Go Out of the Building

The students that develop their own product ideas have to align their products with the market. As already indicated in Sect. 5.4, the contact with experts allows the products to be improved in that dimension. This is promoted essentially by suggesting each team to search a mentor for the project. Again, students must be autonomous in this task but the teaching team can act also as facilitators of contacts or, eventually, as a mentor if their area of expertise and knowledge of the market fits well the project; but that is not expected neither desirable. The mentor can be a potential first client, a business partner, an investor, someone with a good knowledge of the market or the domain. This contact is important to validate the value proposition, to help in developing the proof of concept, and to test the minimum viable product that should be designed and evaluated with feedback from the market throughout the semester. The role of the mentor is to give some advice and feedback and not to coach the project.

In the last edition of the course (2019/20), a team developed an app to suggest outfits based on clothes from different clothing retailers. During the semester, they were able to establish agreements with four well-known retailers, allowing their app to interact with their catalogues (i.e., their databases). This was a successful example of what students are able to achieve by attracting external players to their projects.

In the 2019/20 edition, almost all teams were able to contact and get the support of a mentor of the project, who helped to get data about the market, to give feedback during the development process, and to validate the value proposition.

5.6 Accountability of Students in the Evaluation Process

Whenever there are many students in a team working together, it is always a challenge for the professors to decide how to differentiate the members of each team, according to the individual contributions. In many cases, the easiest solution is to evaluate the collective performance of the team and assign that evaluation to all its members. However, this may be quite unfair in many cases, as students contributed very differently to the final outcome. Thus, we suggest students within the same team to be allowed to decide how to differentiate their individual marks, if they find it appropriate. In fact, providing this power to the students is adequate, since they are the ones best entitled to make a fair evaluation of the performance of each team member.

Transferring this responsibility for the students makes sense, since they should be able to collectively arrive at a consensual decision. In the various editions of the course, for almost 100 teams, only once a team was not able to arrive to a unanimous decision. This evaluation process is accomplished through the implementation of a peer evaluation mechanism [26].

Students provide regular feedback to the teachers regarding the peer assessment. At the end, they indicate for each student the delta that should be summed to the collective mark in order to obtain his/her individual mark. This indication should result from a consensual decision. The total of the deltas should sum up to zero. The indication of the deltas should be given before the collective mark is announced, otherwise students are invited to artificially assign the deltas to maximize the total of the marks.

The peer assessment normally functions as a good indication of the team spirit. A team that is well organized and that promotes the collaboration of its members tends to give a "0" as the delta for all. Teams where there are frictions or problems usually have difficulties to collectively define the deltas. In 2017/18, a team was not able to agree on the peer deltas. At the end, the teachers decided to use "0" as the delta for its members. A final advantage of the peer assessment is to detect students with very low contribution to the project. In the 2019/20, a team suggests one of its members to have -4 as his delta. This high value (in the scale 0–20) prompted the teachers to analyze more carefully the situation. After some meetings with the students, it was concluded that student interrupted the participation in the project in the middle of the semester. We eventually decided that he failed to conclude successfully the course.

Table 2 shows that 63% of the teams proposed to change the final marks of some students. On average, the absolute values of the negative deltas tend to be higher than the positive deltas, which imply that a higher number of students are positively affected in their marks by the peer assessment than the ones that are negatively affected. Considering the maximum and minimum changes on average the delta is almost 3 points, ranging between 2 and 4 points. Thus, this instrument is important and it was more used in some editions (i.e., 2018/19) and less in other ones (e.g., 2017/18).

Table 2. Indicators related to the peer assessment process.

Academic year	Max (average)	Min (average)	Teams with changes/total (%)
2015/16	+1,55	−1,67	5/8 (63%)
2016/17	+1,28	−2,19	4/9 (44%)
2017/18	+2,54	−1,45	4/12 (33%)
2018/19	+0,92	−1,36	17/20 (85%)
2019/20	+1,01	−1,71	13/19 (68%)
Total	**+1,20**	**−1,59**	**43/68 (63%)**

5.7 Focus on Business and Communication

Developing a complex project in a team entails producing a significant volume of documentation in different moments. In the initial editions of PSE, students were asked to produce many deliverables, like requirements documents, user's manuals, installation guides, and business plans.

It is now clear that requesting such amount of documentation is counterproductive, because it deviates the students from the primary aims of the course. Currently, the focus is on developing a proper product/system and its business plan, since it forces engineering students to be able to combine their "natural" technical perspective with a business-oriented one. Students are, thus, asked to justify how their technical product is aligned with the business plan they proposed.

Reduction in the number of deliverables allows students to put more effort on communication issues. In fact, the quantity of deliverables was reduced considerably in 2017/18. Initially, students had to submit various elements and technical documents that were replaced by a small report (max. 20 pages). This change intends to put the focus on product development and the design of the business model. Anyway, it should be highlighted that each team is supposed to develop, within its project, other artefacts (like requirements documents, business plan), but that their contents is not fully evaluated (only the related parts that are included in the report).

Pitching is a crucial element of the project, highlighting the idea that communicating efficiently is a crucial skill for a modern engineer. Thus, students are requested to put great care on it. Three pitches are formally performed throughout the semester. The first pitch takes place at an early stage of the project (after three weeks). The second pitch occurs when the project is near the end (two weeks before the end). The final pitch takes place when the project is finished and aims to present the product and its business model to a panel composed of specialists external to the university.

6 Discussion

This section discusses the pedagogical issues related to the ingredients of the PSE course and how its design/application reflect the concerns with the context of VUCA.

The effort to regularly change the PSE course follows the principle that professors must understand their audience (way of reasoning, culture, dreams, and typical reactions). PSE evolved in order to enhance students' motivation. This is a relevant challenge for educators, because a conquered students audience participates in a more enthusiastic way. Universities must prepare people to deal with the future, where unskilled people, obsolete knowledge and ineffective tools have no room.

6.1 External Elements

Interaction between students and external elements raises the chances that the projects have potential to develop products with a better fit to the market. In general, this interaction is positive, because students can improve their products. Additionally, this interaction allows students to test their communication skills, since they need to align their messages to the different persons with whom they speak.

An additional feature of PSE is the focus on pitching. The final pitch usually takes place outside the university (e.g., in a company) and the session is open to the general public. The presence of the media (e.g., journalist of local newspapers in the final pitches session) has already happened in some editions and puts more pressure on students to have the greatest impact with their pitches, not only for professors but also for external elements.

The contact with external elements means the absence of the typical academic guidelines, which are substituted by VUCA. Students must learn to deal with such experience and to learn from it. It is not an easy task and some of our students do not like it. But students adapt themselves very quickly. During the years of the financial crisis the availability to continue with the project after the course was higher than now. VUCA and entrepreneurial skills appear to be linked.

6.2 Personal Issues and Motivations

Preferably, product ideas should be proposed by students, who will thus be more motivated to develop them. The choice of the idea is a difficult moment for almost all teams, for two major reasons. Firstly, in general, students are not used to conceive a software product from scratch. They have experience in technologically developing a piece of software for a specific client. Developing products for a potential set of users entails a set of different challenges, namely the market fit and the comparison with the competitors. Secondly, the choice of the product idea is easily understood as a critical moment of the project. Students rapidly realize that a bad initial choice has tremendous impact in the rest of the activities. So, they want to make a safe decision.

A good product idea (i.e., with business potential) allows the team to work with a realism similar to that experienced in a business context. It is also a motivating factor, as it allows exploring viable development alternatives and promotes the personal satisfaction of the team members. Contrarily, a weak product idea causes frustration and does not allow the technological development to advance, as it is not stimulating to develop something that has no commercial interest. In some editions, some teams have changed their ideas, after five or six weeks, exactly because they feel frustration (or little interest) in developing a project in which they did not see any potential.

Students learn to deal with VUCA whenever they decide about the type of project and inherent trade-offs, particularly, in terms of technological and business characteristics. A project with little technological risk and a classic business model implies that the team has to explore other aspects much more deeply, like for example an excellent user experience, a solid market validation, or a detailed financial analysis. In contrast, a project with a high technological risk or involving a disruptive business model requires a greater focus in these aspects, which justifies a lower investment in others.

During project development, the effort between planning and building needs to be well balanced. Starting to develop too early, but based on a poorly supported product idea, is not recommended. However, thinking too much and for too long about the idea and then not having time to develop a professional product does not work either. Knowing how to manage this balance sheet is fundamental. In this sense, using an iterative/incremental approach, with regular interaction with users, usually proves to be the and adequate decision.

It is recommended for the students to frame their effort according to the 'Lean Startup' development cycle. The goal is to run short development cycles, adopting a combination of experimenting with the product's value assumptions, using minimal versions of the product for that purpose. Thus, many validation cycles are performed until a valid value proposal is reached. Again, contacting potential customers/users of the product should be carried out to accomplish this validation.

Finally, it must be mentioned that one established software company originated directly from the projects developed within PSE: Nutrium (nutrium.io/en). Other startups could also be considered here, but in those cases what was transposed was only the team (not the products). This is a positive side-effect of the course and shows that students do appreciate the possibility to develop commercially their own ideas.

7 Conclusions

This manuscript presents and discusses the main changes that have been introduced to the PSE course, whose aim is to promote entrepreneurship in the field of software engineering. The changes were introduced to address two main aims: (1) to allow students to experiment with new skills, so that they get better prepared to behave in a VUCA context, and (2) to ease the management of the course. The discussion is focused on the main factors that have induced change in the course: number of students per team, project management and leadership, types of projects, contact with external elements, go out of the building, accountability of students in the evaluation process, and focus on business and communication.

Some of the ideas, guidelines and lessons learned can be used or adapted in similar courses that try to promote engineering and entrepreneurship in a VUCA context.

Entrepreneurship education can help students to cope with the characteristics of a VUCA world. The development of market-driven software products in the context of a course may fit particularly well such purpose. Firstly, software engineering education tends to be focused on the technological issues, but this is always not enough.

Indeed, students must understand that when in companies they must build products that are valuable for users. A common mistake is to develop products that were not sufficiently validated by the market. This sensitiveness is important in the competitive markets that face a globalized competition. This validation needs to be repeated regularly, to address VUCA characteristics.

Furthermore, companies exist to make money. Product and services are sustainable if they are profitable. Profitability is a function of the characteristics of the product in terms of price, quality and functionality, but also of the revenue models and these should be consistent with the firm's business model. Software-based products must be designed in accordance with the firm's characteristics and stakeholders' strategies.

The methodology followed in the engineering course presented here instigates students to develop their creativity, agility (fast reaction to changes), communication skills, and capacity to work in teams, which are important competencies for the VUCA world. The participation of business experts that have knowledge in the market domain is also crucial for the correct development of software products and connects students with the reality of the companies.

Acknowledgements. This work has been supported by FCT—Fundação para a Ciência e Tecnologia within the R&D Units Project Scope: UIDB/00319/2020.

References

1. LeBlanc, P.J.: Higher education in a VUCA world: change. Mag. High. Learn. **50**(3–4), 23–26 (2018). https://doi.org/10.1080/00091383.2018.1507370
2. Waller, R.E., Lemoine, P.A., Mense, E.G., Garretson, C.J., Richardson, M.D.: Global higher education in a VUCA world: concerns and projections. J. Educ. Develop. **3**(2), 73–83 (2019). https://doi.org/10.20849/jed.v3i2.613
3. Woodard, H.C., Shepherd, S.S., Crain-Dorough, M., Richardson, M.D.: The globalization of higher education: through the lens of technology and accountability. I-manage. J. Educ. Technol. **8**(2), 16–24 (2011). https://doi.org/10.26634/jet.8.2.1629
4. Diefenbach, S., Deelmann, T.: Organizational approaches to answer a VUCA world. In: Mack, O., Khare, A., Krämer, A., Burgartz, T. (eds.) Managing in a VUCA World, pp. 197–208. Springer, Cham (2016). https://doi.org/10.1007/978-3-319-16889-0_13
5. Fernandes, J.M., Afonso, P.S., Fonte, V., Alves, V., Ribeiro, A.N.: Promoting entrepreneurship among informatics engineering students: insights from a case study. Eur. J. Eng. Educ. **42**(1), 91–108 (2017). https://doi.org/10.1080/03043797.2016.1197891
6. Järvi, A., Taajamaa, V., Hyrynsalmi, S.: Lean software startup: an experience report from an entrepreneurial software business course. ICSOB **2015**, 230–244 (2015). https://doi.org/10.1007/978-3-319-19593-3_21
7. Hamouda, A., Colman, L.: Investing in entrepreneurial skills: creating an entrepreneurial mind-set amongst engineering graduates. In: CISPEE 2018, Aveiro, Portugal (2018). https://doi.org/10.1109/cispee.2018.8593471
8. Friedman, T.L.: The Flat World: Brief History of the XXI Century. Publishing House AST (2007)
9. Korsakova, T.V.: Higher education in VUCA-world: new metaphor of university. Eur. J. Interdisc. Stud. **5**(2), 31–35 (2019). https://doi.org/10.26417/ejis.v5i2.p31-35
10. Brodnick, R., Gryskiewicz, S.: Using positive turbulence for planning and change. Planning High. Educ. **46**(4), 27–40 (2018)

11. Bennett, N., Lemoine, G.J.: What a difference a word makes: understanding threats to performance in a VUCA world. Bus. Horiz. **57**(3), 311–317 (2014). https://doi.org/10.2139/ssrn.2406676
12. Bates, A.: Teaching in a Digital Age: Open Textbook Project. Press Books (2014)
13. Seow, P.S., Pan, G., Koh, G.: Examining an experiential learning approach to prepare students for the volatile, uncertain, complex and ambiguous (VUCA) work environment. Int. J. Manage. Educ. **17**(1), 62–76 (2019). https://doi.org/10.1016/j.ijme.2018.12.001
14. Powell, P.C.: Assessment of team-based projects in project-led education. Eur. J. Eng. Educ. **29**(2), 221–230 (2004). https://doi.org/10.1080/03043790310001633205
15. Delaney, Y., Pattinson, B., McCarthy, J., Beecham, S.: Transitioning from traditional to problem-based learning in management education: the case of a frontline manager skills development programme. Innov. Educ. Teach. Int. **54**(3), 214–222 (2017). https://doi.org/10.1080/14703297.2015.1077156
16. Dym, C.L., Agogino, A.M., Eris, O., Frey, D.D., Leifer, L.J.: Engineering design thinking, teaching, and learning. J. Eng. Educ. **94**(1), 103–120 (2005). https://doi.org/10.1002/j.2168-9830.2005.tb00832.x
17. Okudan, G.E., Rzasa, S.E.: A project-based approach to entrepreneurial leadership education. Technovation **26**(2), 195–210 (2006). https://doi.org/10.1016/j.technovation.2004.10.012
18. Rosca, D.: Multidisciplinary and active/collaborative approaches in teaching requirements engineering. Eur. J. Eng. Educ. **30**(1), 121–128 (2005). https://doi.org/10.1080/03043790512331313886
19. Cagiltay, N.E.: Teaching software engineering by means of computer-game development: challenges and opportunities. Br. J. Educ. Technol. **38**(3), 405–415 (2007). https://doi.org/10.1111/j.1467-8535.2007.00705
20. Johannisson, B., Landstrom, H., Rosenberg, J.: University training for entrepreneurship: an action frame of reference. Eur. J. Eng. Educ. **23**(4), 477–496 (1998). https://doi.org/10.1080/03043799808923526
21. Rasmussen, E.A., Sørheim, R.: Action-based entrepreneurship education. Technovation **26**(2), 185–194 (2006). https://doi.org/10.1016/j.technovation.2005.06.012
22. Latha, S.: VUCA in engineering education: enhancement of faculty competency for capacity building. Procedia Comput. Sci. **172**, 741–747 (2020). https://doi.org/10.1016/j.procs.2020.05.106
23. Du, J., Chen, Z.: Applying organizational ambidexterity in strategic management under a "VUCA" environment: evidence from high tech companies in China. Int. J. Innov. Stud. **2**(1), 42–52 (2018). https://doi.org/10.1016/j.ijis.2018.03.003
24. Fernandes, J.M., van Hattum-Janssen, N., Fonte, V., Ribeiro, A.N., Santos, L.P., Sousa, P.: An integrated approach to develop professional and technical skills for informatics engineering students. Eur. J. Eng. Educ. **37**(2), 167–177 (2012). https://doi.org/10.1080/03043797.2012.666517
25. Perkins, D.: Making Learning Whole: How Seven Principles of Teaching Can Transform Education. Jossey-Bass (2010)
26. van Hattum-Janssen, N., Fernandes, J.M.: Peer feedback: quality and quantity in large groups. In: Avdelas, A. (ed.) SEFI 2012 (2012)

A Trend Analysis of Software Business Research

Sami Hyrynsalmi[1(✉)] and Arho Suominen[2]

[1] Department of Software Engineering, LUT University, Lahti, Finland
sami.hyrynsalmi@lut.fi
[2] VTT Technical Research Center of Finland, Espoo, Finland
arho.suominen@vtt.fi

Abstract. International Conference on Software Business (ICSOB), one of the first software-intensive business specific conference series, was founded in 2010 and during the last decade, it has each year hosted tens of studies addressing various aspects of doing business with software products and services. As the conference has remained rather similar, it acts as a showcase on recent development trends in software-intensive business research. This short study uses all documents (n = 249) published in ICSOB conferences from 2010 to 2019 as a material for a trend analysis of the field. The metadata of all documents were gathered from Scopus and co-word bibliometric analysis was used to illustrate temporal clusters of research. In addition, the paper illustrate most active institutions and authors in the field.

Keywords: Software-intensive business · Bibliometrics · Literature study

1 Introduction

A devoted conference on software-intensive business (SiB), the *International Conference on Software Business* (ICSOB), was launched in 2010 as a home for cross-sectional research of software engineering, information system sciences, and economics [7]. Since its launch, it has became the world's leading venue for SiB research, gathering yearly researchers to discuss their recent results in the field. Meanwhile, the software products and services have become among the world's most valuable assets—seven out of the ten of the most valuable companies in the world are software houses[1]. Thus, understanding the trending topics in the software business Therefore, ICSOB serves as a good avenue for understanding the recent development of SiB research.

[1] Most Valuable Companies in the World – 2020. https://fxssi.com/top-10-most-valuable-companies-in-the-world. Accessed January 8, 2021.

E. Klotins and K. Wnuk (Eds.): ICSOB 2020, LNBIP 407, pp. 175–183, 2021.
https://doi.org/10.1007/978-3-030-67292-8_13

Related Work and Objective. Compared to literature reviews—which aim to summarise the content on reviewed literature [9]—bibliographical studies analyse the literature and its connections itself. Bibliographical studies have been frequently been present in the fields of software engineering and business. For example, in software engineering there is a series of bibliometric studies published [c.f. 6, 8] to understand highly performing individuals and institutions in the field. In addition, Fernandes [3] and Garousi & Fernandes [4] have studied how publication trends have changed in software engineering; furthermore, Garousi & Fernandes [5, Section 2] reviews related bibliometric studies in the field. In software business, e.g., Seppänen et al. [10] and Suominen et al. [11] have used bibliometrics to study the research literature on software ecosystems.

Recently, Jansen [7] presented an analysis of trends in software-intensive business (SiB) field. He identified from the most cited articles four major areas that are visible in SiB: *Software product management*; *Software ecosystems*; *Continuous X, Agile and Technical Debt*; and *Software Startups*. Based on his analysis, Jansen presented software-intensive business hype-cycle, inspired by the Gartner's technology hype-cycle.

Whereas Jansen's [7] analysis has its merits, it uses a more qualitative approach and only look studies published between 2010 and 2016. To have a view, not limited by a priori definitions of research themes, this study looks at themes of SiB research based on co-word analysis. Co-word analysis allows for an objective view of the thematics and linkages of a field of science [1]. Looking at the nature of words to conceptualise scientific concepts [14] previous work has looked at software research using co-word analysis [2]. However, this work, significantly dated, did not look at software business in detail Thus, for drawing more holistic picture of the recent trends in SiB research also qualitative bibliometric analysis is needed. This short paper aims to answer that call.

Materials and Methods. The set of scientific publications to be used in our review was downloaded from the Scopus database in September of 2020. The search used was constructed to focus strictly on articles published as a result of the ICSOB conferences series. This was implemented by searching for the ISSN codes of the conference proceedings series and the individual volume numbers of each conference proceedings[2]. With this technique, all items published and presented in ICSOB (including keynote addresses and prefaces by the editors) are included into the review. The search returned 249 documents, out of which 228 are conference papers and the rest are prefaces as well as workshop summaries.

We downloaded the metadata for all of the publications and analyse the descriptive statistics, such as yearly count, countries and affiliations of authors, of the sample. Then the data was used to run a co-word analysis using VOSviewer software [13]. In co-word is a bibliometric technique used to identify the thematic areas contained in a set of input documents. This enables creating a link between

[2] Search term for this review is `''ISSN (1865-1348) AND (VOLUME (370) OR VOLUME(336) OR VOLUME(304) OR VOLUME(240) OR VOLUME(210) OR VOLUME(182) OR VOLUME(150) OR VOLUME(114) OR VOLUME(80) OR VOLUME(51))''`.

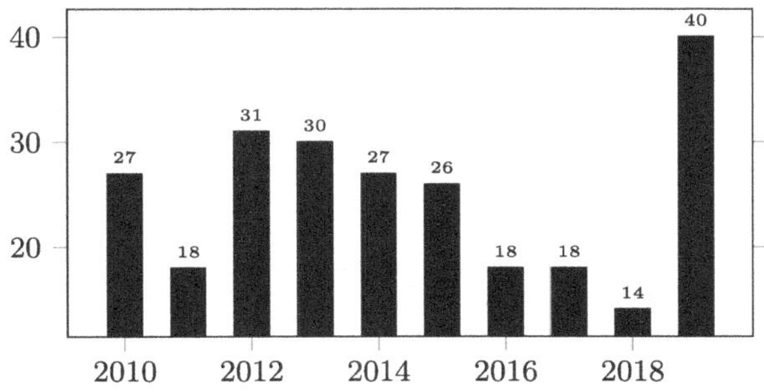

Fig. 1. The number of yearly published documents in ICSOB (September, 2020).

Table 1. Top countries

Country	#
Finland	75
Germany	47
Sweden	44
Netherlands	35
Italy	14
Canada	8
Norway	7
Brazil	6
Denmark	6
United States	6

individual documents in the sample based on their shared words, ultimately leading to a network where links between the documents are weight values based on shared words. Using metadata, we can also visualise the thematic evolution of the sample. The approach allows understanding of the current state, but also the evolution of a field of science. In VOSviewer, the co-word weights are based on shared keywords between the documents. Based on the network created, VOSviewer also applies a clustering algorithm to highlight thematic clusters of publications.

2 Results and Discussion

Descriptive statistics. The ICSOB conference has had on average 25 papers (s = 7.50, N = 10). Having a lower attendance between 2016 to 2018, the conference has attracted a good number of papers broadly focusing on software business. The number of published papers is seen in Fig. 1.

The conference publications are European, mainly from Finland, Germany, Sweden and the Netherlands. Table 1 gives all countries with more than five publications in the conference series. Focusing on the institutions, we see a similar focus to a few organisations, Finland having somewhat broader number of organisations, as seen in Table 2.

ICSOB conference has attracted a broad number of authors, contributing to the conference series ones or multiple times. In total, the publications had 159 authors, with a skewed distribution on the number of contributions made during the conference history. However, 99 authors have contributed more than once. Authors with more than five publications are shown in Table 3.

Co-word Analysis. The results of the co-word analysis is given in two graphs, Fig. 2 and Fig. 3. Figure 2 shows the individual clusters of research published in the conference, while Fig. 3 shows the same graph with a time overlay given in colour. Overall, the conference papers had 1,578 separate keywords being used.

Table 2. Affiliations of publications.

Institution	Country	#
Utrecht University	The Netherlands	31
University of Jyvaskylä	Finland	28
Chalmers University of Technology	Sweden	21
Aalto University	Finland	19
Malmö Högskola	Sweden	13
LUT University	Finland	11
Blekinge Tekniska Högskola	Sweden	11
Free University of Bozen-Bolzano	Italy	10
University of Turku	Finland	9
Tampere University of Technology	Finland	9
SAP AG	Germany	8
Lunds Universitet	Sweden	7
Technische Universität Darmstadt	Germany	6
University of Oulu	Finland	6
Universität Stuttgart	Germany	6

Table 3. Top authors.

Author	#
Jansen, S	25
Bosch, J	20
Brinkkemper, S	12
Olsson, H.H	12
Wnuk, K	10
Luoma, E	9
Abrahamsson, P	8
Hyrynsalmi, S	8
Rönkkö, M	8
Mazhelis, O	7
Wang, X	7
Smolander, K	6
Tyrväinen, P	6

To focus on the main keywords, the analysis was run using the 1,000 most used keywords.

The most used keywords, with no surprise, is 'software engineering' (N = 57), with 'ecosystems' (N = 48) and 'software ecosystems' (N = 40) second and fourth. Among the most used keywords, we can identify some more detailed issues, such as data processing (N = 43), which is actually the third most common keyword. In the top twenty keywords, we can identify a broad range of issues like open source software (N = 18), business models (N = 19) and software products (N = 18).

Focusing on the clusters created in Fig. 2 we can clearly identify a cluster on ecosystems. In addition, we can see two cluster, yellow and blue, focusing on software industry and companies. The yellow cluster seems to focus more on Software Product Management, while the blue on revenue and business models. The central cluster is Software Engineering, and we also see a few isolate clusters, one data processing and one on commerce. These isolate cluster, while relatively large, seem to be very focused. Overall, the co-word analysis resulted in 30 clusters, and our analysis only focuses on the largest clusters.

In looking to understand the evolution of the research published through the conference, in Fig. 3, we can identify that the topic on Software industry level analysis has sustained. However, the graph finds new areas of research such as ecosystem coopetition and governance as well as addressing technical challenges and debt as new areas of research.

Comparing the Results Against Prior Work. In the most completed related work, **(author?)** [7] identified in his analysis four main areas of work in Software-intensive Business among the most cited articles. These areas—Software product management; Software ecosystems; Continuous X, Agile and Technical Debt; and Software Startups—are also visible in our analysis.

Naturally, there are certain differences due to the different approaches used. While for example, software ecosystems is a large and a vibrant topic area in our analysis, the temporal aspect shows clearly recent developments in the research area. For instance, while both analyses has a cluster for software product management, in our analysis—focusing on all related documents of ICSOB conference series instead of the most cited articles—it remains a rather small as well as a historical topic area. This might indicate that software product management research area has been shrivelling up, at least in the context of the ICSOB conference series.

Furthermore, it is worthwhile to note that software startups research does not make a clearly appearance in our analysis. While there are notable software startup research papers published in the studied conference series, the overall number of the studies seem to have remained small. However, this might be seen as a signal of a maturing new research area inside SiB.

3 Key Findings and Conclusions

We summarise our key findings in the following three points:

(i) The keyword-based co-word bibliometric analysis reveals that SiB field is hosting a wide variety of different research streams ranging from more technically focused research (e.g., technical debt, software architecture) to business and management topics (e.g., coopetition, ecosystems, value creation). Thus, the conference series seems to be able to redeem to set goals to work as a plaza for researchers with different backgrounds and research methods. However, the emerging domains are scattered and semantically far from each others. Whether this will be a threat or a promise remains to be seen later. Too diverse conference might expel researchers whereas a diverse forum could also work as an avenue for scholars to innovate new openings.

(ii) The temporal analysis hints that SiB research has been moving from single software company (e.g., productization, requirement engineering and product management topics) focused research through software ecosystems focus towards new rising avenues such as technical debt and coopetition areas. While naturally the older topics remain larger clusters in the analysis, the emergence of new topics hint that the field is able to renew and reinvent itself.

(iii) The author and institution analysis reveal some centralisation to a small group of authors and institutions. While the all studied 249 documents had been authored by 159 authors, as many as 62,2 % of the researchers have authored more than two documents in the studied set. Furthermore, Tables 3 and 2 shows the concentration of the publications among a small set of

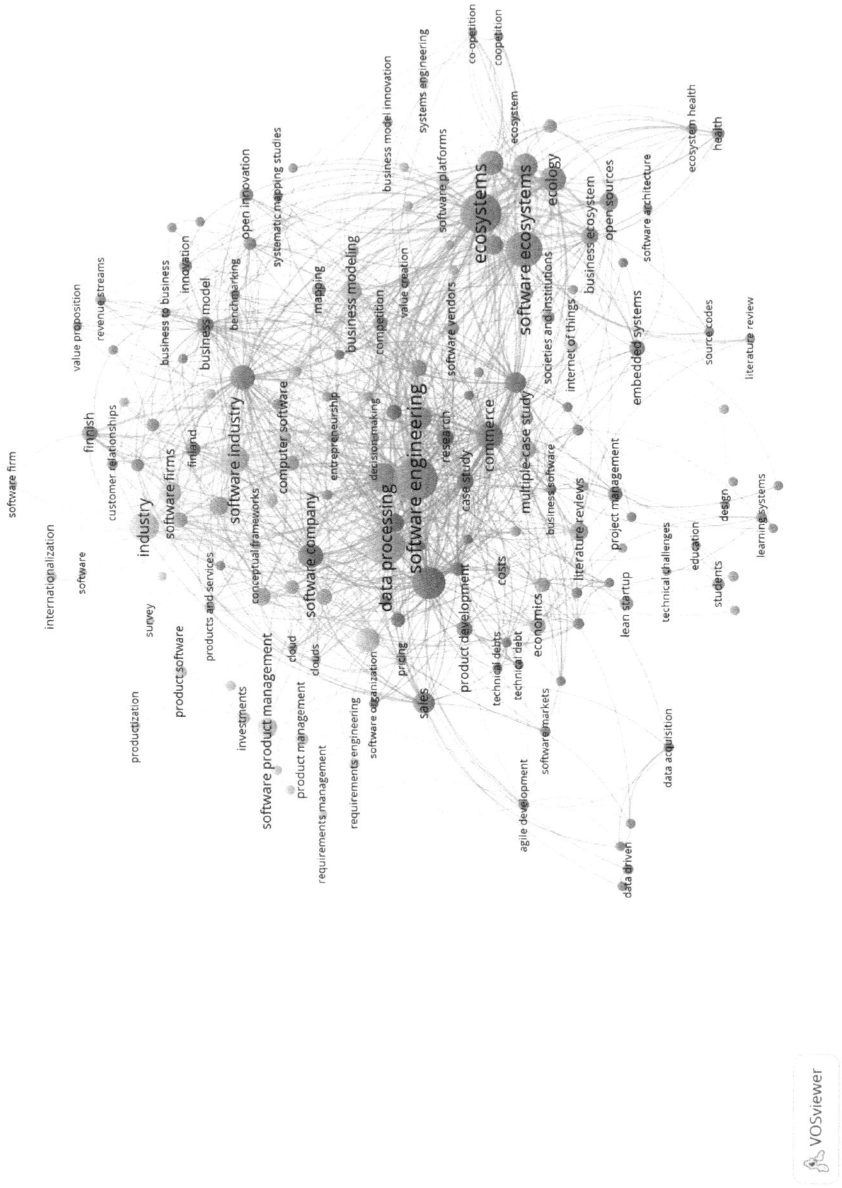

Fig. 2. Historical clusters of the ICSOB 2010–2019 themes.

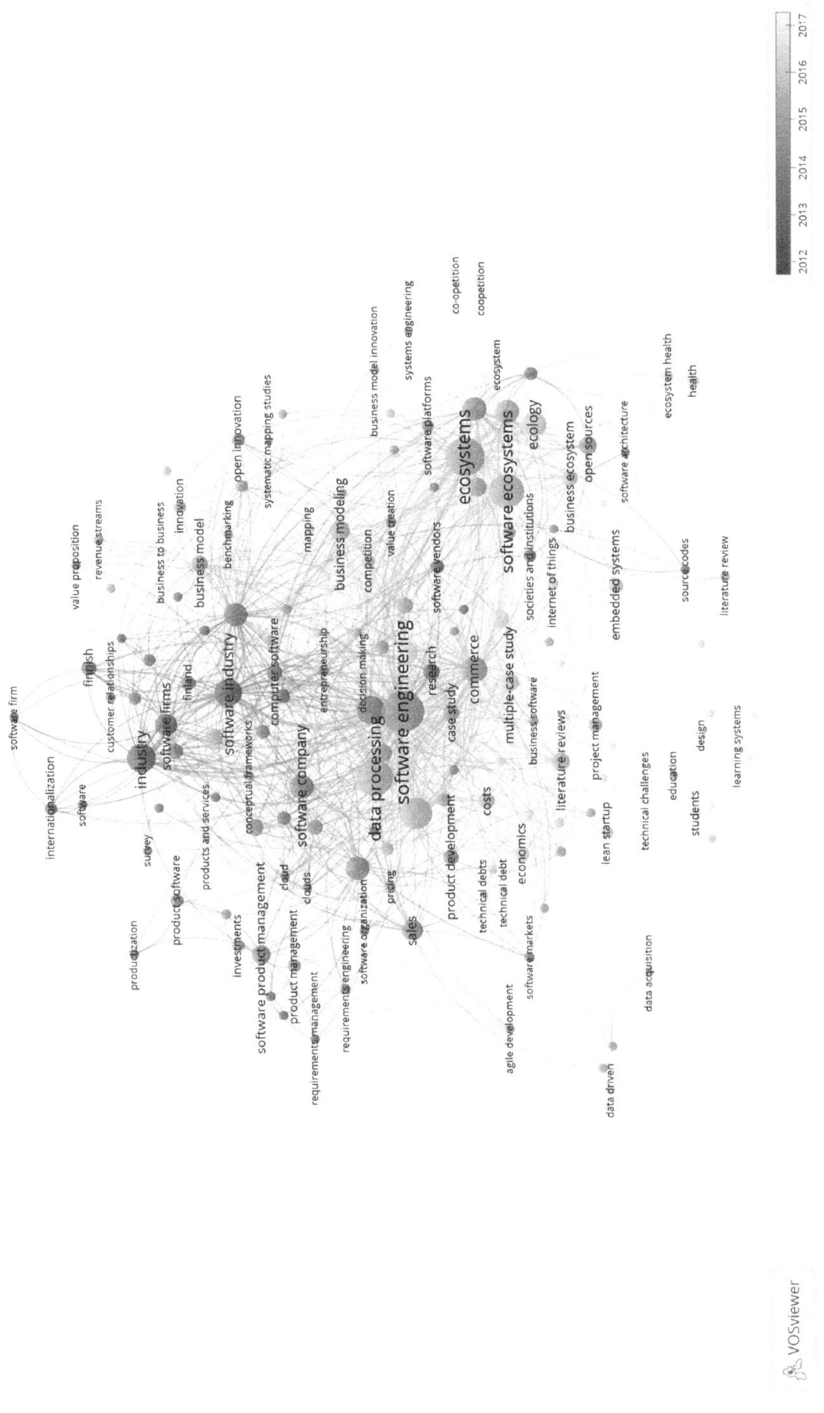

Fig. 3. Historical clusters of the ICSOB 2010–2019 themes with temporal overlay.

institutions and scholars. In order to attract more people to contribute, a shared research agenda could work as a highway for newcomers.

Finally, considering the scattered figure of SiB research—at least based on the ICSOB forum—the field could benefit from a formation of a shared research agenda. For example, the software startup research seems to have benefited from the publication of a shared research agenda back to 2016 [cf 12].

Further work could dive deeper to understand the evolution of the field. For example, a more qualitative analysis could take a look on temporal development of the used research methods and approaches in the field. In addition, the analysis could be strengthened by including also some of the workshop series such as International Workshop of Software-intensive Business (IWSiB), International Workshop of Software Product Management (IWSPM) and International Workshop of Software Ecosystems (IWSECO).

References

1. Callon, M., Law, J., Rip, A.: How to study the force of science. In: Callon, M., Law, J., Rip, A. (eds.) Mapping the Dynamics of Science and Technology, pp. 3–15. Palgrave Macmillan, London (1986). https://doi.org/10.1007/978-1-349-07408-2_1
2. Coulter, N., Monarch, I., Konda, S.: Software engineering as seen through its research literature: a study in co-word analysis. J. Am. Soc. Inf. Sci. **49**(13), 1206–1223 (1998)
3. Fernandes, J.M.: Authorship trends in software engineering. Scientometrics **101**(1), 257–271 (2014). https://doi.org/10.1007/s11192-014-1331-6
4. Garousi, V., Fernandes, J.M.: Quantity versus impact of software engineering papers: a quantitative study. Scientometrics **112**(2), 963–1006 (2017). https://doi.org/10.1007/s11192-017-2419-6
5. Garousi, V., Fernandes, J.M.: Highly-cited papers in software engineering: the top-100. Inf. Softw. Technol. **71**, 108–128 (2016)
6. Glass, R.L.: An assessment of systems and software engineering scholars and institutions. J. Syst. Softw. **27**(1), 63–67 (1994)
7. Jansen, S.: There's no business like software business: trends in software intensive business research. In: Hyrynsalmi, S., Suoranta, M., Nguyen-Duc, A., Tyrväinen, P., Abrahamsson, P. (eds.) ICSOB 2019. LNBIP, vol. 370, pp. 19–27. Springer, Cham (2019). https://doi.org/10.1007/978-3-030-33742-1_3
8. Karanatsiou, D., Li, Y., Arvanitou, E.M., Misirlis, N., Wong, W.E.: A bibliometric assessment of software engineering scholars and institutions (2010–2017). J. Syst. Softw. **147**, 246–261 (2019)
9. Kitchenham, B.A., Charters, S.: Guidelines for performing systematic literature reviews in software engineering. version 2.3. EBSE Technical report EBSE-2007-01, Keele University, Keele, Staffs, United Kingdom, July 2007
10. Seppänen, M., Hyrynsalmi, S., Manikas, K., Suominen, A.: Yet another ecosystem literature review: 10 + 1 research communities. In: 2017 IEEE European Technology and Engineering Management Summit (E-TEMS), pp. 1–8. E-TEMS 2017, IEEE, October 2017
11. Suominen, A., Hyrynsalmi, S., Seppänen, M.: Ecosystems here, there, and everywhere – a barometrical analysis of the roots of 'software ecosystem'. In: Maglyas, A., Lamprecht, A.-L. (eds.) Software Business. LNBIP, vol. 240, pp. 32–46. Springer, Cham (2016). https://doi.org/10.1007/978-3-319-40515-5_3

12. Unterkalmsteiner, M., Abrahamsson, P., Wang, X., et al.: Software startups - a research agenda. e Informatica Softw. Eng. J. **10**(1), 89–124 (2016)
13. Van Eck, N.J., Waltman, L.: Software survey: VOSviewer, a computer program for bibliometric mapping. Scientometrics **84**(2), 523–538 (2010). https://doi.org/10.1007/s11192-009-0146-3
14. Van Raan, A., Tijssen, R.: The neural net of neural network research: an exercise in bibliometric mapping. Scientometrics **26**(1), 169–192 (1993)

A Framework for Designing Self-sustaining Ecosystems with Blockchain

Swayam Shah(✉) and Slinger Jansen

Department of Information and Computing Science, Utrecht University, Utrecht, The Netherlands
s.r.shah@students.uu.nl, slinger.jansen@uu.nl

Abstract. Blockchain is a foundational technology where the idea of a distributed database and trust is established through mass collaboration and smart contracts. It is being claimed to be the next major socio-technical advancement after the invention of the Internet. In this paper we present a framework that supports experts in designing self-sustaining ecosystems leveraging distributed ledger technology. The critical building blocks of the framework are value exchange mapping, determining an evolutionary distributed ledger technology architecture, governance modelling, and token engineering. The goal of the framework is to establish a Minimum Viable Ecosystem that is self-sustaining in itself while having a positive-sum game as the basis to attain organic network effects. The framework has been evaluated through three case studies of prominent distributed ledger technology projects. The results of the case study were positive and evident of the need for such frameworks to help experts to think strategically, critically and precisely.

Keywords: Distributed Ledger Technology · Blockchain · Token engineering · Self-sustaining ecosystems · Socio-technical system

1 Introduction

Problem Statement: Distributed Ledger Technology (DLT) projects have been easy to bootstrap although when it comes to next steps, for going beyond a proof of concept and scaling up while attaining the network effects, numerous projects have failed or substantially devalued. At times, the reason behind the failure is lack of in-depth understanding of intricacies of blockchain systems coupled with unavailability of right tools to help the projects navigate through the complexities to engineer a technically as well as commercially sound product or service. Nonetheless, many blockchain startups and communities lack a well-defined revenue model which makes it difficult to raise external funding. Moreover, there are also instances, where projects decide to completely discard tokenization as it increases complexity in the system, but it backfires as the project loses an important component which can actually facilitate self-sustenance [3].

E. Klotins and K. Wnuk (Eds.): ICSOB 2020, LNBIP 407, pp. 184–192, 2021.
https://doi.org/10.1007/978-3-030-67292-8_14

Self-sustaining ecosystems can be defined as being able to operate itself with negligible interference from the outside world. The value is created, distributed, maintained, exchanged and stored within the ecosystem and follows the principles of anti-fragile systems proposed by Taleb and Douady [8]. Moreover, it aims to establish a Schelling Point which is to have an equilibrium in the network with zero communication or coordination. It is a concept of game theory which people tend to use as default solution in the absence of communication because it seems natural, special, or relevant to them.

Aims and Objectives: The problems discussed in the previous section demand to design a framework which can break down the complexity of DLT systems while enabling stakeholders to create self-sustainable ecosystems.

Moreover, it opens up a wide range of possibilities for creating 'fair' marketplaces where digital assets could be traded, exchanged, gifted or even curated without any mandate from any central entity. Therefore, we evaluate the proposed framework by conducting case-studies with multiple DLT projects. *Additionally, to the best of the authors' knowledge, this is the first attempt towards an artefact that is focused on critical elements of blockchain project which assists in carrying out strategic thinking while establishing a precise project roadmap with the aim to attain self-sustenance in the form of a Minimum Viable Ecosystem(MVE).*

Related Work: The most relevant work carried out before in order to propose a framework to facilitate blockchain ecosystems was 'Token Ecosystem Creation' by Dhaliwal et al. [2]. However, it is precisely focused on token engineering while this study focuses on all critical aspects of any blockchain or a DLT system. Secondly, the research by Pelt et al. [7] and Tan [9], provides a blockchain governance and token economics framework, respectively. These important elements while proposing a holistic framework for strategically navigating through any DLT projects.

Research Process: The research design process followed Design Science Research by Hevner and Chatterjee [6]. Further, for the literature study, the study employed Multivocal literature study by Garousi et al. [5] and to evaluate the proposed framework we followed the guidelines by Yin [11] for conducting multiple case studies.

2 Framework

The conceptual model of DLTs resulting from Multivocal Literature Study, served as an input to further curate the framework. *The framework consist of three phases, namely, Discover, Design and Deploy.* Wherever possible, the steps include suggested tools in the form of state-of-the-art conceptual sub-frameworks or other artefacts which were brought together from academic as well as

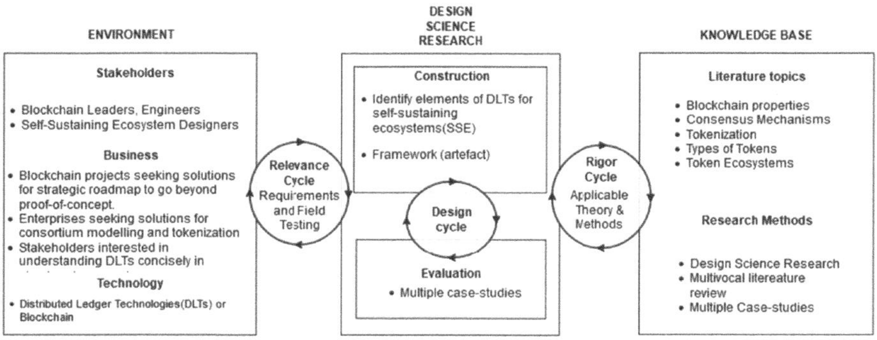

Fig. 1. The design science research framework applied to this study, adapted from [6]

non-academic communities. They were included in the process model to ensure the framework delivers efficacy for DLT projects. *The framework is defined in a manner where governance and token engineering are an integral part of project strategizing.* Moreover, the framework is aligned to our research method of DSR by Hevner and Chatterjee [6], where framework offers a cyclic process for relevance, design, evaluation and rigour as depicted in Fig. 1.

There are two primary requirements for the framework to be operationally feasible and operate at an optimum level, it is assumed that *Self-sovereign identity (SSI)* is integral part of the project and *legal regulations* are being considered at each step of the framework.

It has been observed over the period of time that there is a common practice by experts for approaching DLT projects as starting up a traditional business or startup. But there is more to these projects when approached from the perspective of starting up a new 'country'. The country requires a set of rules (governance) and monetary policies (token economics) to facilitate/attract/retain citizens (network effects) and drive their user behaviour. This approach helps in making the governance, token engineering and network effects as Key Performance Indicators (KPIs) for any Blockchain or DLT project.

The framework (Fig. 2) starts with the '**Discover**' phase which determines the particular characteristics of the ecosystem and the purpose behind the ecosystem followed by **stakeholder mapping** and **value exchange mapping**. The discover phase aims to prepare blockchain leaders with a series of questions while laying out the context, criteria for success, the scope of solution space, and constraints that need to be satisfied. Secondly, **determining DLT architecture** for the project is equally critical as there are key elements to consider such as required level of on-chain transparency, platform access rights, data governance, issuing of digital assets and tokenization. These are a few of the most important considerations required at the beginning of any DLT project. Further, to determine DLT architecture we suggest Decision Support System(DSS) Farshidi et al. [4]. The DSS[1] results in a potential list of possible

[1] https://dss-mcdm.com.

options for DLT architecture as per the initial assumption of the project. The DSS is a useful tool to perform quick initial feasibility check although recommendations are generic and not specific to particular use-case.

The next phase '**Design**' is an emerging concept that consists of building an ecosystem surrounding the market or the business models via use of blockchain or DLTs. It is a complex task, similar to designing and launching a completely new economic system supported by technical infrastructure. It consists of making high-level design choices including governance structures, the token modelling and its parameters. These parameters are needed to be optimized for stakeholders' incentives and the long term sustainability of the associated ecosystem in order to avoid value leakage. The **governance** must be focused on (i) Rules (ii) The collective scope (iii) The decision-making process, and the (iv) Lack of formal control systems. The blockchain governance model curated by van Pelt [10], offers high-level view on the formation and context within the intricacies of blockchain governance. It is divided into five dimensions consisting of roles, incentives, membership, communication and decision making. The next step is the **token engineering**. Token design requires an understanding of the incentives for each participant in the ecosystem, the associated business model, market structure, and network structure. The final model leads to a protocol design that allows the network to sustain itself while prioritizing system security through engineering of optimal incentive and governance mechanisms. *The core elements of token economics are divided into three segments, Market Design, Mechanism Design and Token Design.* **Market design** is the design of the environment which mainly consists of off-chain parameters. **Mechanism design** is the design of the system from off-chain as well as on-chain for optimizing governance, token economy and thereafter, overall ecosystem. **Token design** is the design specific to the token that will be used in the ecosystem ecosystem Tan [9]. Further, the step of '**classifying tokens**' is essential for the token economics and engineering of the tokens. The tokens could be fungible or non-fungible based upon the nature of project. The most critical parameter at the end of Design phase is about '**Analyzing Security Threats**', the research conducted by Debus [1] offers required insights into securing the ecosystem.

The last phase is '**Deploy**'. The '**Testing**' needs to be an integral part of any ecosystem design process to build an optimal feedback loop that helps govern and monitor the system. This deploy phase consists of iteratively testing until all parameters have been optimized with respect to their constraints. The deployment process involves using a combination of mathematical, computer science and engineering principles to fully understand the interactions in our network and its failure points. It is important to note that optimization and testing are present throughout the entire lifecycle in an iterative process, that is, in practice, governance and token models should be continuously optimized for parameters, variable ranges at all stages. There are various methods to test and optimize the network, for instance, regression learning could be used to validate the input selection stage for identifing the variables and parameters of the objective function. Similarly, Monte Carlo simulations and Markov chains that allow quantifying outputs of token gravity to calculate the velocity of the token and its value. Additionally, agent-based modelling and evolutionary algorithms allow for the model to capture possible future interaction of different use cases and users come on the network. The feedback loop created in this process should relay information to deep learning models comprising neural networks, this can assist in optimizing the network and maximize the objective function of the network. The end goal of the proposed framework (Fig. 2) is to achieve *Minimum Viable Ecosystem* that is self-sustaining in itself.

The process from Discover to Design is suggested to be a single way approach as projects are expected to have concrete assumptions and reasoning before starting the Design phase because it is likely to get lost in the hall of mirrors. Although, the Design and Deploy phase are cyclic to keep room for continuous testing and optimization of ecosystem.

3 Case Studies

The case-study partners were selected on the basis of satisfying these criteria: (i) the blockchain project is relevant to the characteristics of SSE (ii) the blockchain project involves a requirement for token engineering. The Table 1 summarizes the case study partner, their field of work, nature of their project along with identifiers. The identifiers were further used in Table 2 to link the case study partner with their prominent comments. Please note that some amendments were made to the framework after these evaluations. These amendments are left out for reasons of brevity.

Table 1. An overview of the conducted evaluation multiple case-studies

Case study	Field of work	Type of project	Identifier
Eclesia	Startup	Digital Collectables	IE-1
Lisk Casino	Community driven	Online Casino (Gambling)	IE-2
SecureSECO	Academic Project	Self-Sustaining Software Ecosystem	IE-3

Table 2. The most prominent comments from the case participants about their experiences with the framework along the five quality dimensions.

Evaluation Characteristics	Rating	Prominent Comments
Operational Feasibility	IE-1: 5/5	IE-1: "The framework could be used by every other DLT project and is relevant to the LeanStack Startup Innovation Framework"
	IE-2: 5/5	IE-2: "It makes you think of all other feasibility aspects"
	IE-3: 5/5	IE-3: "Would be willing to come back to this framework for future DLT projects"

(contniued)

Table 2. *(contniued)*

Evaluation Characteristics	Rating	Prominent Comments
Ease of Use	IE-1: 4/5	IE-1: "Well structured framework which assists in clear thinking about concrete critical steps"
	IE-2: 5/5	IE-2: "DLT ecosystems are complex and this framework helps in breaking down those complexities"
	IE-3: 2/5	IE-3: "Framework is helpful, but DLTs are complex and therefore it gets overwhelming to consider all aspects"
Usefulness	IE-1: 5/5	IE-1: "It helps in thinking about DLT elements that are essential for scaling up"
	IE-2: 4/5	IE-2: "It is a tangible artifacts for blockchain projects"
	IE-3: 5/5	IE-3: "It helps rethinking how blockchain projects operate"
Completeness	IE-1: 4/5	IE-1: "The discover and design phases are accurate and complete although deploy can still be improved"
	IE-2: 5/5	IE-2: "The framework is complete and covers all major aspects"
	IE-3: 5/5	IE-3: "The framework is complete"
Effectiveness	IE-1: 4/5	IE-1: "The framework is relevant to the needs of DLT projects but it can be improved"
	IE-2: 4/5	IE-2: "The aspects discussed in the case study are effective and helps in thinking beyond the proof of concept"
	IE-3: 5/5	IE-3: "It helps in asking the right questions that are crucial for the success of a project"

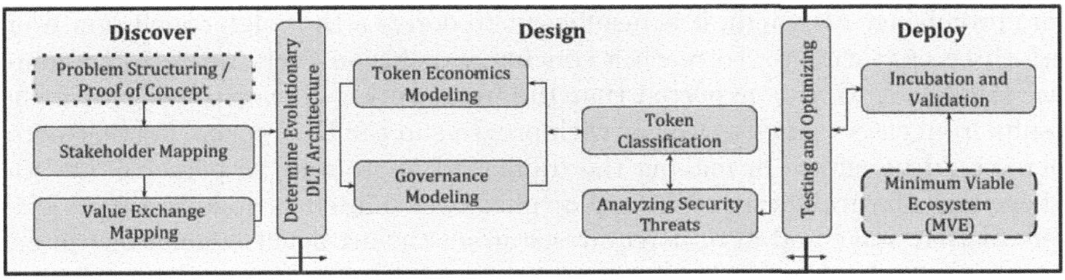

Fig. 2. Revised framework for designing self-sustaining ecosystems

4 Discussion

There was a researched assumption that the DLT community lacks a structured approach while working on a DLT project. Moreover, the aspects such as governance and token economics are rarely considered at the early stage of any DLT project due to their complexity, although these elements determine key design decisions in order to build a Minimum Viable Ecosystem. At the beginning of this research, token engineering was the sole topic to focus on but while progressing and getting a better perception of the range of the topics and gaps in the community, it was decided to further scope our research and propose a holistic framework which is complete in itself while aiming for self-sustenance.

Strengths of Framework: The goal of the framework was to assist DLT projects to efficiently strategize and implement their solutions which includes governance and token engineering as integral part of the process. The case-studies made it evident that the framework is a required tool and important for projects to scale-up. The step for '*value exchange mapping*' was the most discussed element of all the case-studies. The overall results of the case-study received high confidence on the framework in terms of operational feasibility, completeness, effectiveness and usefulness. The framework provides scope for experimentation and exploration throughout the process while aiming for Minimum Viable Ecosystem. Moreover, it fills in the gap for the projects that have already achieved a Proof of Concept for, and are struggling to further scale it up. Here, the framework could be leveraged to attain network effects and scope for new business models. The element such as value exchange mapping which was the most discussed element of the case-study, could benefit from a defined framework which can make value mapping efficient.

Limitations of Framework: During the case-studies, the framework was sometimes perceived as a bit complex but that was also because of the nature of DLT projects. The case-study reference material included all sub-category frameworks regarding governance, token economics, classification of digital assets etc. which can guide the projects but it did add complexity to the main framework. Moreover, the case-studies were conducted with only three partners and results were promising. Although, it is insufficient to derive a thorough conclusion from just three case-studies. To reach a concrete conclusion there needs to be more case-studies. Also, it is expected that the framework will evolve along with the results from case-studies as well as with progress in the DLT space. Furthermore, there could be efforts in making the framework more easy to perceive. On the other hand, the evaluation of the deploy phase was limited as none of the projects were at that stage and also, it requires state-of-the-art agent simulations to get precise results but that in itself is a research and development challenge. Lastly, the framework works as a guiding principle which extensively helps in answering 'why', 'who', 'what', 'when' for the project but has limitations while answering 'how'.

Impacts of Framework: One of the most evident impacts of the framework, during the course of case-studies was that each partner experienced some new territories within the DLTs which were critical for their projects. It enabled rethinking and reconsideration of elements crucial for engineering of DLT projects. Moreover, the framework was received as a complete artefact covering all the required DLT elements for the project. The effectiveness of the framework for each of the project was impeccable as it enabled them to think about every dimension in a DLT project. Each of the partners stated that they would use the framework for their existing work and would be willing to come back to it, in any other future DLT endeavours. Lastly, the framework is critical for the DLT projects which are struggling to move beyond a proof of concept or a minimum viable product.

5 Conclusion

Hence, the framework was curated while studying the intricacies of DLTs and identifying the key elements of DLTs which dictate the design decisions to achieve self-sustenance. These key elements were further structured into three phases of Discover, Design and Deploy. The Design and Deploy are the iterative phases. Furthermore, the framework was rigorously evaluated with ongoing DLT projects as a part of multiple case studies. The results affirmed the need for such artefacts which can help in strategizing the engineering decisions of next-generation socio-technical ecosystems while making them commercially viable.

Future Work: The case studies were limited to three in this study, although more case studies would provide concrete insights along with upgrading the framework itself. The framework was perceived as bit complex and overwhelming so future could be in attempt to make it simpler and concise. Other interesting future work would be modelling of token economics through agent based simulations which would allow designers to bypass any theoretical limitations and model the agents as per the assumptions directly while taking into account every possible constraint.

Acknowledgement. This research is inspired from the work of Dhaliwal et al. [2] and Tan [9].

References

1. Debus, J.: Consensus methods in blockchain systems. Technical report, Frankfurt School of Finance & Management, Blockchain Center (2017)
2. Dhaliwal, E., Gurguc, Z., Machoko, A., Le Fevre, G., Burke, J.: Token ecosystem creation a strategic process to architect and engineer viable token economies (2018)
3. Drljevic, N., Aranda, D.A., Stantchev, V.: Perspectives on risks and standards that affect the requirements engineering of blockchain technology. Comput. Stand. Interfaces **69**, 103409 (2020)

4. Farshidi, S., Jansen, S., España, S., Verkleij, J.: Decision support for blockchain platform selection: three industry case studies. IEEE Trans. Eng. Manage. **67**(4), 1109–1128 (2020)
5. Garousi, V., Felderer, M., Mäntylä, M.V.: Guidelines for including grey literature and conducting multivocal literature reviews in software engineering. Inf. Softw. Technol. **106**, 101–121 (2019)
6. Hevner, A., Chatterjee, S.: Design science research in information systems. In: Design Research in Information Systems. Integrated Series in Information Systems, vol 22. Springer, Boston (2010). https://doi.org/10.1007/978-1-4419-5653-8_2
7. van Pelt, R., Jansen, S., Baars, D., Overbeek, S.: Defining blockchain governance: a framework for analysis and comparison. Inf. Syst. Manage. **38**, 1–21 (2020)
8. Taleb, N.N., Douady, R.: Mathematical definition, mapping, and detection of (anti) fragility. Quant. Financ. **13**(11), 1677–1689 (2013)
9. Tan, L.: Token economics framework. SSRN 3381452 (2019)
10. van Pelt, R.L.: Blockchain governance: a framework for analysis and comparison. Master's thesis (2019)
11. Yin, R.K.: Case Study Research: Design And Methods, 2nd edn. Sage Publications, Thousand Oaks, CA (1994)

The Startup Scratch Book – Opening the Black Box of Startup Education

Pekka Abrahamsson(✉), Mari Suoranta, Sonja Lahti, and Kai-Kristian Kemell

University of Jyväskylä, 40014 Jyväskylä, Finland
{pekka.abrahamsson,mari.suoranta,kai-kristian.o.kemell}@jyu.fi, sohilaht@student.jyu.fi

Abstract. Teaching entrepreneurship and startups is a challenging task. Approaches using real or simulated entrepreneurship as a teaching method are also common in startup education. However, as educators and researchers, we typically only observe the outcomes of the startup journey between weekly lectures and other meetings, whereas the actions taken by the student teams can seldom be observed. This makes the process a black box. All valuable learnings, realizations, and big ideas happen in the students' minds, and little evidence exists to say what happened during the course. As a result, we are entirely missing out on the most critical elements of the learning process. To remedy this issue, we propose a new tool for startup education: The Startup Scratch Book. Based on extant literature and our experiences in the area, we have devised this novel approach to learning diaries in startup education. We discuss the specifics of this proposed approach in this paper.

Keywords: Startup · Software startup · Entrepreneurship education · Learning diary · Methodology

1 Introduction

Software startups are an important economic force globally today. Startups are often associated with innovativeness and with success stories where a garage-based team grows its business into a global corporation. These types of stories have resulted in both research and industry interest towards startups. Researchers and companies alike have sought to understand what a 'startup' really is and what makes them different from other business organizations. Startups have been studied from various points of view, with one point of focus being how startups operate, resulting in approaches such as the Lean Startup Method [16] and Internal Startups [8].

In a similar fashion, this interest towards startups has also made its way into entrepreneurship education. Startup-specific courses can now be found in various disciplines. This also includes IT ones, given how technology-focused startups tend to be.

It seems to be common in startup education to utilize approaches that focus on learning by doing [2, 3]. This is hardly unheard of in entrepreneurship education in

E. Klotins and K. Wnuk (Eds.): ICSOB 2020, LNBIP 407, pp. 193–200, 2021.
https://doi.org/10.1007/978-3-030-67292-8_15

general, as many such course take approaches that focus on teaching students "for" entrepreneurship, preparing them to do so in practice, or "through" entrepreneurship in a simulated or real manner [17]. These types of teaching approaches often result in courses that are not organized in the typical lectures (and exercises) into an exam manner. New types of assignments and grading criteria are needed to evaluate work happening in a real or simulated startup during the course [2, 3].

Research on startups thus far has sought to understand how startups work. This is also of interest from the point of view of education and educators. In courses focusing on learning "through" entrepreneurship, the educators are typically only able to observe the outcomes of the startup journey. Between lectures and other types of meetings, such as mentoring ones, the student teams typically work independently. This results in a situation where the work itself carried out by these teams becomes a black box where only the outcomes of the work can be observed.

In this paper, we propose a data collection tool for startup education, the Startup Scratch Book (SSB). The SSB is a novel approach that draws from the established learning diary approach used in education. We discuss what the tool is and how it could be used in startup education, as well as what potential benefits it could yield.

2 Theoretical Background

In this section, we discuss existing research relevant to this topic. In the first subsection, we discuss entrepreneurship education and startup education. In the second subsection we discuss the use learning diaries in education. In the third subsection, we discuss the Business Model Canvas, as it was used as a part of the research model.

2.1 Entrepreneurship Education and Startup Education

Startup education is often carried out in a manner that makes it a subset of entrepreneurship education, with the focus on the entrepreneurial point of view on startups. Though some entrepreneurship courses also discuss startups, courses focusing specifically on startup entrepreneurship are common. These courses are common in IT disciplines as well [2, 3], given how many startups focus on software or hardware. Even if a startup does not sell software, software is typically at the center of its business and plays a key role in delivering value (e.g. Uber delivers value through an app).

Sirelkhatim and Gangi [17], based on a literature review in the area, categorize entrepreneurship education into three categories: teaching 1) "about" entrepreneurship, 2) "for" entrepreneurship, and 3) "through" entrepreneurship. The first one refers to conventional teacher-centric education where the focus is on theory. The second and third refer to more practice-focused education, where teaching "for" entrepreneurship is about preparing students for entrepreneurship and teaching "through" entrepreneurship either real or simulated entrepreneurship during the course. This typology arguably applies to startup education as well. As Chanin et al. [2, 3] remark, startup education rather commonly utilizes teaching "through" (startup) entrepreneurship approaches. As are often associated with characteristics such as inexperienced team and lack of resources, they are arguably easier to found or simulate in an educational setting with students – and, in fact, many startups are founded by students.

Past studies, such as that of Rasmussen and Sørheim [14], have linked action-based entrepreneurship education (i.e. learning by doing, which can be likened to teaching "through" entrepreneurship) with an increased number of new businesses founded by course participants. If the aim is to foster entrepreneurship among students, such teaching approaches may be preferable to traditional lecture-based ones.

2.2 Learning Diaries in Education

Learning diaries are widely used tools in education. In a course utilizing learning diaries, the students write down their learning experiences into this diary, e.g. one entry per lecture. Rather than simply writing down what was discussed in a lecture, students are encouraged to reflect on the learning experience, thinking about it critically and evaluating the implications of what they have learned. Indeed, learning diaries focus on developing the reflection and critical thinking skills of the students [13]. Learning diaries have been found in past studies to increase the metacognitive skills and attitude of students, their time management skills [4], as well as their engagement and motivation, and to help them better understand their learning processes [12].

For educators, learning diaries function as a way of grading students, as well as a way of tracking what the students are learning. In larger courses, they can be resource-intensive to evaluate, however, given the amount of textual content in each diary [6]. Typical assessment criteria for learning diaries include: (1) length, (2) presentation and legibility, (3) number or regularity of entries, (4) clarity and quality of observation, (5) evidence of speculation, (6) evidence of willingness to revise ideas, (7) honesty and self-assessment, (8) thoroughness of reflection and self-awareness, (9) depth and detail of reflective accounts, (10) evidence of creative thinking, (11) evidence of critical thinking, (12) a deep approach to the subject matter, (13) representation of cognitive skills, (14) relationship of the entries in the journal to any relevant coursework, theories etc., (15) match of the content and outcomes of journal work to course objectives, learning outcomes for the journal or purposes that the journal is intended to fulfill, and (16) questions that arise from the reflective processes and on which to reflect further [10].

2.3 Business Model Canvas

The Business Model Canvas (BMC) [11] was used as one framework in the Startup Scratch Book as discussed in the following section. The BMC takes on the form of one sheet of paper (hence canvas). This sheet is then split into boxes (See Fig. 1 in the next section), each of which contains one element of a business model. The user of the canvas fills it out to get a better picture of their current or hypothetical future business idea. The BMC has become particularly popular among startups where filling out a lengthy business plan, especially early on, can quickly become fruitless work when the approach changes following a so-called pivot.

3 Model for the Startup Scratch Book

The Startup Scratch Book (SSB) is summarized into a model describing its key elements in Fig. 1 below. The SSB combines elements of traditional learning diaries and scrap books. While they contain reflection in the form of text written specifically for the SSB, the SSBs also focus on recording the learning process through various other types of data. These data can be anything from sketches to notes to survey data.

The model for the SSB (Fig. 1) consists of two layers. On the first layer are four building blocks (relevance, depth, reflection, and presentation), while on the second layer is the content of the scratch book, where the Business Model Canvas is used as a framework. Each building block contains sub-elements which also function as assessment criteria. These are discussed in detail in the following subsections.

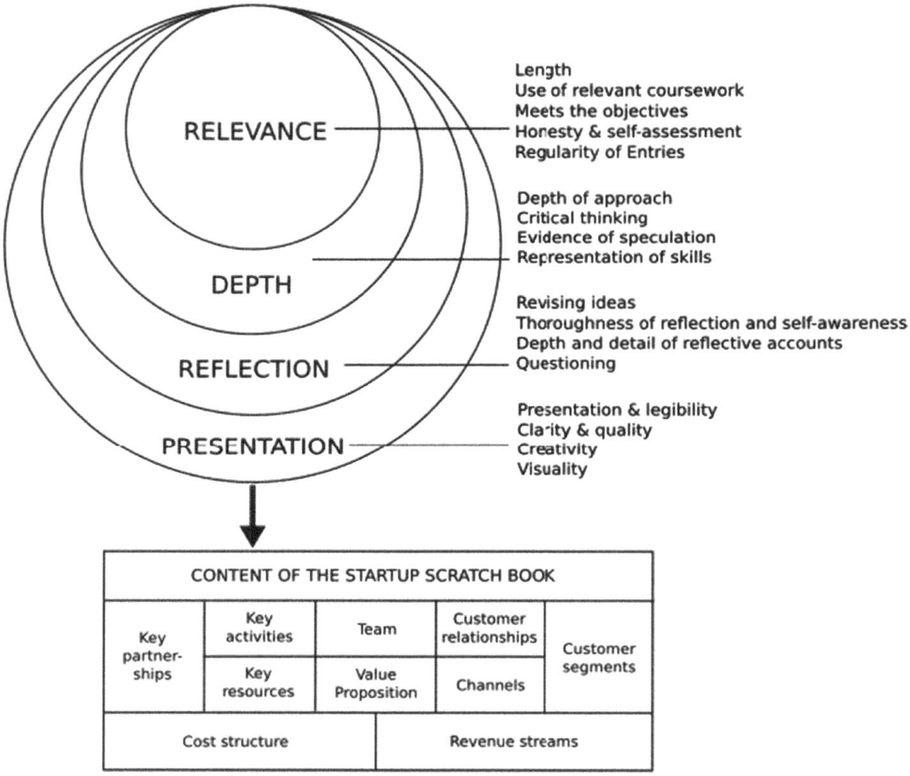

Fig. 1. Model for the Startup Scratch Book.

Aside from its educational goals, the purpose of an SSB is to record as much of the work done in a startup as possible. An SSB contains all the material of a startup from user surveys and the data collected via said surveys to pitch decks and sketches. It provides a large and varied set of data to anyone interested in studying startups, especially in educational settings.

3.1 Relevance

Relevance is the foundation of the scratch book. It is judged based on five criteria. First, the length of the SSB is defined in course requirements (e.g. 100 pages). Secondly, the use of relevant coursework refers to the use of academic literature, frameworks etc. that have been discussed during the lectures or in the course requirements. Thirdly, the SSB should meet any other objectives defined for it.

The fourth criterion, honesty & self-assessment, can be difficult to evaluate objectively. As Maloney et al. [9] discuss in relation to learning diaries, both physical and psychological factors can result in dishonest reflection. To tackle these challenges, it is important to discuss the SSB and its role thoroughly with the students. Honesty is evaluated primarily through the regularity of the entries and how the reflection is carried out. To this end, the fifth and final attribute of relevance, regularity of entries, is evaluated based on how the SSB proceeds chronologically.

3.2 Depth

Depth refers to how in-depth the text goes and how accurate the descriptions are. Moon [10] discuss the depth and detail of the reflection as one evaluation criterion for learning diaries, and it is used as such here. In evaluating depth in SSBs, the presence of critical thinking and any related speculation, and the depth of thought and reflection are focused on. Finally, discussing skills known beforehand or learned during the course and how they were used in the startup process is one factor in evaluating depth, although not mandatory.

3.3 Reflection

Reflection is also a separate building block of its own. Moon [10] argue that reflection is of high quality when it is analytical or integrative and links factors and perspectives. Revising ideas refers to the process being visible in the text, and that ideas and their implementations are revised as the startup progresses. Thoroughness, here, refers to the reflection being visible in the text and it being many-sided and comprehensive. Questioning is about showing in the text that the ideas and sources are questioned in some way when considered worth questioning.

3.4 Presentation

Presentation includes criteria related to the visual aspects of the work as well as its layout. Legibility includes citing any source materials correctly and the text being honest. Clarity and quality are typical assessment criteria in learning diaries [10] and they are used here as well; the content should be understandable and of good quality. Creativity refers to displaying creativity in the ideas depicted in the SSB and their implementation, as well as the layout of the SSB itself. Visuality refers to the visual presentation of the SSB, such as pictures, tables, and any other visual elements and how they are represented.

3.5 Content

The content required in the SSBs should be defined in the course requirements. Aside from other SSB content, it includes the content of the business model canvas. All of the building blocks of the BMC should be covered in an SSB. In addition to the traditional building blocks of BMC, the SSB should also include the team perspective, the potential inclusion of which we have discussed in another paper (see [7]).

4 How to Use the Startup Scratch Book?

The Startup Scratch Book (SSB) is a tool for entrepreneurship courses, and specifically startup entrepreneurship ones, that utilize a learning "through" entrepreneurship approach (as described by Sirelkhatim and Gangi [17]). I.e., for courses that teach through real or simulated entrepreneurship. It is a novel approach to utilizing learning diaries in startup education. Aside from functioning as a learning diary, it is a way of recording the startup journey during such courses. Indeed, rather than focusing exclusively on content manually written for the learning diary, the SSB also includes different types of documents created during the startup journey (e.g. notes, sketches ...).

To this end, aside from being intended to provide the benefits of learning diaries to the students, the SSB is a data collection method for gathering rich data while also serving as a way of tracking the work done by the student teams in the course. Any weekly or other course deliverables are included into the SSB, such as a filled BMC, or data from customer surveys. For students, this serves as a way of showing the work they have done during the course. For teachers (and researchers), this also provides a closer look into the startup journey in the form of a rich set of data that can be adjusted based on research needs.

In evaluating the SSBs, the model we discussed in the previous section is to be used (summary in Fig. 1) There are five building blocks to be evaluated and each of these is discussed in detail in the previous section. In our course, we have defined the minimum length for the SSBs to be 100 pages. This can be adjusted based on what kind of data one wishes to include into the SSBs. In our example use case, we left it up to the students to include whatever they wanted to past the required content.

Due to the proposed length of the SSBs (100+ pages, team effort), we encourage those using the SSBs to monitor the progress of the teams. If regular updates are made, this is ultimately not a daunting amount of data, given that the SSB does *not* consist exclusively of traditional learning diary content in the form of written reflection. Nonetheless, it is arguably a daunting task to produce an SSB a week or a day before the deadline, and as such the teams should be working on it regularly – as is the case with any learning diary.

5 Discussion and Conclusions

Based on extant literature from various areas of research, such as lean startup methodologies [16], the Business Model Canvas [11], startup [2, 3] and entrepreneurship education [17], and learning diaries (e.g. [10]), we propose a novel approach to learning diaries in startup education: the Software Startup Scratchbook. We have discussed the theoretical foundation of this tool in detail in Sect. 3, and how it could be used in practice in Sect. 4. The SSB is a tool that could help capture the overall learning process of creating a new business, including the challenges associated with it. It also serves as a tool for reflecting on the process and what has been learned during it.

Indeed, aside from being a data collection method, the SSB is still an educational tool. Our motto for SSB is that "If it is not recorded in the book, it does not exist." We hypothesize that the students become mindful of their cognitive processes, actions, and material they read and discover, the customers they talk to, and everything that happens in their startup process over the several weeks of the course. Thus, the effects of the SSB should be better when compared to traditional learning diary outcomes. I.e., as traditional learning diaries have been argued to do [4, 12], using the SSB could help students develop their metacognitive skills and attitude, time management skills, and/or their engagement and motivation, and/or help the better understand their learning process. However, this is pending empirical validation.

Aside from educational goals, the SSB functions as a data collection method that produces a large amount of rich data. Given the breadth of data provided by the SSB, it can serve as a primary or supporting data source for various types of studies. On the other hand, one key challenge in using learning diaries is trust [5, 9]. A lack of trust can stem from physical and psychological limitations [9]. E.g. a student might be afraid of receiving a lower grade due to being critical about the course.

However, in this paper, we have only presented a *proposal* for this tool, and described how it could be used in practice. We have, thus far, utilized it in practice ourselves in a Lean Startup course as the University of Jyväskylä. We have developed the tool iteratively, listening to student feedback and using existing literature to improve it. Yet, it is still pending formal, scientific empirical validation in terms of its learning outcomes and how it functions in practice. While we plan to do so ourselves in the future, those interested in the SSB as a potential data collection approach are encouraged to do so as well. To this end, future studies on the SSB should seek to either improve the SSB model further, or to look at how SSBs could be utilized as primary or supporting data in startup research. So far, we submitted the SSB to the 6th Teaching Innovation & Entrepreneurship Excellence competition, and it can now be found in the book [15] featuring all the finalists.

Finally, though SSB could certainly be used outside the educational context as well, producing one can be time-consuming. For a course deliverable that decides a major portion of the grade of a project-based course, resource-intensiveness is to be expected. On the other hand, convincing startup practitioners to produce SSBs for research purposes is likely to be a challenging task.

References

1. Abrahamsson, P., Suoranta, M., Lahti, S., Kemell, K.-K.: The startup scratch book changes the way we teach, research and learn in startup education. In: Remenyi, D. (ed.) 6th Teaching Innovation & Entrepreneurship Excellence Awards 2020 - An Anthology of Case Histories. Academic Conferences International, Reading, United Kingdom (2020)
2. Chanin, R., et al.: Software startup education around the world: a preliminary analysis. In: CEUR Workshop Proceedings (No. 2305). RWTH Aachen University (2018)

3. Chanin, R., Sales, A., Pompermaier, L., Prikladnicki, R.: A systematic mapping study on software startups education. In: Proceedings of the 22nd International Conference on Evaluation and Assessment in Software Engineering 2018, pp. 163–168 (2018)
4. Dignath-van Ewijk, C., Fabriz, S., Buttner, G.: Fostering self-regulated learning among students by means of an electronic learning diary: a training experiment. J. Cogn. Educ. Psychol. **14**(1), 77–97 (2015)
5. English, L.M.: Ethical concerns relating to journal writing. New Dir. Adult Cont. Educ. **90**, 27–35 (2001)
6. Hyppönen, O., Lindén, S.: Opettajan käsikirja: opintojaksojen rakenteet, opetusmenetelmät ja arviointi (2009)
7. Kemell, K.-K., et al.: Business model canvas should pay more attention to the software startup team. In: Proceedings of the 46th Euromicro Conference on Software Engineering and Advanced Applications (SEAA/DSD) (2020)
8. Kemell, K.-K., Risku, J., Strandjord, K., Nguyen-Duc, A., Wang, X., Abrahamsson, P.: Internal software startups – a multiple case study on practices, methods, and success factors. In: Proceedings of the 46th Euromicro Conference on Software Engineering and Advanced Applications (SEAA) (2020)
9. Maloney, S., Tai, J.H.-M., Lo, K., Molloy, E., Ilic, D.: Honesty in critically reflective essays: an analysis of student practice. Adv. Health Sci. Educ. **18**(4), 617–626 (2013). https://doi.org/10.1007/s10459-012-9399-3
10. Moon, J.A.: Learning Journals: A Handbook for Reflective Practice and Professional Development. Routledge, Abingdon (2006)
11. Osterwalder, A., Pigneur, Y.: Business Model Generation: A Handbook for Visionaries, Game Changers, and Challengers. Wiley, Hoboken (2010)
12. Park, C.: Engaging students in the learning process: the learning journal. J. Geogr. Higher Educ. **27**(2), 183–199 (2003)
13. Pavlovich, K., Collins, E., Jones, G.: Developing students' skills in reflective practice: design and assessment. J. Manag. Educ. **33**(1), 37–58 (2009)
14. Rasmussen, E.A., Sørheim, R.: Action-based entrepreneurship education. Technovation **26**(2), 185–194 (2006)
15. Remenyi, D.: Innovation in Teaching of Research Methodology Excellence Awards 2020: An Anthology of Case Histories. Acpil, Reading (2020)
16. Ries, E.: The Lean Startup: How Today's Entrepreneurs Use Continuous Innovation to Create Radically Successful Businesses. Crown Business, New York (2011)
17. Sirelkhatim, F., Gangi, Y.: Entrepreneurship education: a systematic literature review of curricula contents and teaching methods. Cogent Bus. Manag. **2**(1), 1052034 (2015)

SECOGov: A Software Ecosystem Governance Approach to Support IT Architecture Activities

Benno Eduardo Albert[1], Cláudia Maria Lima Werner[1], and Rodrigo Pereira dos Santos[2](✉)

[1] COPPE/UFRJ – Federal University of Rio de Janeiro, Rio de Janeiro 21945-970, Brazil
{benno,werner}@cos.ufrj.br

[2] Department of Applied Informatics, UNIRIO – Federal University of the State of Rio de Janeiro, Rio de Janeiro 22290-240, Brazil
rps@uniriotec.br

Abstract. Organizations have established relationships to create software ecosystems (SECO). Suppliers face challenges when provisioning and maintaining products and technologies in a competitive market, while software-consuming organizations face challenges when performing IT architecture activities, i.e., to choose, adopt and maintain software products and technologies in such a dynamic marketplace. However, the lack of structured knowledge hinders SECO management and monitoring in this scenario. In this paper, SECOGov approach is presented to support IT architects in activities to assist a software-consuming organization to: monitor the market; map relationships with suppliers, software products, and technologies; manage software licenses; and visualize strategic information on IT architecture evolution to adjust production. A tool was developed and a study with 16 IT architects in a large organization of the oil & gas sector was conducted to evaluate its feasibility, as well as utility and ease of use. It was observed that SECOGov is feasible to support IT architecture activities, more specifically regarding monitoring technology adoption.

Keywords: Software ecosystems · Software asset management · Governance · IT architecture · Tool

1 Introduction

IT organizations establish relationships through the acquisition of products and consulting contracts, for example, creating software ecosystems (SECO) [15]. Software-consuming organizations must choose, adopt and maintain products and technologies that serve as tools to support employees' tasks and deliver products and services to achieve business goals. These elements, known as software assets [19], are affected by changes on suppliers' market strategy, or mergers and acquisitions. A better understanding of ecosystems to support decisions has been investigated [12]. However, the lack of structured knowledge hinders SECO management and monitoring [16]. Designing and maintaining IT architecture increase the organization's formal self-knowledge so that information is available to ensure business goals [3]. In this scenario, IT managers and

E. Klotins and K. Wnuk (Eds.): ICSOB 2020, LNBIP 407, pp. 201–209, 2021.
https://doi.org/10.1007/978-3-030-67292-8_16

architects apply spreadsheet analysis and distributed documents, as well as market information based on technology research institutes (e.g., Gartner and Forrester), to maintain the organization's IT architecture [2]. However, they mostly use external information to support IT architecture activities, disregarding information inherent to organization's software assets, without a specific tool support [13].

There is a lack of research to support these activities from a strategy that combines market information (inter-organizational) with those obtained from a structured organizational software asset base (intra-organizational), as reported by Alves et al. [1] and recently verified in our observational study on real cases [19]. Strategies refer to governance frameworks [6], e.g., ITIL [18], ISO 27002 [9] and COBIT [11, 17], or focus on Software Asset Management (SAM) by ISO/IEC 19770 [10, 14], towards decisions that take advantage of the ability to be agile and efficient when compared to competitors [4]. Based on such issues, in this paper, SECOGov approach is presented to help IT architects in activities that enable a software-consuming organization to: monitor the market; map relationships with suppliers, software products, and technologies; manage software licenses; and visualize strategic information on IT architecture evolution to adjust production. The contribution is to provide a tool for SECO governance based on software asset management mechanisms that support IT architecture activities. The strategy addresses intra-organizational and inter-organizational views together to assist IT architects in achieving the organization's business goals.

As related work, Baars and Jansen [3] propose a framework for analysis of SECO governance to improve performance and health so that the organization can gain strategic advantage over competitors. However, it does not consider the relevance of the presented factors and lacks validation by experts and case studies. On the other hand, research institutes produce monitoring reports of technology evolution in the market from surveys with experts, e.g., Gartner Hype Cycles and Forrester Tech Horizon Charts [8]. ThoughtWorks Technology Radar is another report for monitoring technology maturity that, in one view, groups techniques, tools, platforms and languages. Despite the fact that business leaders want to use technology to innovate, several IT departments still rely on traditional methods to track and introduce emerging technologies. In the case of SAM processes [10], there is a partial aid to SECO governance. ISO/IEC 19770 does not support IT architecture activities, such as choosing, adopting, and maintaining technologies. This gap motivated an approach to address SECO governance and SAM mechanisms together, as proposed in this work.

2 SECOGov Approach

From the gap identified in our previous work [19], we developed SECOGov based on related work on SAM and SECO governance. Its mechanisms were organized into two views: (1) ***intra-organizational view***, which establishes a governance process for the software assets incorporated into the organization's IT architecture, inspired by Niemann [16], Gartner [7], and ISO 19770 [10]; and (2) ***inter-organizational view***, which allows monitoring the evolution of markets, suppliers, technologies and products, inspired by Forrester [6] and ISO 19770 [10]. In SECOGov, seven mechanisms are proposed and integrated to support IT architecture activities in the SECO context.

The intra-organizational view consists of the first *four* mechanisms, while the intra-organizational view consists of the last *three*: (1) ***Manage Software Taxonomy*** focuses on defining a taxonomy to structure and maintaining the most appropriate categories to catalog their software assets according to relationships in the ecosystem; (2) ***Manage Software Architecture*** focuses on defining which software assets are standardized for each category so that it is possible to quickly find what tool is standard for a given technology; (3) ***Manage Standard Software Configuration*** focuses on defining which software assets are part of a set of package that meets a specific profile or role within the organization; (4) ***Manage Software Licenses*** focuses on managing available/used licenses; (5) ***Monitor SECO*** focuses on managing information on SECO in which an organization plays from reports of research institutes, consultancies or management teams; (6) ***Analyze Technology Maturity*** focuses on carrying out analyses and inferences from SECO to set up, achieve business objectives and prepare for changes; and (7) ***Select Product or Technology*** focuses on allowing a quick check SECO information and verifying which technology should be revised. Table 1 presents a comparison between related work and SECOGov based on the mechanisms for supporting both intra- and inter-organizational views.

Table 1. Related work against SECOGov mechanisms. ● = implements | ◒ = partially implements | ○ = do not implement

		FORRESTER [6]	GARTNER [7]	ISO 19770 [10]	NIEMANN [17]	SECOGov
"Intra" view	Manage Software Taxonomy	○	●	●	●	●
	Manage Software Architecture	○	◒	●	●	●
	Manage Standard Software Configuration	○	○	●	◒	●
	Manage Software Licenses	○	○	●	●	●
"Inter" view	Monitor SECO	●	○	○	○	●
	Analyze Technology Maturity	●	○	○	○	●
	Select Product or Technology	●	○	●	○	●

SECOGov requires a repository with storage, search and retrieval, documentation, publication and classification modules focused on exploring and maintaining software assets data and information on the ecosystem. As such, a tool support was implemented in Brechó Library[1], called Brechó-SECOGov. Brechó is a web system to support a reuse management process. A user playing as an IT architect role accesses Brechó as administrator. To support his/her activities, some entities were identified and modeled: (1) ***Category*** groups components (e.g., Database Management System); (2) ***Component*** refers to a software asset (e.g., Microsoft Office); (3) ***Distribution*** refers to a set of related assets (e.g., Microsoft Office for iOS); (4) ***Release*** refers to a set of versions (e.g., Microsoft Office 2013 for Windows); (5) ***Package*** groups artifacts to users (e.g., Microsoft Office 2013 installation files to iOS); (6) ***Service*** enables web services (e.g.,

[1] http://reuse.cos.ufrj.br/brecho/user/localeAction.do?language=en.

online service for a collection of images for Microsoft Office 2013 for Windows); (7) ***License*** allows the definition of rights and duties on packages and services (e.g., floating license); (8) ***Analysis*** enables the registration of SECO reports on categories or components (e.g., document "Analysis of Office Suites Evolution"); (9) ***Configuration*** groups assets to support users (e.g., "Configuration for Project Manager" including Microsoft Project); and (10) ***SECOGov Component*** refers to a dynamic form that has SECO relevant information on the software asset.

As an example, let the need of an IT architect be the registration and query of information on different ecosystems. Thus, the IT architect needs to look at the list of software assets. Brechó-SECOGov registers assets by entering information on a specific product or technology in the ecosystem. At "My Components" icon, it is possible to filter and sort assets according to their different characteristics, by clicking on a column's headers on the generated table (Fig. 1). An asset can be added or edited in two stages. In the first stage, *name*, *description*, *categories* and *settings* are provided, being the last two fields requested for the mechanisms *Managing Software Taxonomy* and *Managing Standard Software Configuration.* In the second stage, the SECOGov form requests specific data, such as *supplier*, *nature (acquired, developed, evaluation etc.)*, *maturity date*, *assets produced*, and *URI.* It is also necessary to establish whether the asset is a standard for the category to which it is associated, checking the *standard* column at Brechó-SECOGov, referring to *Manage Software Architecture.*

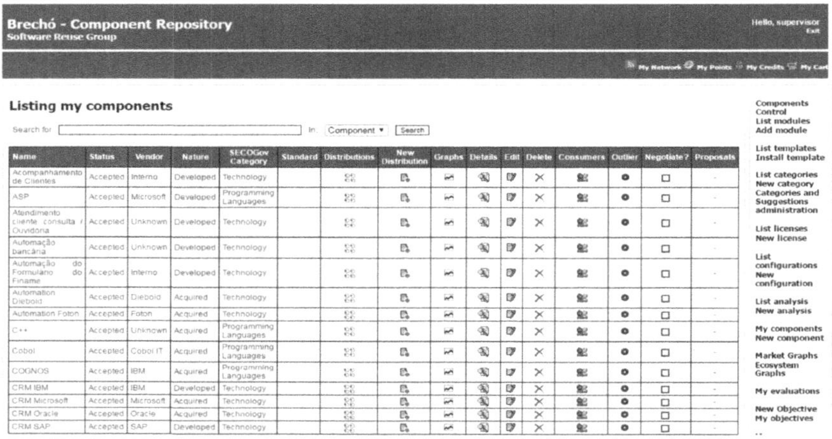

Fig. 1. Brechó-SECOGov main control panel.

For each software asset, three graphs of SECO analysis are available: (a) *use and disuse distribution*, i.e., availability of licenses for each version (*Managing Software Licenses*); (b) *asset trace* with respective category and associated assets; and (c) *productivity* comparing to other software assets that produce a particular asset, filtered by time. In turn, it is possible to check SECO information from the organization from two graphs: (a) *degree of technological dependency* in relation to suppliers; and (b) *distribution of licenses* purchased by the organization for the assets categories. To monitor the participation of an organization in different ecosystems, a SECO Analysis Module was created. When editing an analysis (*Monitor SECO*), SECO information is requested, such as the *title of the analysis, origin/source, author, description, justification, impact on the business, benefit rate, market penetration, maturity, suppliers, time for adoption, recommendation for adoption*, and *comparing products*. To trace the evolution of an analysis over time, it is possible to assign it to categories and/or assets. The analysis list may be ordered with focus on the most important parameters: *benefits rate, maturity, time for adoption (years)*, and *recommendation for adoption*.

3 Evaluation

SECOGov approach and tool were evaluated in a feasibility study. Technology Acceptance Model (TAM) [5] supported the tool's evaluation as regards to easy of use and utility [8]. The main goal was to evaluate SECOGov as a support to IT architecture activities, i.e., choose, adopt and maintain products or technologies offered in the market. Moreover, the tool's ease of use and utility were evaluated. These objectives are presented according to the GQM (Goal-Question-Metric) in Table 2.

Table 2. Objectives #1, #2 and #3.

Analyze	*SECOGov approach and tool*
for the purpose of	*characterizing* (#1) *evaluating easy of use* (#2) *evaluating utility* (#3)
with respect to	*IT architecture activities in the SECO context*
from the point of view of	*IT architects*
in the context of	*a large software-consuming organization*

The main question refers to checking if the participants would be able to understand the relationship of a software-consuming organization with the ecosystems to which it belongs. This perception was measured by metrics of effectiveness and efficiency. Effectiveness measures the ratio between the results obtained and the intended objectives (i.e., number of correct tasks in relation to the proposed set). In turn, efficiency measures the ratio between the results obtained and the resources used (i.e., number of correct tasks relative to time in minutes). Five items were set to check IT architecture activities with and without the tool: (a) difference in the *execution time*; (b) difference in the number of *correct answers* (tasks) after the execution; (c) difference in the *perception of accuracy* of the information recorded by the participants; (d) difference in *effectiveness*; and (e) difference in *efficiency*.

A pilot was conducted with three participants. They performed a set of IT architecture activities with and without the tool support. A field to report the perceived accuracy of the information provided by the participant was added to each task to measure how confident the participant was on performing each of them. After some bug fixes in the tool and review on the study's instrument, the evaluation was conducted with 16 participants working in the IT architecture department of a large software-consuming organization in the oil & gas sector. At first, the participants signed a consent form and filled the characterization form. This allowed us to distribute them into two groups of equal size, keeping the profile of both groups as balanced as possible.

Next, both groups received a text explaining the basics of SECO. The group that would use the tool (G1) also received a brief training on Brechó-SECOGov (about 10 min) in order to use the tool to perform the tasks. The second group (G2) used the organization's IT governance tooling itself (i.e., documents and spreadsheets). Finally, each participant evaluated the SECO governance approach used. Participants in G1 also evaluated the tool regarding ease of use and utility. Regarding academic education, 6% of the participants hold a PhD degree and have already conducted a post-doctoral stage, 6% were PhD students, 50% hold a Master's or Specialization degree, 6% were Master's or Specialization students, and 32% reported having a Bachelor's degree in the field of Computer Science.

In a scale from 0 to 5, where 0 is "*no*" (no experience), 1 is "*studied in class or in a book*" (very low degree), 2 is "*practiced on projects in the classroom*" (low degree), 3 is "*used on personal projects*" (medium degree), 4 is "*used in few projects in the industry*" (high degree), and 5 is "*used in many projects in the industry*" (very high degree), the background was extracted: (i) *Software engineering*: 37% reported very high degree of experience, 25% reported high degree, 19% reported medium degree, and 19% reported very low degree; (ii) *IT Architecture*: 38% reported very high degree of experience, 50% reported high degree, and 12% reported medium degree; (ii) *SAM*: 13% reported very high degree of experience, 19% reported high degree, 37% reported medium, 25% reported very low degree, and 6% had no experience; (iv) *IT Governance*: 25% reported very high degree of experience, 13% reported high degree, 19% reported medium degree, 37% reported low degree, and 6% reported very low degree; and (v) *SECO*: 13% reported very high degree of experience, 12% reported medium degree, 19% reported low degree, 25% reported very low degree, and 31% had no experience. On a 0–2 scale, where 0 is "*I have no familiarity*", 1 is "*have some familiarity*", and 2 is "*I'm very familiar*": (a) 19% were very familiar with IT Governance tools; most (56%) had some familiarity, while 25% were not familiar with such tools; (b) only 13% were very familiar with SAM tools; most (50%) had some familiarity, and 37% were not familiar with such tools; and (c) 31% had some familiarity with SECO view/analysis tools, while most (69%) were not familiar with them.

Next, the results were analyzed based on: (e) the answers provided by the participants; (ii) the duration of the tasks; and (iii) the feedback written in the evaluation form. A statistical analysis was conducted to better understand the results with the aid of Minitab Statistical Software. Measures of central tendency and dispersion were calculated, as shown in Fig. 2.

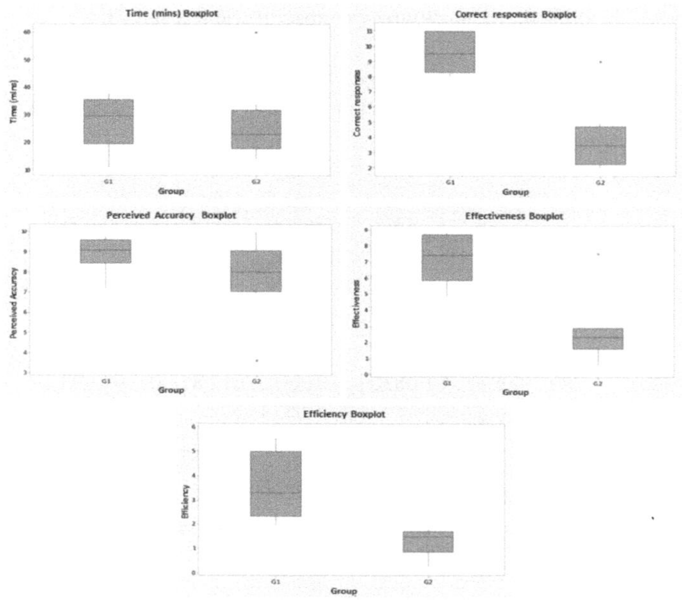

Fig. 2. Boxplot charts comparing G1 e G2.

We used the Mann-Whitney nonparametric test and CI to calculate *p*-value, as shown by Table 3. Considering 95.9% confidence interval (CI) and *p*-value of 0.05, medians and estimates, it was found that the time was not a difference factor between G1 and G2 ($W = 73.5$ and *p*-value of 0.5995). The perceived accuracy of the answers was also not significantly different between the groups ($W = 81$ and *p*-value of 0.1893). However, the use of the tool provided higher effectiveness ($W = 97$ and *p*-value of 0.0028), higher efficiency ($W = 97.5$ and *p*-value = 0.0023) and a larger number of correct answers ($W = 97$ and *p*-value = 0.0028) in G1, in comparison to G2, for the selected arrangement, in the applied context and in accordance with the statistical parameters adopted in this study.

It was revealed that 75% of participants who used the tool had accomplished all tasks (G1), compared to only 37.5% of those who have not used it (G2). A total of 75% of participants in G1 was satisfied with the outcome of the experiment, against 50% in G2. Most participants in both groups (75% in G1 and 87.5% in G2) stated that the proposed "intra" and "inter" views based on the SECO context could benefit or support IT architecture activities, motivating new studies in the field. Finally, the study has indicated that Brechó-SECOGov is easy to use. However, some opportunities for improvement were identified, such as revising the amount of information in the main control panel. Regarding utility, the study has indicated that Brechó-SECOGov fulfilled its goal. As such, participants did not requested improvements in the tool on this subject and indicated that it could be used as a SECO governance tool to support IT architecture activities.

Table 3. Mann-Whitney nonparametric test and CI.

Variable	Group	N	Median	Punctual estimation n1 – n2	95.9 CI for n1 – n2	W	n1 – n2 test versus n1 ≠ n2 significant to	The test is significant (adjust for ties)
T (min)	G1	8	29.5	4.0000	(−13.00; 14.00)	73.50	0.5995	0.5992
	G2	8	23					
Correct answers	G1	8	9.5	6.0000	(4.000; 8.000)	97.00	0.0028	0.0025
	G2	8	3.5					
Perceived accuracy	G1	8	9.083	1.0830	(−0.250; 2.334)	81.00	0.1893	0.1886
	G2	8	8.008					
Effectiveness	G1	8	0.7917	0.5000	(0.3334; 0.6666)	97.00	0.0028	0.0025
	G2	8	0.2917					
Efficiency	G1	8	0.3492	0.2179	(0.0761; 0.4174)	97.50	0.0023	0.0023
	G2	8	0.1583					

Some threats to validity were identified. As ***internal validity***, results depend on the organization's available participants, who were requested to carefully fill the forms and to not exchange information. Unpredicted difficulties with the forms and the tool were mitigated with a pilot and a brief training to G1. In addition, tasks were arranged in a growing sequence of complexity to avoid effects on thinking and execution. As ***external validity***, this study considers part of a mass of data from a real large organization and new studies should be run. As ***constructo validity***, some specific measures were chosen to collect data from the tasks (with the same weight) and a random selection of participants was not possible given the profile (IT architect in industry). Finally, as ***conclusion validity***, the sample size is not ideal from a statistical point of view. However, this is a difficulty for empirical studies in software engineering, especially in industry. So, the results of this study are considered as indications.

4 Final Remarks

This paper presented SECOGov as an approach to support IT architecture activities of software-consuming organizations in SECO, joining governance mechanisms and a SAM strategy to combine intra- and inter-organizational views. A feasibility study indicated that SECOGov provides higher effectiveness, efficiency and number of correct tasks for the selected arrangement and statistical parameters. Future work refers to include requirements management to support *Select Product or Technology* and integrate research institute services to automate *Analyze the Technology Maturity*.

Acknowledgments. This study was financed in part by CNPq and the Coordenação de Aperfeiçoamento de Pessoal de Nível Superior - Brasil (CAPES) - Finance Code 001.

References

1. Alves, C., Oliveira, J., Jansen, S.: Software ecosystems governance - a systematic literature review and research agenda. In: ICEIS 2017, Porto, vol. 3, pp. 215–226 (2017)
2. Axelsson, J., Franke, U., Carlson, J., Sentilles, S., Cicchetti, A.: Towards the architecture of a decision support ecosystem for system component selection. In: Annual IEEE International Systems Conference (SysCon), Montreal, pp. 1–7 (2017)
3. Baars, A., Jansen, S.: A framework for software ecosystem governance. In: Cusumano, M.A., Iyer, B., Venkatraman, N. (eds.) ICSOB 2012. LNBIP, vol. 114, pp. 168–180. Springer, Heidelberg (2012). https://doi.org/10.1007/978-3-642-30746-1_14
4. Bosch, J.: Speed, Data, and Ecosystems Excelling in a Software-Driven World. CRC Press, Boca Raton (2017)
5. Davis, F.D.: User acceptance of information technology: system characteristics, user perceptions, and behavioral impacts. Int. J. Man Mach. Stud. **38**(3), 475–487 (1993)
6. Forrester: The Forrester Wave™ Methodology Guide. Forrester Research (2013)
7. Gartner: Evaluating global-class software ecosystems. Technical report (2007)
8. Howison, J.: Governance in software ecosystems: achieving desirable architectures-in-use through strategies for insight into and influence over end-user development. In: IFIP 8.2 OASIS Workshop, Auckland (2014)
9. ISO: International Organization for Standardization (ISO): ISO 17799 (2005)
10. ISO: ISO/IEC 19770-1: Information technology - IT asset management - Part 1: IT asset management systems – Requirements (2017)
11. ITGI: IT Governance Institute: CObIT 4.1 Excerpt, Executive Summary (2011)
12. Jansen, S.: A focus area maturity model for software ecosystem governance. Inf. Softw. Technol. **118**(2020), 106219 (2020)
13. Jazayeri, B., Schwichtenberg, S., Küster, J., Zimmermann, O., Engels, G.: Modeling and analyzing architectural diversity of open platforms. In: Dustdar, S., Yu, E., Salinesi, C., Rieu, D., Pant, V. (eds.) CAiSE 2020. LNCS, vol. 12127, pp. 36–53. Springer, Cham (2020). https://doi.org/10.1007/978-3-030-49435-3_3
14. Kenefick, S.: Software Asset Management. Gartner Technical Professional Advice (2011)
15. Manikas, K.: Revisiting software ecosystems research: a longitudinal literature study. J. Syst. Softw. **177**(2016), 84–103 (2016)
16. Niemann, K.: From Enterprise Architecture to IT Governance: Elements of Effective IT Management. Vieweg, Wiesbaden (2006)
17. Niemann, M., Eckert, J., Repp, N., Steinmetz, R.: Towards a generic governance model for service-oriented architectures. In: AMCIS 2008 Proceedings, paper 361 (2008)
18. OGC: Office of Governance Commerce (OGC): IT Infrastructure Library (2020)
19. Santos, R.P., Werner, C., Finkelstein, A.: Ecosystems effects on software-consuming organizations: an experience report on two observational studies. In: 12th European Conference on Software Architecture (ECSA), WDES, Madrid, pp. 1–7, no. 23 (2018)

Engineering Federated Learning Systems: A Literature Review

Hongyi Zhang[1(✉)], Jan Bosch[1], and Helena Holmström Olsson[2]

[1] Department of Computer Science and Engineering,
Chalmers University of Technology, Hörselgången 11, 412 96 Göteborg, Sweden
{hongyiz,jan.bosch}@chalmers.se
[2] Department of Computer Science and Media Technology,
Malmö University, Östra Varvsgatan 11, 205 06 Malmö, Sweden
helena.holmstrom.olsson@mau.se

Abstract. With the increasing attention on Machine Learning applications, more and more companies are involved in implementing AI components into their software products in order to improve the service quality. With the rapid growth of distributed edge devices, Federated Learning has been introduced as a distributed learning technique, which enables model training in a large decentralized network without exchanging collected edge data. The method can not only preserve sensitive user data privacy but also save a large amount of data transmission bandwidth and the budget cost of computation equipment. In this paper, we provide a state-of-the-art overview of the empirical results reported in the existing literature regarding Federated Learning. According to the problems they expressed and solved, we then categorize those deployments into different application domains, identify their challenges and then propose six open research questions.

Keywords: Federated learning · Machine learning · Software business · Literature review

1 Introduction

Nowadays, the development of mobile devices, connected vehicles, and data collection sensors has brought explosive growth of data, which highly power the traditional Machine Learning methods [1]. However, those common methods usually require centralized model training by storing data in a single machine or a central cloud data center, which leads to many problems such as data privacy, computation efficiency [2], etc.

Due to the development of computing and storage capabilities of distributed edge devices, using increased computing power on the edge becomes an applicable solution [3]. In a Federated Learning system, local model training is applied and data created by edge devices do not need to be exchanged. Instead, weight updates are sent to a central aggregation server to generate a global model. The

E. Klotins and K. Wnuk (Eds.): ICSOB 2020, LNBIP 407, pp. 210–218, 2021.
https://doi.org/10.1007/978-3-030-67292-8_17

system solves the problem that models in a traditional Machine Learning approach can only be trained and delivered on a single central server. The theory of Federated Learning has been explored in [4,5]. After the concept was first applied by Google in 2017 [6], there have been several Federated Learning architectures, frameworks and solutions proposed to solve real-world issues.

The contribution of this paper is threefold. First, we provide a state-of-art literature review within the area of Federated Learning systems. We identify and categorize existing literature into different application domains according to the problems expressed and solved. Based on the challenges and limitations identified in our literature review, we propose six open research questions for future research. This review can recommend a new option for industries and AI software engineer to solve the problems of traditional AI/ML systems, like expensive training equipment, computation efficiency, data privacy, etc. Furthermore, the difficulties are pointed out in this review when deploying the Federated Learning components into real systems.

This paper is structured as follows. In Sect. 2, we describe the research method we applied. In Sect. 3, we summarize the results from the literature review. In Sect. 4, we outline the challenges of current Federated Learning systems. Finally, we conclude the paper in Sect. 5.

2 Research Method

This research is conducted following the guidelines presented by Kitchenham [7]. The purpose of our review is to present an overview of contemporary research on the empirical results and solutions regarding Federated Learning that has been reported in the existing literature. In this paper, we address the following research questions:

- **RQ1.** What are the application domains where Federated Learning technique is applied?
- **RQ2.** What are the existing Federated Learning systems as reported in the published literature?
- **RQ3.** What are the main challenges and limitations identified in those reported systems?

2.1 Search Process

To provide a state-of-the-art literature review of Federated Learning in the software engineering research domain, we searched papers from several high-ranked journals/conferences. During our search process, in order to include all the papers which are related to our research questions, we started by selecting relevant terms, namely "Federated Learning", "Distributed Learning", "Collaborative Learning" to cover all papers which are related to Federated Learning and continued with "Case Study", "Application", "Solution" and "Framework" to identify papers that report on empirical study results.

The journals that were included in our search process are top-ranked software engineering and computer science journals such as IEEE Transactions on Software Engineering (TSE), Communications of the ACM (CACM), Machine Learning (JML), etc. [8]. In addition, we used the same queries to search for relevant conference papers and literature in the well-known libraries, such as IEEE Xplore Digital Library, ACM Digital Library, Science Direct and Google Scholar.

2.2 Inclusion and Exclusion Criteria

Each paper that matched the search criteria was reviewed by at least one of the authors of this paper. During the selection, we firstly checked the keywords and the abstract to only include papers within Federated Learning field. After that, we searched and analyzed the application scenario in the body of the paper to identify the specific engineering problems solved by applying Federated Learning. We only selected the papers that report on Federated Learning with empirical results, e.g.. Federated Learning on user action prediction, wireless systems, health records, etc. In summary, we included the paper where engineering Federated Learning systems are the main topic of the paper.

2.3 Results of the Literature Search Process

This section summarizes the results of our literature search process. Although there were about 253 different papers that initially matched the search criteria entered in the search engines of the journals and conferences listed in Sect. 2.1, we found only 28 papers satisfying the inclusion criteria we specified. Those papers solve at least one engineering problem and present their empirical findings/results in the abstract or in the body of the paper. The selected papers are marked by "▲" in the reference section. Based on problems addressed and solved in each paper, we categorize them into six application domains. In our search results, there are 4 papers ([9–12]) in telecommunication field, 6 papers ([6,13–17]) relates to mobile applications, 4 papers ([18–21]) relates to automotive, 5 papers ([22–26]) in IoT and 4 papers ([27–30]) relates to medical solutions. The rest of the papers ([31–35]) are related to other fields like air quality monitoring, image-based geolocation recognition, etc.

3 Existing Federated Learning Systems

In this section, and in accordance with the RQ2, we present the existing Federated Learning systems reported in papers we selected. In the rest of the section, in order to provide clear descriptions, we present each domain in more details.

Telecommunication. A typical telecommunication system usually contains numerous components and distributes to different places. In our results, most of the research focuses on constructing an efficient learning framework for federated model training. Wang et al. [9] define an "In-Edge AI" framework which enables intelligent collaboration between devices and the aggregation server to exchange learning parameters for better model training in energy and computation constraint user equipments. Kang et al. [11] introduce reputation metrics for reliable worker selection in mobile networks. The solution enhances system safety while keeping the same prediction accuracy. Yang et al. [12] propose a novel over-the-air computation based approach for fast global model aggregation via exploring the super-position property of the wireless multiple-access channel, which solves the problem of limited communication bandwidth in wireless systems for aggregating the locally computed updates.

Mobile Applications. Because of the explosive growth of smartphones and the evolution of the wireless network, a statistical Machine Learning model can significantly improve the mobile applications. However, due to the private data produced by personal-owned mobile devices, data privacy and security is also an essential topic in this domain. In order to apply Machine Learning techniques to human daily life, Yang et al. [6] and Ramaswamy et al. [13] apply Federated Learning techniques on the Google Keyboard platform to improve virtual keyboard search suggestion quality and emoji prediction. Leroy et al. [15] conduct an empirical study for the "Hey Snips" wake word spotting by applying Federated Learning techniques. Ammand et al. [16] implement a federated collaborative filter for personalized recommendation system. Liu et al. [17] propose "FedVision", an online visual object detection platform, which is the first computer vision application applied Federated Learning technique.

Automotive. Automotive is a prospective domain for Federated Learning applications. Samarakoon et al. [18] suggest a distributed approach of joint transmit power and resource allocation which enables low-latency communication in vehicular networks. The proposed method can reduce waiting queue length without additional power consumption and similar model prediction performance compared to a centralized solution. Lu et al. [19] and Saputra et al. [20] evaluate the failure battery and energy demand for the electronic vehicle (EV) on top of Federated Learning. Their approaches show the effectiveness of privacy serving, latency reduction and security protection. Zeng et al. [21] propose a framework for combining Federated Learning algorithm within a UAV swarm. The framework proves that it can reduce the number of communication rounds needed for convergence compared to baseline approaches.

IoT. Internet of Things is a distributed platform which contains numerous remote sensors and devices. Different from the wireless system, devices within IoT are power-constrained. In our search results, most research in this domain focuses on data privacy and system efficiency problem. Zhou et al. [22] propose a real-time data processing architecture of the Federated Learning system on top of differential IoT. Zhao et al. [23] design an intelligent system which utilizes customer data to predict client requirements and consumer behaviour with Federated Learning techniques. However, the authors use the blockchain to replace the centralized aggregator in the traditional Federated Learning system in order to enhance security and system robustness. Mills et al. [25] design an advanced FedAvg algorithm which greatly reduces the number of rounds to model convergence in IoT network. Savazzi et al. [26] present a fully distributed or server-less learning approach in a massive IoT network. The proposed distributed learning approach is validated in an IoT scenario where a machine learning model is trained distributively to solve the problem of body detection. Sada et al. [24] give a distributed video analytic architecture based on Federated Learning. It allows real-time distributed object detection and privacy-preserving scheme for model updating.

Medical. Federated Learning has propelled to the forefront in investigations of this application domain. Vepakomma et al. [27] propose "splitNN" which enables local and central health entities to collaborate without sharing patient labels. Huang et al. [28][30] present an approach of improving the efficiency of Federated Learning on health records prediction. Brisimi et al. [29] give an approach to a binary supervised classification problem to predict hospitalizations for cardiac events on top of Federated Learning, which demonstrates faster convergence and less communication overhead compared to traditional machine learning approaches.

Other. In our research, we also identified some other application scenarios. Sozinov et al. [34] evaluate federated learning for training a human activity recognition classifier which can be applied to recognize human behaviour such as sitting, standing, etc. Sprague et al. [33] gives a groundwork for deploying large-scale federated learning as a tool to automatically learn, and continually update a machine learning model that encodes location. Verma et al. [32] provide strategies and results in building AI models using the concept of federated AI across multiple agencies. Hu et al. [35] propose an inference framework "Federated Region-Learning" to PM2.5 monitoring. The results demonstrate the computational efficiency compared to the centralized training method. Hao et al. [31] evaluate an efficient and privacy-enhanced Federated Learning scheme for industrial AI solution.

4 Discussion

In the previous section, we can observe that although Federated Learning is a newly-emerging concept, it has the potential to accelerate the Machine Learning process, utilize the advantage of distributed computing and preserve user privacy. However, there are several challenges and limitations associated with the techniques identified and described in the literature review. One of the biggest problems is the system failure tolerance, the majority of the Federated Learning systems presented in our reviewed paper apply a centralized architecture where edge devices are directly connected to a single central server and exchange model information. As [9] describe, this may make the system face the risk of single-point failure and influence the service availability of the learning system.

Furthermore, system efficiency is still a crucial problem for Federated Learning system. There are some proposed approaches to save computation power and communication resources for Federated Learning systems [12,25,31]. However, the conclusion needs to be further verified in real-world industrial deployments with the largely increased number of edge nodes. Besides, our review also identifies challenges of the methods to separate training devices, since systems reported in our reviewed papers usually utilize all the devices to participate training, which leads to the waste of the computation resources.

In addition, model validation has to be further improved. Especially for those safety-critical systems, such as automotive and medical applications [19,29,30], the quality of the models in all edge devices should be guaranteed.

Besides, due to the increasing number of edge devices, the mechanism of handling devices joining and leaving is one of the limitations in current Federated Learning systems. As [4] presents, the most common way is to simply accept new drop broken connections. This may lead to further problems of system performance such as model performance and model convergence.

Finally, although Federated Learning systems have the advantage of privacy-preserving, systems still have to face the risk of various security issues such as Denial-of-Service, malicious model updates, etc., which is also a major limitation and future direction for Federated Learning systems [23].

According to these challenges, we then propose six open questions for future research:

1. How to guarantee continuous model training and deployment in an industrial Federated Learning system?
2. How to efficiently update model weights and deploy global models?
3. How to split edge device sets for model training and testing?
4. How to guarantee model performance on all edge devices?
5. How to handle devices leaving and joining in different industrial scenarios?
6. How to protect Federated Learning systems from malicious attacks?

5 Conclusion

To stay competitive, more and more companies have introduced AI components into their products. However, although machine learning methods can improve software service quality, many companies struggle with how to minimize the system training cost and a reliable way to preserve user data privacy. Due to the model-only exchange and distributed learning features, Federated Learning is one option to solve those challenges. In order to provide concrete knowledge of this kind of learning approach to the industry, in this paper, we provide a literature review of the empirical results of Federated Learning systems presented in the existing literature. Our research reveals that there are several Federated Learning systems used for different application scenarios. Those scenarios are categorized into six different application domains: telecommunication, mobile applications, automotive, IoT, medical, other. Also, we note that the emerging trend of applying Federated Learning to mobile applications and identify several prospective domains. We summarize our findings in this article that works as a support for researchers and companies when selecting the appropriate technique. Furthermore, based on the challenges and limitations of current Federated Learning systems, six open research questions are presented.

In our future work, we plan to expand this review to include closely related, and highly relevant research papers. Also, we plan to validate our findings in the industry and explore the open research questions we propose in this paper.

References

1. Bishop, C.M.: Pattern Recognition and Machine Learning. Springer, Heidelberg (2006). ISBN 978-0-387-31073-2
2. L'heureux, A., Grolinger, K., Elyamany, H.F., Capretz, M.A.: Machine learning with big data: challenges and approaches. IEEE Access **5**, 7776–7797 (2017)
3. Beck, M.T., Werner, M., Feld, S., Schimper, S.: Mobile edge computing: a taxonomy. In: Proceedings of the Sixth International Conference on Advances in Future Internet, pp. 48–55. Citeseer (2014)
4. Konečný, J., McMahan, H.B., Yu, F.X., Richtárik, P., Suresh, A.T., Bacon, D.: Federated learning: strategies for improving communication efficiency. arXiv preprint arXiv:1610.05492 (2016)
5. McMahan, H.B., Moore, E., Ramage, D., Hampson, S., et al.: Communication-efficient learning of deep networks from decentralized data. arXiv preprint arXiv:1602.05629 (2016)
6. ▲ Yang, T., et al.: Applied federated learning: improving Google keyboard query suggestions. arXiv preprint arXiv:1812.02903 (2018)
7. Kitchenham, B.: Procedures for performing systematic reviews. Keele, UK, Keele University **33**(2004), 1–26 (2004)
8. Feldt, R.: ISI SE journals (ranked). http://www.robertfeldt.net/advice/se_venues/
9. ▲ Wang, X., Han, Y., Wang, C., Zhao, Q., Chen, X., Chen, M.: In-edge AI: Intelligentizing mobile edge computing, caching and communication by federated learning. IEEE Netw. **33**(5), 156–165 (2019)
10. ▲ Tran, N.H., Bao, W., Zomaya, A., NH, N.M., Hong, C.S.: Federated learning over wireless networks: optimization model design and analysis. In: IEEE INFOCOM 2019-IEEE Conference on Computer Communications, pp. 1387–1395. IEEE (2019)
11. ▲ Kang, J., Xiong, Z., Niyato, D., Zou, Y., Zhang, Y., Guizani, M.: Reliable federated learning for mobile networks. arXiv preprint arXiv:1910.06837 (2019)
12. ▲ Yang, K., Jiang, T., Shi, Y., Ding, Z.: Federated learning via over-the-air computation. IEEE Trans. Wirel. Commun. **19**(3), 2022–2035 (2020)
13. ▲ Ramaswamy, S., Mathews, R., Rao, K., Beaufays, F.: Federated learning for emoji prediction in a mobile keyboard. arXiv preprint arXiv:1906.04329 (2019)

14. ▲ Hard, A., et al.: Federated learning for mobile keyboard prediction. arXiv preprint arXiv:1811.03604 (2018)
15. ▲ Leroy, D., Coucke, A., Lavril, T., Gisselbrecht, T., Dureau, J.: Federated learning for keyword spotting. In: ICASSP 2019–2019 IEEE International Conference on Acoustics, Speech and Signal Processing (ICASSP), pp. 6341–6345. IEEE (2019)
16. ▲ Ammad-ud din, M., et al.: Federated collaborative filtering for privacy-preserving personalized recommendation system. arXiv preprint arXiv:1901.09888 (2019)
17. ▲ Liu, Y., et al.: FedVision: an online visual object detection platform powered by federated learning. arXiv preprint arXiv:2001.06202 (2020)
18. ▲ Samarakoon, S., Bennis, M., Saad, W., Debbah, M.: Federated learning for ultra-reliable low-latency V2V communications. In: 2018 IEEE Global Communications Conference (GLOBECOM), pp. 1–7. IEEE (2018)
19. ▲ Lu, S., Yao, Y., Shi, W.: Collaborative learning on the edges: a case study on connected vehicles. In: 2nd {USENIX} Workshop on Hot Topics in Edge Computing (HotEdge 2019) (2019)
20. ▲ Saputra, Y.M., Hoang, D.T., Nguyen, D.N., Dutkiewicz, E., Mueck, M.D., Srikanteswara, S.: Energy demand prediction with federated learning for electric vehicle networks. arXiv preprint arXiv:1909.00907 (2019)
21. ▲ Zeng, T., Semiari, O., Mozaffari, M., Chen, M., Saad, W., Bennis, M.: Federated learning in the sky: joint power allocation and scheduling with UAV swarms. arXiv preprint arXiv:2002.08196 (2020)
22. ▲ Zhou, W., Li, Y., Chen, S., Ding, B.: Real-time data processing architecture for multi-robots based on differential federated learning. In: 2018 IEEE SmartWorld/SCALCOM/UIC/ATC/CBDCom/IOP/SCI, pp. 462–471. IEEE (2018)
23. ▲ Zhao, Y., Zhao, J., Jiang, L., Tan, R., Niyato, D.: Mobile edge computing, blockchain and reputation-based crowdsourcing IoT federated learning: a secure, decentralized and privacy-preserving system. arXiv preprint arXiv:1906.10893 (2019)
24. ▲ Sada, A.B., Bouras, M.A., Ma, J., Runhe, H., Ning, H.: A distributed video analytics architecture based on edge-computing and federated learning. In: 2019 IEEE International Conference on DASC/PiCom/CBDCom/CyberSciTech, pp. 215–220. IEEE (2019)
25. ▲ Mills, J., Hu, J., Min, G.: Communication-efficient federated learning for wireless edge intelligence in IoT. IEEE Internet Things J. **7**, 5986–5994 (2019)
26. ▲ Savazzi, S., Nicoli, M., Rampa, V.: Federated learning with cooperating devices: a consensus approach for massive IoT networks. IEEE Internet Things J. **7**(5), 4641–4654 (2020)
27. ▲ Vepakomma, P., Gupta, O., Swedish, T., Raskar, R.: Split learning for health: distributed deep learning without sharing raw patient data. arXiv preprint arXiv:1812.00564 (2018)
28. ▲ Huang, L., Yin, Y., Fu, Z., Zhang, S., Deng, H., Liu, D.: LoAdaBoost: loss-based AdaBoost federated machine learning on medical data. arXiv preprint arXiv:1811.12629 (2018)
29. ▲ Brisimi, T.S., Chen, R., Mela, T., Olshevsky, A., Paschalidis, I.C., Shi, W.: Federated learning of predictive models from federated electronic health records. Int. J. Med. Inform. **112**, 59–67 (2018)
30. ▲ Huang, L., Shea, A.L., Qian, H., Masurkar, A., Deng, H., Liu, D.: Patient clustering improves efficiency of federated machine learning to predict mortality and hospital stay time using distributed electronic medical records. J. Biomed. Inform. **99**, 103291 (2019)

31. ▲ Hao, M., Li, H., Luo, X., Xu, G., Yang, H., Liu, S.: Efficient and privacy-enhanced federated learning for industrial artificial intelligence. IEEE Trans. Ind. Inform. **16**, 6532–6542 (2019)
32. ▲ Verma, D., Julier, S., Cirincione, G.: Federated AI for building AI solutions across multiple agencies. arXiv preprint arXiv:1809.10036 (2018)
33. ▲ Sprague, M.R., et al.: Asynchronous federated learning for geospatial applications. In: Monreale, A., et al. (eds.) ECML PKDD 2018. CCIS, vol. 967, pp. 21–28. Springer, Cham (2019). https://doi.org/10.1007/978-3-030-14880-5_2
34. ▲ Sozinov, K., Vlassov, V., Girdzijauskas, S.: Human activity recognition using federated learning. In: 2018 IEEE International Conference on ISPA/IUCC/BDCloud/SocialCom/SustainCom, pp. 1103–1111. IEEE (2018)
35. ▲ Hu, B., Gao, Y., Liu, L., Ma, H.: Federated region-learning: an edge computing based framework for urban environment sensing. In: 2018 IEEE Global Communications Conference (GLOBECOM), pp. 1–7. IEEE (2018)

Evaluating the Software Problem Representation on the Basis of Rationale Trees and User Story Maps: Premises of an Experiment

Konstantinos Tsilionis[1(✉)], Joris Maene[1], Samedi Heng[2], Yves Wautelet[1], and Stephan Poelmans[1]

[1] KU Leuven, Leuven, Belgium
{konstantinos.tsilionis,yves.wautelet,stephan.poelmans}@kuleuven.be
[2] HEC Liège, Université de Liège, Liège, Belgium
samedi.heng@uliege.be

Abstract. User stories describe system requirements from the users' point of view using structured natural language. These artifacts mostly assist the development team in agile projects where sets of them express the expected features of the to-be software. Nevertheless, when faced with large user stories' sets, further structuring needs to be introduced to make the software problem more understandable/clear. Indeed, the latter can hardly be understood on the basis of huge flat lists of sentences. The present paper describes the premises of an experiment destined to evaluate whether novice modelers can understand the requirements problem better through a visual representation (called Rationale Tree) built out of a user stories' set. It does so by comparing, on the same objective, the Rationale Tree method to the industry-adopted User Story Mapping technique with a modeling exercise. This was performed with the participation of two student groups where one used the former technique while the other one employed the latter. The ultimate goal of this exercise is to identify the actual performance of the Rational Tree in delivering understandability to the requirements problem (when input is provided in the form of a complex user stories' set) in order to identify possible bottlenecks and improvement opportunities within the method itself.

Keywords: User stories · User story · Rationale Tree · User Story Mapping · Agile requirements engineering

1 Introduction

User stories are requirements expressions written in natural language, generally structured around three dimensions, i.e. the WHO, the WHAT and (possibly) the WHY [9]. They are usually manifested in the format 'As a <type of user >, I want <some goal> so that <some reason>' [1]. Even though the user

E. Klotins and K. Wnuk (Eds.): ICSOB 2020, LNBIP 407, pp. 219–227, 2021.
https://doi.org/10.1007/978-3-030-67292-8_18

stories' simple structure is beneficial in describing globally the features of the to-be system especially when developed in an agile manner, still delineating thoroughly every aspect of the software requirements specification problem from a list of user stories remains challenging.

The *Rationale Tree* [8,10] is one way of dealing with this challenge; it represents a conceptual modeling-based method to visually represent elements extracted from a user stories' set and to link these elements. The method uses parts of the i* strategic rationale diagram constructs [12] and visual notation to build various trees of relating user story elements in a single project with the purpose of identifying depending user stories, identifying Epic ones and group them around common Themes. In essence, this visually-aided method aims to recognize and reduce any occurring modeling redundancies during the stages of requirements' analysis and design at the start of a software development project. The Rationale Tree was introduced theoretically in [10]; it was applied on real life cases in [8] and its ability as a stand-alone method to improve the understanding of user stories' set has been tested on novice modelers in [6,11]. On the other hand, *User Story Mapping* [3] is an industry-adopted user stories' structuring method based on listing, under the scope of an epic user story, all of the related lower-level functions described in ordinary user stories.

The study aims to overview whether a conceptual modeling-based approach such as the Rationale Tree offers a better resolution to the elicitation of user requirements when compared to a simpler user stories' structuring approach (User Story Mapping). Under this scope, an experiment – whose premises are presented in this paper – was organized with the participation of master-level students taking on the role of novice modelers. Half of these students were asked to perform a modeling exercise (see Sect. 2) based upon a case study's user story set by using the Rationale Tree method. At the same time, the other half of the group had to undergo the structuring of the same user story set but using the User Story Mapping technique. This paper overviews the ability of the first group to produce a rationale tree of acceptable quality and the one of the second group to produce a user story map of acceptable quality. Further analysis will be the subject of a following communication.

2 Research Approach and Sampling Technique

For the purposes of this study, we performed a *modeling exercise* (referred also as the *drawing exercise*) with the participation of a student group. Our goal was to capture the modeling capabilities[1] of novice modelers when employing the Rationale Tree method in order to discover possible benefits and/or drawbacks derived from its application. Since a generic class of novice modelers could be instantiated by many possible roles and task-specifications within the software development industry there was no available comprehensive sampling frame to rely on. Consequently we decided to use non-stochastic purposive sampling in

[1] Modeling capability will denote the capacity of novice modelers to produce qualitative artifacts while employing a specific user stories' structuring method each time.

the form of typical cases [4] representing our participating students. In particular, our sample consisted of the Master program of Business Administration with a specialization track in Business Information Management from the 'Katholieke Universiteit Leuven' (Brussels Campus). This group totaled seventy-two students previously educated in general business and economics subjects other than the Information Technology field. Their limited experience in the domain of software modeling and requirements engineering was suitable in order to test the level of general comprehension and learning transferability of the Rationale Tree (compared to the User Story Mapping) as represented by the quality of the artifacts produced by the students when exercised in a specific case study with a defined user stories' set.

3 Design of the Modeling Exercise

The exercise began by introducing a mix of open-ended and closed questions intended to: a) collect background information concerning the participating students, and b) survey their previous knowledge corresponding to the domain of software modeling. For this introductory part, the students had to write down their primary occupation at the time the exercise was taking place and their previous experience with software modeling. This last question asked the students to elaborate on the specific modeling languages they were accustomed to and how they acquired this kind of knowledge. Following, the format of the questions changed from open-ended to a Likert style as they became more specific to the structure of user stories, the Rationale Tree method and the User Story Mapping technique. In particular, students were asked to what extend they were aware of these techniques (in general) and to what extend they were accustomed to specific features incorporated in these techniques (i.e., 'are you familiar with the i* modeling language?'). Due to size limitations, all the information collected from these questions is presented in Appendix 1[2].

Next, the entire group was split randomly into two equally-sized smaller groups. The first group[3], amounting to thirty-six students, had to employ the Rationale Tree method throughout the entire endeavor. The exercise began by introducing a detailed theoretical explanation of the method accompanied by a solved example to instigate further the students' understanding. Next, each student was given the same case description ('Company X' case, see Fig. 1) and had to identify/correspond the user stories' dimensions to the modeling elements of the Rationale Tree. Following, each student individually had to draw a *RT diagram*[4] based on the information provided from the previously determined user stories' set. The second student group[5], comprised also of thirty-six students, had to follow exactly the same procedure to perform the modeling exercise; they were, however, instructed to employ the User Story Mapping technique throughout

[2] All Appendices are available at: http://dx.doi.org/10.17632/b4zyddbrbc.1.

[3] The first student group will also be referred to as the 'Rationale Tree group'.

[4] 'RT diagram' denotes the artifact produced by employing the Rationale Tree method.

[5] The second student group will also be referred to as the 'User Story Mapping group'.

their entire endeavor. In this aspect, this particular group was provided with a theoretical explanation about the User Story Mapping technique accompanied by a solved example with the ultimate goal of each student producing a *USM*[6]. A full description of the tasks and expectations involved in this drawing exercise is given in Appendix 2. Both groups were given the same time to perform this drawing exercise (one hour). An experimental design in the aforementioned form is justified in [5] as it is purposed to analyze the students' ability to respond to complex software engineering cases given that their viewpoint provides an alternative conceptual framework, a wider scope and a rich set of data.

The case study used for this modeling exercise was retrieved from [6] and referred to the case provided by a 'Company X' remained unnamed for privacy reasons. This particular case study (presented in Fig. 1) was reviewed and optimized using the Quality User Story framework [2,6]. The latter represents a linguistic approach to engage in a first-level evaluation of the quality in a set of user stories. Overall, the framework establishes a set of fourteen criteria addressing the syntactic, the semantic, and the pragmatic content of the text that should define high-quality user stories [2]. Therefore, a quality-enhanced user story set, after the implementation of the aforementioned framework, was used in the present exercise in order to build a 'golden standard' for the RT diagram. The 'golden standard' method refers to the construction of an 'ideal' artifact created by our research team. Every correct element and link was awarded with points. The RT diagrams produced by the Rationale Tree group approaching this 'ideal'

Company X has developed a web application where users can analyze DNA samples. If End Users want to make use of the analysis's platform, they need to sign into the web application. Before signing in, they need to complete a registration process via a personal activation code, generated by the partners. Because the information used and shared on the platform is of high confidentiality, the End User has the choice to enable a two-factor authentication during the registration. If enabled, every time an End User wants to log in to the platform, he/she receives a two-factor authentication.

1. As an End User I want to change my personal information So that I can correct errors in my personal information.
2. As an End User I want to receive an activation code So that only known customers can register.
3. As an End User I want to register myself So that I can sign in with a user account.
4. As an End User I want to register an account with a valid activation code of a customer, my personal information and a secret password.
5. As an End User that is unauthenticated, I want to read and accept the terms and conditions upon registration of an account So that I will act in compliance with the regulatory requirements.
6. As an End User I want to be able to log in with a two-factor authentication so that my log in is more secure.
7. As an End User I want the application to ask for my authentication So that only authenticated End Users can sign into the platform.

Fig. 1. The 'Company X' case study for the drawing exercise.

[6] The 'USM' abbreviation denotes the artifact of the User Story Mapping technique.

solution the most, were awarded with the most points (see Sect. 5). This golden standard was then 'converted' into a USM to compare and evaluate optimally the artifacts received by the User Story Mapping group also.

4 Hypothesis

As justified before, the comparison between the different features of the Rationale Tree and the User Story Mapping started by providing a thorough theoretical explanation of each approach before the actual drawing exercise takes place. Whether the notions were sufficiently understood was measured by the quality of the artifacts extrapolated from the answers of the students. Conversely to the User Story Mapping technique, the Rationale Tree contains links and decompositions making it more difficult to be comprehended by novice modelers. The latter incorporates also a broader choice of elements with semantics open to interpretation, adding thusly to its overall complexity. Hence, *our main hypothesis:*

'The artifacts resulting from the drawing exercise are of lower quality in the Rationale Tree group than the User Story Mapping group.'

The quality in the artifacts produced by these two student groups represents the level of comprehension of the requirements problem, as presented in the case study and its accompanying user stories' set, when assisted by the employment of the two aforementioned user story structuring techniques.

5 Evaluation Methods for the Students' Artifacts and Validation of the Hypothesis

This section is devoted to the evaluation and comparison of the students' drawn artifacts. We used two evaluation methods to assess the **RT diagrams**: The first one (the *Three Criteria* evaluation method [11]) consisted of the evaluation of three main criteria namely completeness, conformity and accuracy. A score was allocated to each model element and link identified in each of the RT diagrams reproduced by the respondents. *Completeness* checked whether the respondents have modeled all WHAT and WHY dimensions in a complete way, receiving a point for each modeled element. *Conformity* referred to the respondents ability to identify which modeling construct would represent each user story dimension. For each conformed element half a point was given. *Accuracy* referred to the correct identification of a number of fundamental links as identified from the golden standard artifact. For each correctly identified link, four points were given. If the link was present but the wrong type of link was used, only one point was given. The second evaluation method (the *Golden Standard* [6]) was based on an 'ideal' artifact, created by the research team, whose every correct element and link was awarded with the maximum of points. The RT diagrams provided by the students approaching this 'ideal' solution the most gathered the most points. The **USM**

artifacts were evaluated based on five identified criteria namely completeness, consistency, accuracy, correctness and accuracy. Appendix 3 provides a detailed description of each evaluation method as well as the grading system per criterion.

5.1 How Well Can the Rationale Tree Group Identify Correctly the WHO-, WHAT-, WHY-Dimension of the User Stories' Set?

Before commencing with the actual evaluation of the produced artifacts for the two groups, we analyzed whether the identification of the WHO-, WHAT-, and WHY-dimensions within the user stories' set was easily feasible for the participating students. We started with that because a proper identification of the user stories' dimensions is not an easy task for novice modelers.

Judging from the students' choices, the **WHO-dimension** was identified correctly by 73% of the students assigned to the Rationale Tree method. However, this particular group had difficulty in identifying elements of the **WHAT-** and **WHY-dimension**. Indeed, Table 1 shows the participants' augmented difficulty in distinguishing between *Task* and *Capability* on the one hand, and *Soft-* and *Hard-Goal* on the other. We therefore consider that the differentiation between the former mentioned elements can be ambiguous for novice modelers when using the Rationale Tree method.

Table 1. WHAT-, WHY-dimension analysis for Rationale Tree group.

MBA student	Task	Capability	Soft-goal	Hard-goal	Not present
US2WHAT	45.9	**48.6**	5.4		
US2WHY	2.7	5.4	**51.4**	40.5	
US3WHAT	**94.6**	5.4			
US3WHY	21.6	16.2	**56.8**	5.4	
US4WHAT	29.7	**70.3**			
US4WHY					100
US5WHAT	**59.5**	40.5			
US5WHY	10.8		43.2	**45.9**	
US6WHAT	16.2	**81.1**	2.7		
US6WHY			13.5	**86.5**	
US7WHAT	**62.2**	35.1	2.7		
US7WHY	2.7	5.4	**54.1**	37.8	

*__Bold elements__ indicate the most occurring element within that sample.

5.2 How Well Can the User Story Mapping Group Identify Correctly the WHO-, WHAT-, WHY-Dimension of the User Stories' Set?

Judging from the students' choices, the **WHO-dimension** was identified correctly by 62.9% of the students assigned to the User Story Mapping technique. Table 2 reveals that for this particular group there was also a lot of variability in the identification of elements which points towards the existence of ambiguity in the artifacts' semantics. Students tend to identify the WHY-dimension solely as an *Activity*, which is the highest level used element in the USM. Goal-level tasks are identified solely as activities, although this depends on the context of each case. Our used case (Company X) did not have much details, and due to the hierarchical structure of the User Story Mapping technique, an activity must be followed by a task and finally a detail. This unlike the Rationale Tree where goals, tasks and capabilities can all be used interchangeably.

Table 2. WHAT-, WHY-dimension analysis for User Story Mapping group.

MBA student	Activity	Task	Detail	Not present
US2WHAT	5.7	**57.1**	37.1	
US2WHY	**51.4**	11.4	34.3	2.9
US3WHAT	20	**77.1**	2.9	
US3WHY	**71.4**	25.7		2.9
US4WHAT		37.1	**62.9**	
US4WHY	2.9	2.9		**94.3**
US5WHAT	2.9	**74.3**	22.9	
US5WHY	**62.9**	8.6	25.7	2.9
US6WHAT	8.6	**74.3**	17.1	
US6WHY	**71.4**	5.7	20	
US7WHAT	5.7	**74.3**	17.1	2.9
US7WHY	**51.4**	14.3	25.7	8.6

***Bold elements** indicate the most occurring element within that sample.

5.3 Comparison of the Resulting RT Diagrams and USM Artifacts for the 'Company X' Case

Table 3 compares various descriptive elements related to the acquired points for each drawn artifact, based on their corresponded evaluation method. We observe that the means are similar for the artifacts produced by both groups. Standard deviation is lower for the resulting USM. Hence, the artifacts resulting from the modeling exercise were similar in quality regardless to which group the students were assigned to, which is an element that leads us towards the rejection of our *main hypothesis*.

Table 3. Descriptive statistics of three evaluation methods.

		% of points on USM	% of points on RT diagram based on Golden Standard evaluation	% of points on RT diagram based on Three Criteria evaluation
N	Valid	35	37	37
	Missing	37	35	35
Mean		.5281	.5536	.5522
Median		.5690	.5806	.5965
Std. Deviation		.13698	.20109	.17229
Minimum		.14	.03	.11
Maximum		.71	1.29	.83

6 Conclusion

The present study illustrates a first-level comparison between a relatively-new and conceptual modeling-based method of structuring user stories' sets to the industry-adopted technique. In total, the elements/links presented in the Rationale Tree method were perceived as somehow difficult to identify and differentiate one from another. Our analysis explicitly revealed a prolonged confusion between the elements used to describe the WHAT- and WHY-dimension within a user stories' set such as Tasks/Capabilities and Soft-Goals/Hard-Goals. This is an indication that more thought should be placed in the semantics and rules to facilitate the differentiation between such functional elements. However, despite our initial expectations, the Rationale Tree group produced artifacts similar in quality compared to the ones of the User Story Mapping technique. A factor that might have influenced these results is the use of the particular case study which proved to be difficult in representing the requirements problem no matter the method used by the students. However, the use of this case provided us with the necessary consistency in studying and comparing our results with the ones received from previous studies. Moreover, the complexity of the case adds value to the goal of this exercise which was to be considered as a first-level simulation of the elaborate tasks that modelers have to perform when taking on the task of requirements elicitation and analysis. An even more in-depth comparison of the ability of understanding the software problem and, more particularly, specific key aspects like missing requirements, Epics and Themes on the basis of both techniques will be the subject of a broader communication. Future work also includes reproducing the same kind of experiment but opposing the rationale tree and the use case diagram [7].

References

1. Cohn, M.: User Stories Applied: For Agile Software Development. Addison-Wesley Professional, Boston (2004)

2. Lucassen, G., Dalpiaz, F., van der Werf, J.M.E.M., Brinkkemper, S.: Improving agile requirements: the quality user story framework and tool. Requirements Eng. **21**(3), 383–403 (2016). https://doi.org/10.1007/s00766-016-0250-x
3. Patton, J., Economy, P.: User Story Mapping: Discover the Whole Story, Build the Right Product. O'Reilly Media, Inc., Sebastopol (2014)
4. Saunders, M., Lewis, P., Thornhill, A.: Research Methods for Business Students. Pearson Education, London (2016)
5. Teddlie, C., Tashakkori, A.: Foundations of Mixed Methods Research: Integrating Quantitative and Qualitative Approaches in the Social and Behavioral Sciences. Sage, Thousand Oaks (2009)
6. Wautelet, Y., Gielis, D., Poelmans, S., Heng, S.: Evaluating the impact of user stories quality on the ability to understand and structure requirements. In: Gordijn, J., Guédria, W., Proper, H.A. (eds.) PoEM 2019. LNBIP, vol. 369, pp. 3–19. Springer, Cham (2019). https://doi.org/10.1007/978-3-030-35151-9_1
7. Wautelet, Y., Heng, S., Hintea, D., Kolp, M., Poelmans, S.: Bridging user story sets with the use case model. In: Link, S., Trujillo, J.C. (eds.) ER 2016. LNCS, vol. 9975, pp. 127–138. Springer, Cham (2016). https://doi.org/10.1007/978-3-319-47717-6_11
8. Wautelet, Y., Heng, S., Kiv, S., Kolp, M.: User-story driven development of multi-agent systems: a process fragment for agile methods. Comput. Lang. Syst. Struct. **50**, 159–176 (2017)
9. Wautelet, Y., Heng, S., Kolp, M., Mirbel, I.: Unifying and extending user story models. In: Jarke, M., et al. (eds.) CAiSE 2014. LNCS, vol. 8484, pp. 211–225. Springer, Cham (2014). https://doi.org/10.1007/978-3-319-07881-6_15
10. Wautelet, Y., Heng, S., Kolp, M., Mirbel, I., Poelmans, S.: Building a rationale diagram for evaluating user story sets. In: 2016 IEEE Tenth International Conference on Research Challenges in Information Science (RCIS), pp. 1–12. IEEE (2016)
11. Wautelet, Y., Velghe, M., Heng, S., Poelmans, S., Kolp, M.: On modelers ability to build a visual diagram from a user story set: a goal-oriented approach. In: Kamsties, E., Horkoff, J., Dalpiaz, F. (eds.) REFSQ 2018. LNCS, vol. 10753, pp. 209–226. Springer, Cham (2018). https://doi.org/10.1007/978-3-319-77243-1_13
12. Yu, E., Giorgini, P., Maiden, N., Mylopoulos, J.: Social Modeling for Requirements Engineering. MIT Press, Cambridge (2011)

Author Index

The manufacturer's authorised representative in the EU is Springer Nature Customer Service Centre GmbH, Europaplatz 3, 69115 Heidelberg, Germany. If you have any concerns regarding our products, please contact ProductSafety@springernature.com

Printed and bound by CPI Group (UK) Ltd, Croydon, CR0 4YY
30/09/2026
02225688-0006